Scribe Publications
SO GREEK

Niki Savva was one of the most senior correspondents in the Canberra Press Gallery. She was twice political correspondent on *The Australian*, and headed up the Canberra bureaus of both *The Herald Sun* and *The Age*. When family tragedy forced a career change, she became Peter Costello's press secretary for six years and was then on John Howard's staff for three. Her work brought her into intimate contact with the major political players of the last 30 years.

For Christina,
a shining example of the value of life and how it should be lived.

CONFESSIONS OF A CONSERVATIVE LEFTIE

Niki Savva

SCRIBE
Melbourne

Scribe Publications Pty Ltd
PO Box 523
Carlton North, Victoria, Australia 3054
Email: info@scribepub.com.au

First published by Scribe 2010
Reprinted 2010

Copyright © Niki Savva 2010

All rights reserved. Without limiting the rights under copyright reserved above, no part of this publication may be reproduced, stored in or introduced into a retrieval system, or transmitted, in any form or by any means (electronic, mechanical, photocopying, recording or otherwise) without the prior written permission of the publishers of this book.

Typeset in 11.5/16 pt Minion by the publishers
Printed and bound in Australia by Griffin Press
Only wood grown from sustainable regrowth forests is used in the manufacture of paper found in this book.

National Library of Australia
Cataloguing-in-Publication data

Savva, Niki
So Greek: confessions of a conservative leftie

9781921640278 (pbk.)

1. Savva, Niki. 2. Liberal Party of Australia–Officials and employees–Biography. 3. Journalists–Australia–20th century–Biography. 4. Press secretaries–Australia–Biography. 5. Australia–Politics and government.

994.063092

www.scribepublications.com.au

Contents

So Greek	1
1: Leaving Cyprus, ready or not	7
2: Moving to Mars	15
3: Lucky or what?	35
4: Too much fun	49
5: The good, the bad, and the ugly	70
6: Nothing lasts forever	88
7: 1998: tragedies and triumph	108
8: Killing dragons, getting stoned	134
9: Get out the bloody billycart	158
10: Peter Peter Peter Peter	176
11: Invasion of the body-snatcher	191
12: Economy great; government stinks	208
13: Dear John …	225
14: Murphy's Law XL	247
15: Finally	275
Acknowledgements	287
Index	291

So Greek

It's hard to say when Peter was the most exasperating: when he was wanting to be prime minister, or when he was acting as prime minister.

When he was acting as prime minister, he drove us near mad with his incessant demands. He was so frightened of making a mistake and giving his enemies the ammunition — as if they needed any — to undermine him that he grew completely unreasonable.

In early July 2000, John Howard had gone overseas, and Peter was in charge. There were a myriad things happening, and we had to fly from Melbourne to Sydney late in the day to position for a function the next morning.

Desperate to go to the toilet, I took advantage of a break in calls to duck down the corridor to the ladies.

This is getting dangerously close to too much information but, just as I sat down, a pair of feet appeared outside the door. There was a vacant cubicle next door, so I knew it wasn't a queue.

Gritting my teeth, I waited for Philippa, our receptionist, to speak, suspecting what would come next.

'He told me to come and get you. He wants you to come back right away.'

If there is a stronger word than livid, I was it. I told her I would come back when I was good and ready. Naturally, I dawdled back, and deliberately avoided going into his office.

The quasi-crisis which had prompted this had disappeared by the time I got back, but I had been given one more task: to get him to clear and then to issue, as acting prime minister, a press release written by the Department of Prime Minister and Cabinet paying tribute to war hero and nurse Sister Vivian Bullwinkel, who had died. I took the release with me to Sydney.

Mitch Fifield, his then political adviser, and I went to Peter's hotel suite to clear up a few things before dinner. Two security guards hovered outside.

I pulled out the Bullwinkel press release and showed it to Peter, suggesting a couple of changes because I thought it was a bit stilted and repetitive. He looked at me in that way one does when about to reprove a recalcitrant child, cocked his head, and began: 'Now, Niki …'

I sensed what he was about to say.

A month before, we had had, in the overall scheme of things, a minor crisis to deal with, involving the use of the electoral roll by the Australian Tax Office to send out letters to households extolling the many benefits of the new tax system.

A carefully worded press release had to go out from then attorney-general Darryl Williams, a decent soul with not one political bone in his body, explaining why the government had used taxpayers' money in this manner, so our office was helping with the preparation of the release. We worked late into the night, and from very early the next morning, poring over the formulation, wondering how we were going to get out of this one, and knowing we were going to cop an almighty belting.

That next morning, however, as luck would have it, and as is the way with government, another minor crisis developed. Better still, it didn't involve us! Civil unrest had broken out in Honiara, and the Australian consul there had asked the government to arrange the evacuation of Australian nationals.

John Moore, the defence minister, sauntered down to our office in the morning and wondered, ever so coolly, if he should send a naval vessel to rescue the expats. All of us, simultaneously, knowing that the pictures and story would help bury some of the unpleasantness over the use of the electoral roll, yelled out, '*Yes!*'

Mike Callaghan, our then chief of staff, said later it was the closest thing to 'wag the dog' he had seen in government.

A fresh copy of Darryl Williams' press release, which had been through several drafts, arrived soon after, and I noticed that there were two 'to's side by side in the very first paragraph.

Even though English is only my second language, I had from an early age developed an obsessive compulsion to correct grammatical errors, either verbal or written, whenever or wherever I spotted them. Perhaps subconsciously it was my petty revenge for all those times I had been called a 'wog' — or worse — when I was growing up, by kids paler or slower than me.

My first memory of it was in Grade 6 at Doveton West State School, when I heard the teacher slip up in class. I put up my hand to tell him. He ignored me for a good ten minutes and then finally, wearily, asked me what the problem was.

'Sir, you said "done" instead of "did", before.'

Mr Jackman went all colours, including red and purple, and hurled his piece of chalk across the room. He just managed to stop himself from cursing, and looked as if he wanted to run across the room, put his hands around my throat, and strangle me. Instead, he stopped the lesson and told us all to keep quiet and read our books. The other kids looked at me, mystified. Deep down, I was pleased. It wasn't payback or anything, even though Mr Jackman had once made fun of my pierced ears and earrings. The midwife had used a hot needle to pierce my ears on the day I was born and, fearing the holes would close up, my mother insisted I wear earrings every day.

It was just that if I saw or heard something which I knew was wrong and needed correcting, I had to fix it.

So if there was a lesson there about leaving well enough alone, I had never learned it. After all, I was right, wasn't I? If I believed in leaving well enough alone, I would still be living in that housing-commission estate in Doveton.

And it was right that one of the two 'to's in Williams' press release should go, so I asked his office to fix it.

Williams' office copied the release, sent one down to our office for the treasurer, then headed up to the press-gallery boxes to distribute the rest to the media. Suddenly there was a loud, strangled cry from the treasurer's office. The copy that was about to be boxed was not the right copy, but an earlier version that he had amended. He insisted it be withdrawn.

Tony Smith, Costello's political adviser, raced after Williams' girls and caught them before they got to the boxes.

Peter blamed me for the mix-up because I'd insisted that the typo be corrected.

There was the internal equivalent of a royal commission, spearheaded by Tony, which uncovered the real reason. Williams' office had been working on the press release on two screens, and had mistakenly printed off an earlier version from one of them.

Tony tried to explain to Peter what had happened, but soon gave up. I slammed the door to my office as hard as I could, and sat there fuming at the obstinacy of my boss and at the injustice of it all.

We all knew only too well that once a notion had entered Costello's head (such as this person being a friend, and that one an enemy, or whatever), it was next to impossible to dislodge it. I had, in his mind, almost turned a trivial mistake into a near-calamity by asking for the removal of an extra 'to'.

So there we were, these few weeks later, sitting in the splendour of one of the Intercontinental's best suites, after a day of being on the receiving end of incessant demands while Costello acted as PM — such as him issuing directions to evacuate lavatories — and there I was again, daring to ask for something to be changed.

'Now, Niki … you know what happened last time you wanted to change a typo.'

A blood vessel in my brain felt like it was about to burst.

I was sitting at the dining-room table, with the Vivian Bullwinkel press release in front of me. I lifted both hands above my head and slammed my open palms down as hard as I could on the table's highly polished surface. It made a sound like the crack of lightning and, as the noise reverberated around the room, I screamed at him.

'*It wasn't the fucking typo!*'

Silence. I half-expected the security guards stationed outside to burst into the room, guns drawn.

Peter just stood there, staring at me with a 'What the hell' kind of look on his face. Mitch's jaw dropped.

If there had been something within reach, I would have grabbed it at that instant and hurled it at the federal treasurer, with the express aim of either decapitating or severely maiming him.

Not for the last time, Peter's dilemma was whether to fight or retreat. He chose a middle course — the right call, on this occasion — saying simply, 'You're so Greek.'

You had to laugh.

The Bullwinkel press release went out without amendment. We grabbed our things and went to dinner at Beppis with Frank Devine and Michael Duffy.

Strictly speaking, I'm not Greek. But we both knew exactly what he meant.

CHAPTER ONE

Leaving Cyprus, ready or not

In 1947, when Andreas married Elpiniki, he was given four fields, with the almond, carob, olive, fig, and mulberry trees that grew on them; three houses, including a mill to grind the grains; one cow; one donkey; and one goat. The day after the wedding, when the sheets were inspected and Elpiniki's goodness was revealed, they received another house. Although this was quite a good dowry for the time, the 'houses' were little more than mud-brick rooms. There was no water, no sewerage, no electricity.

The marriage had been arranged, as was the custom, by their parents. Elpiniki's father thought she needed a calm, steadying influence, and believed that Andreas was a good man. Andreas did not need the dowry to induce him. He would have married her for nothing. She was 18 and the prettiest girl in the village of Choli, from a solid if volatile family.

Choli was like many other villages in Cyprus, remote and poor, hidden away in the mountains, safe from predators and closer to what little arable farmland there was in the south-west of the island in the province of Paphos, the birthplace of Aphrodite. Houses in the village were clustered around a communal well and the small church of the Archangel Michael with its famous frescoes that had been built around the end of the fifteenth century, but its population never really grew beyond a couple of dozen families.

Andreas had been to school for three years and Elpiniki for three days. On her third day at school, the teacher had slapped her; after she complained to her father, he kept her at home to help her mother care for her six siblings. She became an exceptional cook; could copy any knitted or crocheted garment or doily, no matter how intricate, simply by counting the stitches; and was razor sharp in both tongue and mind. But she never learned to read and write.

As a young child, Andreas ploughed fields owned by others, and cracked rocks to help build roads around the villages. It was work that literally broke his back. He suffered chronic pain all his life, and X-rays later showed that his vertebrae had suffered damage during his youth.

His life was little different from the lives of hundreds of other children in the surrounding villages. Depending on how you look at these things, his upbringing had been as good or as bad as that of his father, Savvas, who was known everywhere as Saouris, a diminutive of Savva.

Few people in Cyprus are known by the name with which they were christened. It is easier, given that almost everyone is named after a handful of saints, to identify them by their nicknames, which are often cruel and always funny.

For instance, Elpiniki's clan was known as Chimoni, a corruption of the Greek for winter. Apparently, after a particularly large meal to break his Easter fast, her grandfather was walking to the neighbouring village when he spied some wild berries. As he reached to pick them, he lost his footing and fell down a ravine into the freezing waters of a small pond. He began to punch his full stomach with all his might, cursing it with each strike: 'I gave you *flayounes* [Cypriot cheese pies], I gave you *embasies* [meat pies], I gave you *loukanika* [sausages], and it wasn't enough for you. Still you wanted *mersinokoka* [wild berries].'

He was hard and cold. Her father, Nikolas, earned the nickname in his own right, thanks to his drinking, eating, and bad behaviour, and it was passed on to his progeny.

One of his sons came to be known as Farmakas (poison); another, Attiki (jewel); and another, Kokkinos (red hair and blue eyes). Collectively, though, they were known as Chimonies, and they had a fierce reputation. They were short, stout, and very aggressive. Few people dared challenge them.

Elpiniki's maternal grandfather was called Angelli. As his name suggested, he was tall and slim, with blond hair and blue eyes. He looked like an angel.

Andreas was tall and lean, and came from a very different kind of family. Saouris' mother had died when he was a small boy, leaving him and his two brothers to be cared for by their father. Their father remarried, and his new wife — so the family legend went — wanted nothing to do with his other three children. He set about touring the villages to give away his sons. The children were split up among different villages in different states, and Saouris, then only five, was taken in by his late mother's brother, Pappou Krassaris from Arodes, a long way from his birthplace of Agatha, and a donkey-ride away from Choli. Krassaris had 12 children of his own, but he raised Saouri nonetheless, even teaching him to make shoes and chairs.

Cyprus is only a small place, but very mountainous. In those days, travel was not easy, and communication was scant to non-existent. There was no contact between the brothers and, as far as can be established, no further contact between father and children.

Saouris, who was conscripted by the British in the First World War, was travelling by train across Europe when he was confronted by another lanky male who had slung his legs across the aisle, blocking his passage. Saouris yelled at him to get his useless legs out of the way and, when the other soldier refused, he kicked him. They started punching one another, and had to be separated by the other soldiers.

They arrived at their destination, and met up again at the yards where the horses and pack mules were corralled. They were both good with animals and it was their job to look after them, but they were only looking to settle the score between them. They drew daggers, hell-bent on drawing blood. Their comrades separated them again, and they were both hauled before their commanding officer. As he went through their documentation, the commanding officer made a startling discovery. 'Did you know you are brothers?', he asked. They did not.

The man Saouris had fought and had been determined to kill was his brother, Chrisostomos. After decades of separation, the two brothers began weeping, and then kissing and embracing each other. When they returned to Cyprus, they searched out their other brother.

This story was told and retold many times over in the family. There was never any bitterness in the retelling. There was always a lot of laughter over how the two strangers fought; and, with their reunion as brothers, the storytellers would nod at fate and marvel at its many curses and occasional gifts.

So it was that three years after they married, Andreas and Elpiniki were sitting in the *kafeneion* at the neighbouring village of Goudi.

It was autumn, and Elpiniki was peeling a pomegranate, stripping back the red-and-yellow peel to expose the luscious, red fruit beneath.

The men were discussing a story in the local paper. Australia was looking for migrants. 'Andreas,' she said, 'you should apply.'

Her three Angelli uncles — Phillipos, Yiorgos, and Miros — had left Cyprus years before. One died after falling into a ship's furnace, and contact with the others was lost. Phillipos came back to Cyprus once for a holiday. He had been living in America and was planning to move his family to Argentina. His mother and sister, Elpiniki's mother, loved him so much that they didn't want him to leave. They hid his passport and refused to give it back to him. Eventually they relented, but only after he threatened to kill them both. He was so enraged that he never went back, and he never wrote to them again. He was Angelli in name, but definitely not in nature.

Several of Elpiniki's relatives had gone to South Africa. More villagers had left for England.

Elpiniki wanted somewhere so far away that it would be impossible for them to come back. Failure was possible, but there would be no easy fix for it.

Andreas had been renting paddocks from the other landowners, Theodolos and Charalambos, to supplement their small holdings. He had planted snake beans, peas, watermelons, and aubergines. They harvested olives, almonds, and carobs from their trees, and ate little meat, apart from the pig slaughtered each Christmas. The olives, boiled, dried, and then pressed, produced an oil as thick as syrup, and the carobs a syrup like molasses. Almonds were eaten green, before the outer shell had hardened, with a sip of the home-made rocket fuel called *zivania,* or else ripened and strung together, and dipped in grape juice over a period of days to produce a long, preserved sweet roll called *shijouko*.

They had enough to live on in those days but, with two children already, nowhere near enough to prosper. And there were unsettling developments. Andreas was sitting outside his house one day when his brother-in-law Farmakas came running up and threw a shotgun at his feet. 'Get rid of it,' he shouted, and kept running. Andreas looked down into the valley and could see police in hot pursuit on foot. He threw the shotgun into the sewage pit.

Every Cypriot had passionate political views, and Andreas was no exception. He was a socialist and ardently anti-British. His brother Pavlos, ten years younger, was to be captured and tortured by the British later, during the uprising of the mid-1950s, for his involvement with the right-wing ENOSIS movement that sought union with Greece.

Andreas and Elpiniki could see what lay before them — what lay before all of us. The furthest things from their mind were the kinds of challenges they might confront in another country — a new language and an alien culture. All they could see, and it was just as well, was opportunity.

'Would you go to Australia?' Andreas asked Elpiniki that day. 'Yes,' she said. And that was that.

They borrowed eight pounds from another villager, Brothiereas, who had set up a community group to try to help the villagers improve their lot. The next day, Andreas found a car and driver, and went to see Nikos Koundoros, a lawyer in the town of Ktima, who helped him fill out his applications for a visa and a passport.

Months went by without word on his visa. Andreas began to lose hope. He feared that his left-wing political alliances were responsible for the delay. He began to tour the churches lighting candles. He visited the church of his namesake, Apostolos Andreas, on the northernmost tip of the island and the furthest point from Choli, and prayed for his ticket. He went back to cracking rocks for road building. He and Elpiniki became the butt of jokes in the village. They had been taken for a ride by the lawyer in Ktima, they said — serve them right for thinking they could break free of their destiny.

Then, one night, Andreas dreamed of a small church, and saw the Virgin Mary. She told him not to worry, that everything would work out. 'But you have gone around Cyprus to all the churches and you haven't come to mine,' she complained. 'Come and light a candle in my church.'

He had sold the donkey, so the next day he set out to walk the several kilometres to the church he had seen in his dreams in the village of Fitefkia. He went in and lit a candle and some incense, and he prayed again.

Within a week, the lawyer notified him that his visa had arrived. Andreas believed it was a miracle, and he never tired of telling the story.

He and eight other Cypriots, including his good friend Charalambos Theophanous, boarded a tub called the Corsica at the port of Limassol on 12 December 1951, leaving behind his 22-year-old wife with their two children.

On the day he left, the howls of his grief-stricken father could be heard in the next village. His neighbours saw him beating his head against a tree trunk. Saouris was 45 when he had Andreas; his wife, Christina, was 38. She had had other pregnancies and had given birth to other children — perhaps four before him. He was the first to make it into adulthood; the others had died in infancy or early childhood, probably from the same disease that would later claim his own daughter. And here he was leaving. Saouris never saw his son again.

Andreas arrived at Station Pier in Melbourne in February 1952. He was one of 1718 Cypriots to arrive in Australia that year.

It was early evening and, as he looked down from the ship, he couldn't see anyone he recognised. Of the 12 English pounds he had scrounged before his departure, he had one left, so he decided to spend the night on the ship.

Then he heard someone calling out his name. 'Andreas. *Ela kato*.' ('Come down').

It was Panayioti (who in Australia became Peter), the grandson of the man who had fostered his father. The old man Krassaris had written, telling him that Andreas, Saouris' son, was on his way, and urged Panayioti to meet him and look after him.

Peter, who was 21, had three jobs. His younger brother, Chrisanthos, was a few months shy of his 18th birthday and was working as a carpenter. His older brother, Steve, worked in a milk bar at Flinders St. railway station. Their first cousin, Hazel, one of two daughters, had been sent out by her parents when she was just 16.

When Theo Notaras, the father of family friend Georgina Koundouris, had arrived alone in Australia in 1922 he was only 13 years old. By the age of 17 he had a coffee shop in Captains Flat; and by the time Old Parliament House opened in 1927, he owned the

Capital café in Canberra, then ended up acquiring large slabs of the city and the inner suburbs.

It was a common practice amongst Cypriot and Greek families. Children were sent by their poverty-stricken parents to find a better life — which they usually did — but the pain of separation from their parents stayed with them forever. A few never forgave them, regardless of the great wealth they had amassed. One acquaintance was so unforgiving that, when his mother died, he shipped her body to Australia and buried her here, ignoring her wishes to be interred in the village cemetery beside her husband — his father.

As he gathered up Andreas and his belongings at Station Pier, Peter gave the newcomer a few pounds, and took him to the home in Essendon — a grand old mansion with an orchard down the back — of his uncle, Savvas Krassaris, who had arrived in Melbourne in 1924, sponsored by our cousin Tsindos of the famous Melbourne restaurant family. The extended Krassaris family was a bedrock of enduring friendship and support for generations of the Savva family.

CHAPTER TWO

Moving to Mars

Andreas might as well have gone to live on Mars. There was a small, close Greek community already established, but the culture and landscape of 1950s' Melbourne was like that of another planet.

He got a job quickly, as did so many other migrants, at the GM-H plant at Fishermens Bend in the CKD (complete knock-down) section, opening crates full of parts for the new cars being built. He was an accomplished social animal, totally uninhibited by his lack of language or polish, and good-humoured and good-natured — except for the occasional volcanic explosion. He was pretty much a typical Greek (Cypriot).

He played cricket with his Australian workmates, and became a hero one day when he stuck out his hand and caught the ball. He had no idea what he was supposed to do, but realised it had been the right thing when his team-mates jumped all over him in excitement. His action had won the match, and they rewarded him with beers.

He became an even greater hero when one of his workmates fell into a vat and he had the presence of mind to swing a heavy chain across and help haul him out. His boss, Norm, never forgot and made sure that Andreas kept a cushy job at the factory. Later he helped him get a house in a new housing-commission estate on the outskirts of Melbourne. With most other Greeks clustered around the inner city, Andreas moved from Mars and headed for the Moon.

Andreas was a good man, and that is what we wrote on his tombstone when he died, but even good men have their flaws. He discovered the racetrack soon after he arrived. Cyprus didn't even have lawns — except on the British bases, where they were pointed out as a curiosity and indulgence, given the scarcity of water on the island — much less a racecourse. Now, despite his limited English, Andreas quickly learned how to place a bet. The trouble was, he never knew when to stop.

On one memorable day at the Moonee Valley course, he was 800 pounds up by the second-last race. He was ecstatic. In one almighty expression of faith, he bet it all on the last race on a horse running at 33 to one, and lost the lot when it came in second. He didn't even have enough left for the bus fare home, and walked all the way back to the rented terrace he shared with Peter in then decidedly untrendy Carlton. It was either the worst of luck or the best of luck. In those days, 800 pounds probably would have bought three terraces in Carlton, and the family would have been set for life. Or he would have gone back to Cyprus, and the rest of us would never have discovered Australia.

More than two years had passed since he'd left Cyprus. Chimoni's high regard for his son-in-law had evaporated. He told Elpiniki not to expect him to return or to send for her, that he had forgotten her, and that she should divorce him. He pledged to find her another husband. No one believed she was the one who had wanted to leave Cyprus in the first place. These taunts, although hurtful, were not idle. Some men had 'forgotten' their families. Some never brought them out to Australia; others started new families, or — shame heaped on shame — began secret lives with other men.

Andreas had not forgotten, and would cry at family gatherings because he missed his wife and children so much.

Peter, distressed at Andreas' unhappiness, lent him money to help buy the tickets to get Elpiniki and their two children to Melbourne.

As she closed the door on her tiny house in Choli on a hot summer's day, leaving most of her possessions inside, Elpiniki was apprehensive and beginning to regret her impulsive decision to migrate.

Clutching a child in each hand, she farewelled her brother George, who had taken her to the port in Limassol, and boarded the vessel which was to take her to Beirut to link up with the Kyrenia for the voyage to Melbourne. She had only left her village a handful of times before, and here she was leaving her country, her family, and everything familiar behind. What had she been thinking?

She felt anything but reassured when she boarded and saw on the deck two black men chained to a post, wearing only loincloths. *Oh my God*, she thought: *cannibals*.

She relaxed slightly in Beirut. She remembers eating, that night, the best bean casserole she had ever tasted. Food was not just fuel in the Savva household. It provided comfort, distraction, relaxation, and competition (who made the best *kourabiedes*, the best *spanakopita*, the best *baklava* — invariably, it was her). It was always delicious, and it helped forge many friendships.

Her anxiety soon resurfaced when one of the locals walked her back to the hotel where she and the two kids were to spend the night. The man, thinking he was helping, picked me up and slung me onto his shoulders. I began screaming, pulling his hair and slapping him on the head. Elpiniki, cursing Arabs in her best Cypriot dialect, feared he was going to make off with me, and urged Steven, the protective older brother, to hurry and keep up and make sure that the bastard didn't get away.

Steven was five.

The Kyrenia arrived in Melbourne on a beautiful, sunny winter morning in July 1954. Elpiniki could not see Andreas on the dock and returned, crying, to her cabin. She decided she was going to stay on the ship and go back to Cyprus.

Steven remained on deck and then returned excitedly to the

cabin, telling her he had seen our father waiting below. Andreas was wearing the same coat he had worn when he had left Cyprus; even after all that time, Steven had recognised it and him.

Steven was probably the most responsible little boy I have ever encountered. He helped look after us, especially after Mum went to work, making sure we got up in time, had breakfast, and dressed properly for school — even down to tying my shoelaces until I learned to do them myself.

Even after I became the Canberra correspondent for the largest-selling daily newspaper in Australia, and then worked for the treasurer and the prime minister, my rellies never tired of reminding me that as a two-year-old in Choli I had almost fallen down the sewage pit in the yard, and that my brother had had to tie my shoelaces till I was eight years old.

It's a wonder that Steven made it out of childhood, though. Not long after we arrived, he bought firecrackers, which he had never had before, and lit them all at once while he was holding them. His hand swelled mightily, turning black and purple. He was lucky he didn't lose it or some of his fingers. A little while later, he was run over by a cyclist. His injuries were minor, but I always felt sorry for the boy who rode over him and brought him home, only to be greeted by Elpiniki's screams of abuse.

Steven was enrolled in primary school, and I went to kinder in Carlton. I wanted nothing to do with Andreas. He was a stranger to me, and for a long time I hid whenever he was around.

Elpiniki cried a lot in those days, especially when I brought home the group photo from kinder with all the little kids seated on the bench — all of them together down one end, except me, sitting on my own down the other.

Nothing was easy. If she needed eggs, she would take eggshells down to the corner milk bar to get more; if she needed olive oil, she had to go to the chemist, where it was sold in small bottles as if it was for medicinal purposes only — say, to treat constipation.

Every Saturday afternoon, Steve and I went by ourselves to the local cinema. Dad gave us enough for the show — usually an American gangster movie of the Boston Blackie variety or a western — and an ice-cream. The Saturday matinee became a critical part of our English tuition and cultural assimilation.

A year after Elpiniki's arrival, another baby, Christina, was born. Hazel, whom I loved dearly, made our lunches for us while Mum was in hospital — thick slices of white bread with lashings of butter and strawberry jam. I threw them in the bin, much preferring sandwiches stuffed with leftovers from the previous night's dinner, especially *frittata* — eggs and zucchini — with oil oozing through the bread and soaking it. I got away with this for a couple of years, until one day when some Australian kids saw what I was eating: 'Er, yuk! *What* is *that*?' It was Vegemite with cheddar-cheese slices on plain white sliced bread every day thereafter at school for me, and I have never touched either since.

When Christina was brought home to the old Carlton terrace, there was no crib, and she slept in the drawer of an old chest. It was snug and safe.

Andreas had stopped going to the track, although his Saturday afternoons were spent in furious argument with the radio, and we were starting to find our way. Unfortunately, he and Elpiniki never stood a chance.

When Christina was about three months old, Elpiniki noticed that there was something wrong with her. She was terribly pale, and unlike her other babies when she had wrapped them after their bath, Christina did not go that cheery, cherub-like pink colour.

With Peter's help, they took her to the Royal Children's Hospital, which was in those days a run-down collection of buildings in Carlton. They were told — as it would turn out, not for the last time — that she was going to die, so they summonsed a priest, and she was christened in a sink at the old hospital. Christina defied the predictions.

Doctors soon diagnosed her illness as thalassemia major, a life-threatening form of anaemia, the treatment for which requires regular blood transfusions. The doctors soon discovered that there were others like her among the migrant children from the Mediterranean region, and to their eternal credit soon established a self-contained unit to treat them.

The doctor in charge of Christina's treatment was John Colebatch, a brilliant clinician with lousy people-skills. He was one of those Australians who thought that if you yelled loudly enough at people who didn't speak your language, you could eventually make them understand what you were saying.

Elpiniki both feared and respected him. He had saved her daughter's life, but did he have to be so gruff? Christina made an indelible impression on him, too.

Years later, Dr Colebatch spied my by-line in *The Age* when I was chief of the Canberra bureau, and asked his son Tim, the paper's economics editor, if I was related to Christina.

After Christina's birth, we moved from Carlton to Brunswick to live with Hazel and her new husband, Harry. Elpiniki was pregnant again; with the new baby, Mary, there were six of us sleeping in the one room. Steven and I shared a bed, sleeping toe to toe, but for us kids it was not an unhappy time.

It wasn't as if we knew people who were better off than us. Almost everybody we knew was living the same way, and we didn't have television to tell us every night that we were poor, or to show us the luxuries we were missing out on.

There were lots of other kids — Australian, Greeks, and Italians — in the street, and we played outside constantly. The little blonde girl with freckles who lived across the road would press her face close to mine and sing a little song: 'Brown eyes, twinkle eyes. Brown eyes, twinkle eyes.'

Although I understood what she said, I couldn't tell the difference between affectionate teasing and mocking, and decided it was the latter, so I tried to hurt her back by singing: 'Blue eyes, twinkle eyes. Blue eyes, twinkle eyes.' Bet that scarred her for life.

We played hide and seek, and I soon discovered the only place where the other kids couldn't find me: I would lie down flat under cars parked in the street. No one ever found me, and at night when my mother asked me how I got the oil stains on the front of my dress (always a dress, never pants or shorts — not allowed), I would say I fell over.

My parents' problems just kept multiplying: now they realised that there was something wrong with Mary. Mum always said that Mary was her prettiest baby, but she barely moved, she never walked, and she never spoke.

She was taken to the Kew Cottages, a state-run home for mentally or physically severely disabled children, where she lived most of her short life, apart from brief visits home. She died when she was 19 months old. In between taking Christina to hospital, our parents would visit her there, but I only went once.

We walked past cribs with severely disabled children, including one baby with a head three times the size of its body. It was harrowing.

Mary looked 'normal' enough, but we never found out exactly what was wrong with her. The doctors couldn't speak Greek, and my parents couldn't speak English. Years later, when I went to interview the head of the cottages for an article for the *Australian*, he kindly agreed to try to find out. Unfortunately, the records had been destroyed in a fire a few years before.

The language barrier was a constant source of frustration both between us and our parents, and between them and others. My father chased me around the kitchen table once in an absolute rage after I had told him to 'leave me alone, willya'.

'Who is this "willya"?' he yelled. He thought it was a disparaging nickname I had invented for him. I defy anyone to translate 'willya'. I certainly couldn't, making Andreas even madder. Steven rescued me by pushing the table into Andreas, and he soon calmed down. I refined my Boston Blackie English to say 'will you'.

To get by, Greeks in Australia developed their own language. 'Car' became 'caro'; 'refrigerator' became 'friza'; 'bus' was 'busso'; 'block' was 'blocko'; 'market' became 'mariketta'; and so on.

It was simple enough. An 'o' or an 'a' was added to English words, then pronounced with a Greek accent. The trouble was, they bore absolutely no resemblance to the Greek words for the same items.

Children spoke half-Greek and half-English to their parents, and were expected to interpret everything from doctors' instructions to hire-purchase agreements. We opened all of our parents' mail. When the Kew Cottages sent a telegram to inform them of Mary's death, I had to read it out to them. I was eight.

Among adults, illiteracy in both languages was pretty common, so that when the migrants returned to their homelands after decades in Australia, flaunting their concocted Gringlish, even their own family members couldn't understand them. They didn't really belong in their new country, and they were alienated from their old country.

Gringlish continues to filter through the generations. When my goddaughter Elpiniki, besotted by everything pink, was three, she called the fish-roe dip *taramasalata* — 'Barbie food'.

When they weren't running fish-and-chip shops or milk bars, migrants became factory fodder. In the mid-1950s, three new plants had been built alongside one another on a short strip along the Princes Highway at Dandenong — GM-H, Heinz, and International Harvester. They are all gone now, but back then they were booming. They needed workers, and lots of them.

The state government built Doveton. Most of the houses were the product of an instant-construction process: big slabs of concrete were hauled into position by cranes and joined together, and were then given a light wash of paint. When we moved there in 1957, the roads had not been sealed — when it rained, the mud flowed like rivers outside the houses. Mould grew inside the houses from the damp.

But we had our own house. Andreas and Elpiniki rented out the front room, so Steven and I still had to share, but for us this fitted Monty Python's definition of luxury — a toilet attached to the house, and more than one room to revel in.

Andreas turned the backyard into a market garden, filling it with fruit trees and vegetables. He welcomed my help until the day I pulled out what I thought was a weed, but which was in fact a giant radish that he had allowed to go to flower so he could collect the seed. He chased me round the yard, brandishing a beer bottle. There was that volcano again.

Elpiniki would regularly light incense and dried olive leaves in a small urn. The evocative smell would fill every room in the house as she carried it around, while delivering a little chant in a cleansing ritual. It was to both bless the house and everyone in it, but also to ward off the 'evil eye'.

She fervently believes, as do a lot of Greeks, in the evil eye. If someone who she suspects has it visits the house, she will 'smoke' every room as well as the garden after they leave, and spit on anything they admire. It is useless trying to convince her that this is ignorant village behaviour. 'Did you see that plant? After she touched it, it wilted,' she complains. Or she fears that their terrible gaze will inflict even more illness on her family.

Our main blessing, though, was that the Abaloz family lived across the road. Ted was American, of Hispanic–Aztec Indian descent, and Vera was Australian, with a great pair of legs, and wore shorts all summer long.

Andreas and Elpiniki suspended their distrust of all foreigners with the Abalozes, even though they never quite abandoned their bias against other races. They had a hierarchy of ethnics who could be trusted: Cypriots came first; Greeks, second; then came other Mediterraneans, other Europeans, and so on. On the very bottom were the English — unless they happened to be raised in Australia, in which case they were tolerable, but still second from the bottom. It was best not to mention Asians or Africans.

Ted and Vera had three boys, and their oldest, Bruce, soon became my best friend. Wearing our wellies, Bruce and I would tramp the wetlands behind our homes, collecting leeches in jars. Bruce would harangue Ted until he drove us and the leeches to the local hospital, where we 'donated' them for snakebite treatment.

Or we would strip the bark off trees, and put spiders and other bugs in bottles so that Bruce could euthanase them with methylated spirits, and study them at home.

Ted would drive everyone to work, and when the inevitable medical emergencies arose with Christina, he would drive our parents into the city — a good 20 miles away — in his Vauxhall soft-top convertible.

In gratitude, whenever my mother baked, I would carry a plate of something across the road to Vera. Sometimes it was *baklava*; sometimes a kind of shortbread dipped in syrup that was flavoured with a few drops of rosewater and rolled in crushed nuts. Vera and the boys were fascinated by the smell. 'Has this got perfume in it?' they asked, and I doubted that those particular delicacies were ever eaten. In the 1950s, rosewater and orange-flower water were not the height of food fashion that they are today.

Elpiniki showed them how to make meatballs deep-fried in olive oil. The Abaloz boys still cook them that way.

Andreas and Elpiniki never tired of saying that we (foreigners generally, and Greeks particularly) taught Australians how to eat. Before us, it was meat pies and sausage rolls. Thanks to us, Australia was a cornucopia. Anglos, on the other hand, complained that we smelled of garlic or onions (better known as Cypriot fruit). Rather that than dogs' breath, my rellies countered.

Vera was also a great cook. She would bake heavenly apple-sponges so light that they floated off the plate, and would send them over. Then, one amazing day, when Bruce and his brothers, Larry and Richard, brought their sandwiches to eat on our porch, Elpiniki caught a whiff and asked for a taste. They obliged, and she demanded to know what it was so she could get some.

Vera bought Elpiniki her first jar of Vegemite. Maybe Australians did know a thing or two, too.

Food, glorious, food! There is nothing like it to bond or bind.

When the Abaloz boys hit their teens, the family moved out and was replaced by the Walkers. In one of those bizarre coincidences, their son John later became town clerk at Mark Latham's Liverpool City Council.

Bruce, a histologist who managed the lab in the zoology department at Melbourne University, reckons there was a burst of energy around that little corner in Doveton that just propelled people along.

If Christina needed to go to hospital and it was school-holiday time, we would all go into town together. We were needed to interpret anyway. More often than not, Elpiniki couldn't afford to buy train tickets for all of us, so we sneaked on board. Whenever she got caught by the ticket inspectors, she would say she'd got on at Richmond, the last stop before town — rather than at Dandenong, where we'd really boarded, which was the first stop on the line — so she wouldn't have to pay as much.

Once, we all got hauled into the inspector's office for questioning. Of course, I started bawling, and that set Mum off, too. It was easier for them to let us go.

Andreas and Elpiniki did leave Steven and me at home one day, when Christina became ill and Ted had to drive them into town. When it seemed to us that they were late getting home, we set off to find them. Christina had had to stay in hospital, and our parents nearly went mad when they got home and found their other two children missing. Ted drove round searching for us until he finally found us a few miles from home, sitting on a bench outside the

Dandenong town hall, catching our breath before heading off to the station to get the train into the city.

Not long before Mary died, with the medical bills piling up, Elpiniki went to work at GM-H. She was the first Greek wife of our acquaintance to work in paid employment. Andreas was uncomfortable about this; but, with four kids — two of them with serious illnesses that needed constant medical attention — there was no choice. There was no universal health-care system back then.

Elpiniki was 29 when she started work, and she felt like her life was over. She had left Cyprus because she didn't want to work on the farms, and here she was on the assembly line, drilling holes in bits of metal for refrigerators. 'I am too old,' she would say over and over.

Christina was three. We found a Greek family, the marvellous Zaffiris, near our school where the mother, Catholiki, could babysit while we were at school.

Steven built a billycart, using wheels from Christina's old pram. He would dress her, put her in it, and pull or push it up the hills for the three-kilometre trip to school, drop her off at the Zaffiris house, then pick her up after school and take her home. I would tag along beside them, hugely impressed by Steve's strength and ingenuity.

We learned, very young, how to be self-sufficient. We learned to just get on with it, no matter what and, perhaps more importantly, that whingeing would never get us anywhere. It was a waste of time and energy.

What was becoming increasingly difficult, however — for me, anyway — was getting by in two completely different worlds. When the door closed at home, I was reticent and generally obedient: the perfect Greek daughter. At school, I was competitive, talkative, and downright disrespectful. I was two people in one shell — a split that has been accommodated, but never reconciled.

The number of things I wasn't allowed to do kept increasing. And the older I got, the bigger the cultural divide seemed to be.

I wasn't allowed to ride a bike; wasn't allowed to wear slacks; wasn't allowed to wear bathers; wasn't allowed to wander around barefoot, in case people thought we couldn't afford shoes; and wasn't allowed to visit Australian kids in their homes. Playing with Bruce was now frowned upon — only heaven knew where it might lead. There would definitely be no dating for me.

One of my mother's male relatives offered to give me $500 if I stayed a virgin until I married. And it was assumed that I would marry someone my parents chose for me — as their parents had done. If it couldn't be a Cypriot, preferably from our home state of Paphos, a Greek would have to do.

School was an escape from the restrictions and the ever-present worry of Christina's illness, and I loved it.

Doveton High had only been going for three years when I began there. As well as taking in kids from the housing-commission estate, it also drew them from around the district, including from Berwick, Pakenham, and Beaconsfield.

There was a nasty little gang of boys that hung around the breezeway, the open corridor between the boys' and girls' toilets. They would try to stick their rulers up the girls' skirts and panties if they were unsuspecting enough to walk past them.

They had been at my primary school, and I knew to steer clear of them from bitter experience. In Grade 3 at Doveton Primary, one of them, Peter, once threw a jam tin around the playground like a Frisbee, and it had sliced across the top of my nose. Our teacher's favourite saying was 'MYOB' — Mind Your Own Business. She had it plastered across the top of the blackboard; so, despite my bleeding wound, I got little sympathy at the time.

The gang leader at Doveton High was Henry Morhun, a skinny, blond kid with a scarily manic laugh. He and his friends terrorised the playground for almost three years. Morhun would later rape and murder a 16-year-old girl, and be sent to prison, 'gaoled at the Governor's pleasure'.

Eventually, one of the girls, Shirley Crow, complained to her parents. In October 1963, the school made it to the front page of the now-defunct Melbourne *Truth*, which salivated over just such stories. The headline, proclaiming the discovery of a 'Sex College', led to a police investigation ordered by the chief secretary, Arthur Rylah, and the removal of the principal and most of the teachers.

It turned out to be the best thing that ever happened to the school, and definitely to me.

The new principal, Mr E.R. Johnson, was a strange character, tall, with steel-grey hair and deep, black circles under his eyes. He would walk up and down the corridors, peering into the classrooms to make sure that students and teachers alike were behaving. We called him Lurch, after the butler in the Addams Family.

He was ramrod straight and ran the school the same way, with the help of Mrs Large, the equally strict deputy headmistress, who would insist on giving us graphic lessons on the need for hygiene whenever, as she claimed, she could smell girls menstruating. This was useful but embarrassing.

Mr Johnson and Mrs Large would not tolerate even the slightest bit of nonsense.

Walking through the school kitchen one day, I saw a plate of rock cakes on the table, grabbed one, and ate it. When I made the mistake of blabbing to the other girls about my exploit, they promptly dobbed me in, so I was hauled in for a lecture on the evils of stealing. Rock cakes have been off my menu, too, ever since.

The teachers were either mad or brilliant.

The music teacher called us all bastards, and the maths teacher grabbed Forrest Redlich by the lapels and hauled him into the corridor, smashing him against the steel school lockers just because Forrest had told him his fly was undone. Forrest thought he had done him a favour. And he had, because we couldn't concentrate on anything the teacher was saying — we were so fixated on the area below his belt.

Thank heavens they weren't all like that. Joy Brown brought literature to life; Tom Comerford recreated the Renaissance in modern European history; and Max Oldmeadow, who would later be elected the federal Labor member for Holt, provided us with a solid grounding in Australian history.

When I went to thank Mr Comerford on my last day at school, he told me that while it might have been a pleasure to teach me that year, the year before it definitely had not been.

I couldn't blame him: I'd talked and interjected incessantly. He brought in slides of his European holiday once, and flashed up a scene of the narrow, dark alleyways of Florence. I scoffed out loud. 'Huh. That shows us a lot, doesn't it?'

He'd rolled his eyes and patiently explained that, actually, it did tell us a lot about the history and architecture of the place. In fact, having been inspired by him, I discovered Michelangelo and went on to visit that most beautiful of Italian cities a number of times; it remains my favourite place in the world.

Miss Brown, a gentle creature and therefore more vulnerable to my bad behaviour, almost fell over backwards whenever I got an answer right, and she came close to fainting when she read out the results of the vote for head prefect: me.

As head prefect and house captain, I wasn't what you might call a perfect role-model. I struggled to control myself in class, interrupted the teachers constantly, and took obvious joy from their discomfort.

Mr Johnson caught me flirting with the boys, and called me in to his office to chastise me. As punishment, he demanded an essay.

Lyndon Johnson had visited Australia some time before, and Harold Holt's immortal line, 'All the Way with LBJ', was still reverberating as the Vietnam War escalated. So I called my essay 'All the Way with ERJ', delivering a mock apology to the headmaster for my transgression, and promising to do all he asked of me.

He called me in again, and showed grace and humour that I had never suspected existed, and which I probably didn't deserve. He loved my little send-up. When he asked me what I wanted to be, I said a journalist. I had always loved reading and writing, and was always getting into trouble at home for reading when I should have been doing my chores. Vera used to send over her used magazines and books, and any of her sons' old comic books for me and Steven to read. I discovered Superman when I was eight, and realised that a job existed where I could write, get paid for it, and have fun, too. And, with a bit of luck, get out of Doveton and into Metropolis.

Months later, George Ackland, the editor of the local paper, the Dandenong *Journal*, came to the school to see another pupil, Werner, who had a similar ambition. Mr Johnson remembered our conversation, and arranged for me to see George as well.

George suggested I contribute articles to his bi-weekly while I was still at school. I did, and at the end of the year he offered me a cadetship.

I was not the only one at the school who loved writing. Forrest Redlich would fill countless exercise books with graphic stories, and hand them over to me and my friend Ros Walker for review.

'Tone down the sex and violence, and you'll do really well,' was my considered if pompous opinion.

Forrest went on to become, among other things, the executive producer of *A Country Practice*, one of Australia's best-loved television series. He followed up with the edgier, but less popular, *E Street*.

At home, life was much the same.

My brother had started playing Aussie Rules football, showing some talent. We would go to watch him play on Saturdays, and would stay as far away from my mother as possible, as she screamed in both Greek and broken English at anybody who dared touch her son. She would start walking on to the oval if the umpire was a bit slow to act, threatening to hit them all — and she would have, too.

A highlight of our teenage years occurred when the president of the Richmond Football Club, Graham Richmond, turned up at our house in Doveton one day with one of the all-time greats of the game, Jack 'Captain Blood' Dyer, to sign up Steve for the Tigers' under-19 team.

A back injury and conscription helped put an end to Steve's football career; but, over the years, my bragging that I had served Captain Blood a beer in our lounge room impressed more people than the fact that I knew the prime minister.

Andreas' love of politics, passed on to all his children, ensured furious debate around the dinner table every night. Whatever position he took, we would take the opposite. It was not Greek to agree; that was boring. If he was anti-American — which he always was — we were pro. If he was pro-Soviet — which he was — we were anti.

As is also the Greek way, the discussions were loud, irrational, and impassioned. Any stranger listening would have thought we were fighting. We were not; we were talking normally.

Christina was still making regular visits to the Royal Children's Hospital for blood transfusions. Mum and Dad found it difficult to take the time off work to take her, so Steve and I, then in our mid-teens, would alternate. We would catch a bus to the train station in Dandenong for the 45-minute trip to Flinders St., and then take a tram to Parkville.

Except that, most times, we would make a detour to the city. Steve would take her to the movies to see his favourites, like *How the West Was Won*, or I would take her to the chick flicks like *Charley Girl*, or the lunchtime discos where we danced like crazy for an hour before heading for the hospital. If she didn't have to stay in to be transfused, we would put it down to our fun morning. She loved it all.

In the early years of her treatment, doctors would cut down into her veins for the transfusions, only later developing the prick into the vein with the needle. The cut-downs meant that some of her veins became useless, and over the years the remainder became stressed.

We would have to wait and see what her haemoglobin count was and if she needed to be admitted. 'Did they find a good vein today?', we would ask anxiously. When they refined the treatment, she would be transfused regardless every six weeks.

Steven and I had little idea of the severity of her condition. We had no clue that it was life threatening; no knowledge that the very transfusions that saved her could also kill her. We just knew she was special.

At first, doctors told Andreas and Elpiniki that she would not live through her infancy, and then that she would not make it through her teens. Later, when she passed that milestone, they confidently predicted that she would die in her twenties.

We never really discussed her illness until she was a lot older and I had read a few articles about it that scared me. She got cranky with me when I tried to ask doctors about her condition, and instructed them not to discuss it with me.

By the time Christina was in her twenties she knew more about thalassemia than the people who were treating her. A lot of them resented it. I am sure they hurt her more than was necessary when she told them what they were doing wrong. More than anything, she wanted to be a nurse, but the doctors vetoed it because they thought she would be too susceptible to infection.

So she decided to help patients in a different way. She was instrumental in setting up the Thalassemia Society in Victoria, and later roped me in to help secure funding to set up an office and keep it going. I would call my friend and fellow Greek Petro Georgiou, and ask if he could prevail on his friend Jeff Kennett for some money to keep the centre going. They always came through.

She raised money for research that she hoped and prayed would one day find a cure. She was also tireless in getting information to Greeks and other Mediterraneans about the need for blood tests before marriage, and would do the circuit of doctors and surgeons' conferences, lecturing on the needs and problems of thalassemia patients.

She had a full-time job, she would party, and she would travel. She had inherited Andreas' gambling gene. There wasn't a card game she didn't know, or a Greek dance she hadn't learned the steps to. If we went out to the Greek nightclubs, she would insist we stay out till daylight, finishing the night with a coffee and sweet at the sugar shops in the Greek part of town.

I would worry about Andreas and Elpiniki going off, but she didn't give a fig. They would get over it, and there was fun to be had.

She was brilliantly chatty, could recall jokes, and tell them and be funny.

If I was having trouble sleeping at any time during the 15 years we shared a room, or later when we travelled together, I would say to her: 'Talk me to sleep, will you, darlin'.' And off she would go until I dropped off. Now, when I'm on my own, I turn on the radio. It's nowhere near as amusing or informative, but it blots everything out.

She loved cooking and eating, either at home or out, reading, the movies, and Australian Rules football. When she was a little kid, the Krassaris boys took her to Windy Hill and hoisted her onto their shoulders to watch the Bombers play. She was hooked.

She was an essential part of the glue that bound our family together. She insisted that all traditions be maintained, down to the last detail. One year at Christmas I cooked a turkey with mushroom and pine-nut stuffing. That was it — we had to have it every year thereafter, with no variations, along with an ice-cream cake made to look like a plum pudding layered with fruit soaked in rum.

At Christmas, other Greeks would fire up the coals and get the lamb on the spit. In Choli, they would slaughter a pig. At Doveton, and much later when the family moved up the road to Hallam, the Savvas would sit down to stuffed turkey with roast potatoes, pumpkin, and parsnip, no matter what the temperature was. Our concession to the old country was to crumble fetta on top of a salad with everything in it, including avocado.

Elpiniki's younger brother and wife visited one year. She was incredibly finicky about her food, and when I was making the stuffing she suggested I chop some parsley into it. Thinking this would induce her to eat it, I did. Christina was furious. 'Since when did we put parsley in the pine-nut stuffing?' she yelled, glaring at both me and our aunt. She knew our aunt wouldn't eat any of it anyway, and she was right. There was no point wasting time trying to please people you knew were never going to appreciate your efforts.

In fact, there was no time to waste at all. Christina's will to live was matched by her determination to live every day to the fullest. She refused to put up with any nonsense from anybody. It made her incredibly direct, and she had a clear social conscience. She was the one person I could count on to tell me exactly what she thought, even when I didn't want to hear it.

She was both my conscience and my compass.

THREE

Lucky or what?

With a brief peck on the cheek from Elpiniki to wish me luck, and carrying my portable typewriter, I set off to begin my cadetship at the Dandenong *Journal*, feeling much the same as I would almost every morning for the next 30 years. I couldn't wait to get to work. They were paying me $26 a week, and I would have done it for nothing.

It wasn't Metropolis, but I had taken a giant leap into an exciting new world, full of characters even more colourful than the fictional ones in my comic books, and it was largely thanks to the man we'd called Lurch.

The Journal, part of a chain of suburban papers then owned by fledgling tycoon Rupert Murdoch, was a great local paper that took its community role seriously, and employed a substantial team of reporters to cover the district from Springvale to Pakenham. I was the one and only cadet, a little lump of fresh meat for the men to tease and mould.

Frank Quill was especially good at it. Frank, a boxing nut, subbed my copy, and provided vivid word-pictures to help drive home his messages about which words to use and when. There should be a Frank Quill in every office to whip reporters, public-relations consultants, and advertising copywriters into shape.

'Buildings are not erected, Niki,' he said early on. 'The only time you use "erect" is to describe a man's penis in the act of making love.'

This drew a flush of bright crimson from me, and set off muffled laughter from everyone else.

Des Carroll also got into the swing of things after I poked my tongue out at him. 'The tongue is a sexual instrument, Niki, so don't stick it out unless you mean to do something with it.' More muffled laugher; more shades of crimson from me.

Crude, yes. Unforgettable, definitely.

Working there was an absolute gift.

George Ackland drove me everywhere, introduced me to people, taught me to recognise a story when I thought there wasn't one, and helped me write them.

Hugh Buggy, a legendary figure in Australian journalism, was in charge of a column called Hotline answering queries from readers. It was a long way from where he had been on *The Argus* and other major dailies, covering the notorious criminal John Wren and infamous murder cases such as the Pyjama Girl, but he would turn up religiously in his felt hat and three-piece suit, looking as if he had just walked off a 1930s' movie set, ready to deal with the pressing issues of garbage collection or potholed footpaths. He called Rupert 'the young master'.

Hugh is credited with having invented the term 'bodyline' to describe the ruthless tactic used by the visiting English cricket side in 1932–33, but every time it came up he would just shake his head and swear that it wasn't him. Given everything else he admitted to, I see no reason why he would deny this if it was true.

He handed over typed notes every day on the murder investigations he covered (which stood at 200) and the hangings he witnessed (9). He seemed utterly unaffected by any of it.

On one assignment, he went out in a rowboat with police to recover a body. They slung a rope around the corpse to tow it back to shore, and Hugh was told to hang on to the rope, but to be careful not to jerk it around in case the head came off — they needed it for identification. Hugh, then in his seventies, found humour in the grotesque, and couldn't stop laughing as he told the story.

He gave me a book for my birthday and inscribed it thus: 'Madamoiselle Muffet. Many happy returns. Sir Huys de Bughouse Professor Emeritus of Journalism. Read marked passages carefully and DIGEST.'

The book was *The Truth About a Journalist* by Sydney A. Moseley, published in 1935, and bears no resemblance to the life and style of journalists today, or even then, but encapsulated the approach of Hugh's days when the story was bigger than the reporter.

Marg Stork, who still does a column for *The Journal*, was a gentle and dedicated soul responsible for the social pages and local news. She was a motherly counterpoint to the deliberately roughhouse approach of the men.

A couple of days a week I would visit Rowley Moody, a gifted sub-editor, for free tuition on journalism and life. Rowley, who had worked on *Truth*, had ruined his life and wrecked his career, thanks to alcohol.

Often he was drunk, but it didn't stop him from saying that, to get ahead in journalism, women should never drink and never swear. He modified the no-swearing bit to say that women should only ever swear in exceptional circumstances, so any foul language or point they were trying to make could be guaranteed to have maximum impact.

There were many times I wished I had listened to Rowley about drinking and swearing, but the other lessons stayed.

When people died, they were dead — they weren't allowed to pass away. Politicians could not get away with saying 'At this point in time', or 'At the present time'. They were ruses to get more space; 'Now' was more than enough. 'Prior to' also was an attempt to crib more air time or column inches; 'Before' was ample. If someone asked how you were, you had to say 'Well', not 'Good' — they were asking after your physical well-being, not your moral health. And people were hanged; pictures and paintings were hung.

It was always 'different from', not 'different to'; there was a difference between 'disinterested' (impartial) and 'uninterested' (not interested); 'may' was seeking permission and 'might' represented a possibility.

Everything a reader needed to know had to be in the first paragraph, using as few words as possible to answer the basic, implicit questions raised by any newsworthy event: *who* did it, *what* happened, *where* did it happen, *when* did it happen, and *why*. Rowley drummed into me the fact that the first paragraph might be the only one that made it into the paper.

Also, he taught me never to expect people to read beyond the first few paragraphs, and to write as if a nine-year-old was reading it, because that was the average mental age of most newspaper readers. And so on.

It was heaven for pedants, who nowadays should be declared an endangered species, given the complete bastardisation of the language — thanks to the failure by schools to teach grammar or spelling, the corrupting influence of television and now, sadly, the neglect of newspapers.

Cadets on city dailies complained that they were stuck with compiling the tides and the weather. On *The Journal* I got to try everything, including laying out the social pages, and met or interviewed everyone who mattered. Lots of famous people were either from Dandenong or came to visit it — everyone from John Farnham to Gough Whitlam.

The mayor held separate receptions for both Gough Whitlam and John Gorton when they came through to campaign for the federal election in 1969. I never joined, but I had been to a few meetings of Young Labor, which was being set up in the area by Rob Jolly. Partly because of this, and partly because I had started my cadetship on *The Journal*, I was invited to both cocktail parties, along with my fellow Young Labor friend and former school chum, David.

Gough came over to say a brief hello, greeting me with, 'Ah, the fourth estate!'

'Yes, but definitely not a fifth column,' I replied, still in my teens and, as ever, a smart alec.

Whitlam soon left, finding more interesting company, but Gorton spent almost the entire cocktail party talking to David and me. We decided later that, although Whitlam was awesome, Gorton was a much more likeable character. Still, it didn't stop David from ringing through a hoax bomb-threat to the town hall where Gorton was holding his rally.

Much as I loved *The Journal* and everyone on it, my ambition was to work on one of the city dailies. Thanks to what I later found out was a glowing reference from *The Journal's* managing editor, John Wood, I managed to land a job on *The Australian* in late 1970.

Rowley gave me a magnificent dictionary, which I took to work and placed on my new desk. Sadly, it disappeared in a matter of days. That was one lesson he didn't teach me and that I had to learn the hard way. Hugh gave me a couple of first-edition books; later, one was nicked from my house during a party, and the other was destroyed by fire.

I went from covering local councils to the royal commission into the West Gate Bridge disaster. The bridge had collapsed on 15 October 1970 while still under construction, killing 35 workers. The commission had attracted the biggest single collection of QCs and technical experts then seen in Melbourne.

The evidence on the box-girder-style bridge was highly technical, with debate about the suitability of the design and its construction at the centre of the inquiry to determine why the bridge had collapsed. The commission had begun well before I was told to cover it. I knew nothing about engineering, much less about bridge design, but luckily *The Australian* was only interested in the highlights, and I eventually got the hang of skating over the detail and sticking to the main points.

On the last day of the hearing, I dictated my story from a phone in the press room. The reporter from *The Age* was tapping away on a typewriter at exactly the same time. Next day, our stories bore an incredible similarity. It was kind of comforting to know that I was not alone in my ignorance, but it was one more lesson on journalistic behaviour. It's not always ethical.

As the youngest reporter, I also invariably got the celebrity round.

Jack Lord, the star of the top-rating show *Hawaii Five-O*, was in town. His bio from the PR people said he liked gardening, so I went to the hotel florist, which sported a large bowl of banksias. I bought one for him, thinking that an unusual specimen of Australian flora would arouse his interest.

He was an odd-looking fellow, short and slight, and a little effeminate — unlike his tough-guy TV persona — with very pale skin and incredibly black hair. No matter. Pleased with my ingenuity, I thought I was set for a nice little colour story and photograph on page three of *The Australian*, the slot usually reserved for those kind of things.

As I held out my banksia and asked him to pose for the photographer, he recoiled: 'I can't be photographed with that. It's too phallic.'

At first I couldn't understand what he said. Thanks to Frank and Des on *The Journal*, I knew what 'phallic' meant, but Lord pronounced it 'phay-lic', so I kept pushing the banksia at him.

'No, no. It's too phaylic.'

He looked so anxious that I thought he was going to run away. Finally I got the message, and stopped pointing it at him. We didn't get the pic, but I got a funny story, and the paper ran it with a cute cartoon of Snugglepot and Cuddlepie, and a caption which had the little bush characters wondering what to make of Lord's take on their habitat.

Things began to pick up. The Rolling Stones were in town,

and I was assigned to cover their one-and-only press conference at Montsalvat, the artists' retreat on the outskirts of Melbourne. Newspapers were running stories telling parents to lock up their daughters, as the Stones were heading to town. There was good reason for the warning.

But, as I was getting ready to drive out to Montsalvat, the Melbourne bureau chief, John Dunne, called me in to give me another assignment that had to take priority.

What could be bigger than the Rolling Stones? Who could be more important than Mick Jagger? Unless it was the Pope, who was also coming to Melbourne for the Eucharistic Congress. *It better be a one-on-one*, I thought to myself.

My heart sank when Dunne told me that I had to go and interview Dorrie Evans at the Southern Cross Hotel. Or, rather, the actress Pat McDonald, who played Dorrie Evans in *Number 96*, who was about to be rewarded with a Logie for best actress. It was television's night of nights and, as *TV Week* was part of the stable, *The Australian* had to give the awards a good run the next day. We knew who the recipients were, even before they were announced.

The magazine had already been printed, and *The Australian* had decided to give Pat, the soapie's resident snoop and, to my mind, the show's least likeable character, star billing.

I'm not sure why I'd been given the job. The blokes made a few bawdy remarks as they took off for home or round the corner to the pub. It was Friday evening, and almost everyone had disappeared. The copygirl, Mandy Wilson, left for Montsalvat while I went to the Southern Cross to interview Dorrie bloody Evans.

At Montsalvat, Mandy walked up to Charlie Watts to ask him if he was in town for the Eucharistic Congress, and he told her to get fucked. That could have been me!

The consolation prize was a bunch of tickets to the Stones concert. I went with my sister and a journalist friend, Adam Hankin, who was a dead spit for Rudolf Nureyev. Adam had left

The Australian and gone to *The Sun News-Pictorial*, where the editor welcomed him aboard by saying: 'You're not on a poofter intelligentsia rag now, you know.' Adam loved ballet; when he went to interview Nureyev, the Russian dancer himself remarked on their likeness, and they had their photo taken together.

Adam had Nureyev, and I had Dorrie bloody Evans.

Not even the concert appeased me. I remembered the Stones as specks on the stage. Christina said we were so close that she could see Mick's eye makeup.

The Australian's early glory days were, unfortunately, about to end. Rupert Murdoch tired of its editor, Adrian Deamer, and the paper's small 'l' liberal approach, and replaced him with Bruce Rothwell. Rothwell, in turn, instigated a purge. On a visit to Melbourne, Peter Smark told us that they were busily drawing up a list at head office in Sydney of which journalists to sack. Several in the Melbourne bureau would have to go.

'They're tossing a coin over you,' Smark told me. 'It's between you and Deb Garland.' Deb was a lovely older woman, very experienced, but highly strung and probably approaching the end of her career.

'They think you have talent, and if they sack you, you can always get another job.' In other words, they knew that if they sacked Deb it would be curtains on her reporting career.

What a cruel business it is. They sacked Deb.

A few months later, showing youthful insouciance, I asked for and got six months' leave of absence and went to Cyprus. I had wanted to go to England as well, but my father wouldn't hear of it. Andreas insisted — straight to Cyprus and straight back. Soon he would regret even that.

Andreas and Elpiniki had scraped together the money and gone the previous year. Andreas' parents had died years before; Elpiniki's were still alive, although her father, Nikolas Chimoni, had had a stroke, was bedridden, and couldn't talk. I wanted to see him before he died.

When they came back to Australia, Andreas swore he would never return to Cyprus. Nothing had changed; nothing would ever change. The villagers were still poor, the people who owned everything when he was there still owned everything, and he hated it.

They fired up their siblings, and several of them later emigrated.

Almost from the moment I arrived there, I loved it, and I didn't want to come back. My parents couldn't fathom it. They had done everything to get out of there. What could I be thinking?

Christina, who visited later, also loved it but, unlike me, never had any doubts about our parents' wisdom in leaving. She knew that if she had been born there, she would not have survived childhood. When she visited as an adult, she had to take a relative with matching blood-type to hospital with her to donate blood for her transfusions. There was no blood bank. Nothing was ever easy for her, but nothing ever stopped her from doing what she wanted.

On my first return visit, it was obvious that little had changed in the village. Electricity had been connected, so they had televisions and fridges. But there was no sewerage: the toilet was still a pit out in the yard, with a wooden or tin shed on top, and a piece of hessian slung across the front as the door. Snakes often found refuge inside.

Grandmother's house consisted of one room, with a concrete floor. Lizards and scorpions abounded, and snakes hid in the rock walls.

There were no showers and no bathrooms. Elpiniki had warned her mother that I would want to bathe every day, so every day my grandmother would boil a huge stockpot of water, then mix it in another pot with cold water until it was the right temperature. I would sit inside on a low stool by the front door with my soap and a tin can, lathering up and rinsing, and the water would run out onto the stoop. She would wait outside for me to finish, laughing with her passing neighbours about my obsession with washing myself every day.

In the village, I spent most of the time with my cousins and aunties, learning to shoot an air gun, watching them cook in the mud-brick ovens outside, or keeping them company, listening to their stories while they harvested. I realised why Elpiniki wanted to escape the farm work. Just sitting out in the 40-degree heat for a short time gave me migraines.

After sunset we walked between the villages, drinking in the smell of wild herbs.

In the little seaside town of Ktima lived my father's brother Pavlos, with his wife and three daughters. They were a minute's walk from the beach, and two minutes away from the old port where a sixteenth-century Venetian castle still stood guard against potential invaders. The church around the corner had a small, smooth marble post in the yard where they claimed the Apostle Paul had been tied and given his 40 lashes. Down the road they had discovered centuries-old Roman mosaics.

During the day, Uncle Pavlos worked at the local factory, where they made wine and brandy, and at night he waited on tables set under stars at a rustic taverna overlooking the ocean. The stage was a couple of posts with a thatched roof. There was a *bouzouki* player who sang as the men — and only the men — danced. We had siestas in the middle of the day, after we shopped and parried with the gypsies at the market wanting to tell our fortunes for a few coins, and then at night we went to the taverna.

Or during the day we would visit friends and family, drinking the muddy coffees with sweetly preserved baby walnuts, figs, or cherries.

One day we managed to visit, in their separate houses, eight sisters, each one of whom had made preserved apricots. The preserves were all delicious — even the one made by the hostess who kept looking at me and giggling because she thought I looked as if I could be the daughter of the president, Archbishop Makarios. When they weren't laughing at how I looked, they laughed at the way I spoke, as I confused my genders and trotted out my Gringlish. How embarrassment, as Effie would say.

It was breathtakingly beautiful, culturally rich, sunny, and simple. What was not to like?

Occasionally there was a bit of push and shove on the taverna dance floor between the right-wingers and left-wingers — those who longed for union with Greece and saw it as their only defence against Turkey, and those who wanted a separate Cyprus.

In my parents' youth, Greek and Turkish Cypriots lived in the same villages, but they were separated in the mid-1950s by the British, in a move that only bred resentment.

One day, my aunt Christina and I missed the bus into the nearby town of Polis. She wasn't worried; we would thumb a ride. A truck stopped and picked us up. My aunt was very quiet on the trip, and she told me later that our helpful driver had been Turkish. There was little contact between the races, but at the local level there was not much tension that I could see or feel.

My time on the island was drawing to a close when an acquaintance visited my uncle Pavlos with a proposition. A young man, quite wealthy, who worked at the titles office and had seen me around the town, had become besotted and wanted to marry me. Just like that. He looked decent enough, and at that stage I had no desire to return to Australia. So I said okay. Just like that.

There was one small detail, according to the man acting as the marriage broker: I could not go into the marriage with nothing, especially given the wealth of the prospective groom. My parents had to provide a house — the old dowry system was still thriving. Families with more than one daughter worked all their lives to amass enough money to arrange good marriages for them. Fields, mud-brick houses, a few trees, and a collection of animals were no longer enough. Love seldom entered the equation.

It had to be a modern house, cement rendered, with marble-tiled floors, running water and flushing toilets, and fully furnished.

I told him there was no way my parents could afford it. The broker insisted that I ring them anyway, so he could report back to my suitor.

My uncle and I went down to the local telephone exchange and called Andreas. They were shocked: of course, there was no way they could provide such a house, or anything like it. This was more confirmation for my father of how hopeless Cyprus was.

The broker did not take it well. 'I put this together, and I can pull it apart,' he warned. Next day, the marriage was off. *Them's the breaks*, I thought. I didn't really mind.

What I really minded, when I found out a few years later, was that he had 'pulled it apart' by telling the young man of my sister's illness, and warning him that any children would be born with the same complaint.

The broker himself later migrated to Australia. He had a lovely wife and good kids, but I never forgave him for his scummy behaviour, especially for the hurt he inflicted on my sister when she inevitably found out — not from me — what he had done.

My love affair with Cyprus continued a few years later after my childhood friend Natalie Philippou had married Andreas Alexiou, a lawyer from Paphos, and again after I frightened Bob Hawke into reversing a decision to halve the number of Australian police in the United Nations peacekeeping force there by reminding him — in print — of the number of Greeks in his electorate.

Cyprus' love affair with me fractured, though, after I went there with Paul Keating for the Commonwealth heads of government meeting in 1993. This time, it wasn't Keating's fault.

The Cyprus Broadcasting Corporation interviewed me about my return there, and in the course of it I said how disappointed I was that, when the Cypriot delegation had entered the conference room, the band had struck up the Greek national anthem. Why didn't Cyprus have its own national anthem?

There was a huge response to these remarks, most of it

unfavourable. A few of my cousins vowed never to speak to me again. Australia was still ruled by Britain (at least Cyprus had become a republic), and here was I lecturing them about their anthem! And what was wrong with the Greek national anthem anyway?

Back in Melbourne, life went on as before: Australian at work, Greek at home. I was still a general reporter, still the most junior, and often rostered to work the 5.00 p.m. to 1.00 a.m. shift, where my sole task was to ring the news editor in Sydney at midnight when *The Sun* and *The Age* appeared, to tell him what stories we had missed that day.

Then I got a break. David Jack, who had taken over as bureau chief, said that the paper needed someone with good shorthand to go to Canberra to cover Parliament. Gough Whitlam had been elected, and there was an immense workload. Was I interested in working there for a few months? Was I ever!

After the sex scandal at Doveton High, Andreas had stopped short of removing me from the school, and had insisted instead that I drop out of the professional classes and go into the all-girl commercial classes that taught shorthand and typing, so all the young ladies could become secretaries. In a way, then, this sudden career opportunity was his fault.

Andreas and Elpiniki were beside themselves. Absolutely not, under any circumstances, ever, was I going to leave home unmarried. As the oldest girl in our extended family, I was expected to set an example and to not humiliate my family.

By this time, my mother's sister, her brother, and father's brother had migrated to Australia with their families. Andreas had built a bungalow out the back to accommodate my uncles until they could get on their feet.

They were arriving and I was leaving? No way.

The fights were long and loud and extremely emotional. In his anger and desperation, Andreas threatened that if I left home, if people asked, he would say that I was not his daughter. It was a cutting piece of emotional blackmail. It hurt. I felt for them, and for Christina.

I went anyway. The freedom to pursue a career, to have a liberated social life, and to be on my own was intoxicating. For years thereafter, whenever I rang, they would ask when I was coming home. Although I couldn't bring myself to say it, the answer was never.

The separation did little or nothing to resolve my internal conflict. Years later, an American woman asked me what I felt I was in my heart of hearts — Australian or Cypriot?

Even though there is little of the old Cyprus left now, thanks to the influx of cheap tours from England and the Scandinavian countries, it is a state of mind and heart, not of place. I couldn't answer her question then, and I still can't.

Andreas had a favourite saying: cursed was the man who knew two countries. It sounds better in Greek, because it conveys the full meaning of the love of two homelands, and the relentless conflict of emotions and loyalty. As an adult I grew to understand exactly what he meant, and as an adult I also came to see it as a blessing, as well as a curse. It makes for a richer, if more complicated, existence — that's for sure.

CHAPTER FOUR

Too much fun

By February 1974, when I moved to Canberra to take up my new post, Gough Whitlam had been in power for 14 months, and Labor's winning election-slogan might as well have been: 'It's time to party like there's no tomorrow.'

The corridors of Old Parliament House, the ministers' offices, the non-members' bar, the Wellington Hotel, and the houses of the senior correspondents (provided at the most expensive addresses by their newspapers) rotated as venues for all-night carousing, drinking, and sex — if anybody could manage the latter, after all the alcohol.

Fridays were declared 'a Friday'. This usually meant a brief appearance in the office before a long lunch, and a brief appearance after lunch, before repairing to the Wello and then to dinner. If you were slow with either chopsticks or wit at the Lotus, the *Mirror's* Peter Barron ate your lunch and made you part of the menu.

On one memorable day a few years later — well, as memorable as it could be, given the circumstances — we set a record of 17-and-a-half hours for lunch. It started at the Bacchus Tavern, and continued on at Charlies.

During one election-campaign visit to Adelaide, a radio journalist nicknamed Sebastian Dangerfield (after the infamous character in J.P. Donleavy's *The Ginger Man*), boarded the press bus at five in the morning, reeking of alcohol and clinking when he moved. He had emptied all the bottles from the hotel mini-bar into his briefcase, so he could polish them off during the day.

If this sounds like there was never much work done, that was not the case.

There was lots of work. There was lots of everything. If there was a paradise for journalists and political junkies, Old Parliament House was it. That lifestyle, an endless cycle of work and play, continued on past the Whitlam years, and only began to abate after we moved to the new Parliament House in 1988. A combination of factors slowed us down — especially age and the ailments that go with it, and the new building's deliberately designed separations of MPs, the executive, and the media. Then a different breed of journalist appeared. They jogged, they hardly drank, and they insisted on a life outside the gallery. The non-members' bar in the new building was forced to close because of little or no patronage, and is now a child-minding centre. It's true that the new journos' extra-curricular activities were more restricted by tighter and more frequent deadlines, but in the main they were incredibly earnest. And just that little bit duller.

When I arrived in Canberra, the Press Gallery was mostly male, mostly middle class, and mostly Anglo-Saxon — all the things I was not. There were only three women working full-time in the gallery and two as sessionals, covering Parliament when it sat. The best of the young male journalists fought to get there to make their mark.

It was a combustible combination of ambition and testosterone. Growing up, I had been teased gently and cruelly about my ethnic origins; but, in the peculiar environment of politics and journalism, 'woman' plus 'wog' equalled 'exotic', and I became a bit of a target. Being conspicuous also made it easier to get stories.

Anything went.

Journalists who went to exotic locations with Gough came back with equally exotic stories. One had hired a mariachi band to serenade him and his companions in Mexico. Someone else had claimed back 'hire of bikes' (a crude euphemism) on expenses from his newspaper. Others had spent days in a daze in Jamaica after inhaling too much of the local weed.

In his drinking days, and before he found religion, Chris Forsyth walked end to end along a Mercedes from bonnet to boot. Forsyth offered me a job as the notorious, anonymous Whip on *Truth*, which I took up part time, with Laurie Oakes as co-author, for a few months.

One Sunday afternoon I had to ring a prominent Labor politician at home to ask him if it was true that he had punched a glamorous female reporter in the face at a party in Melbourne. He didn't deny it — he just threatened to sue if we ran the story.

Political correctness had not been invented, and male journos as well as Labor staffers were, deliberately or not, heavily into racist and sexist rhyming slang. I was a Werris (Werris Creek, Greek); others were forbys (four-by-two — you can guess the rest); and so on.

For a time they called me Ethniki, which was funny, and which they claimed had been coined by Gough, but I could never confirm this.

They kept calling the National Party MP Ralph Hunt, 'Mike's brother'. I wrote a gossip item about Hunt for a column Robert Drewe was then editing, and used his nickname. It got a run. I didn't have a clue what it meant, and just thought it was a bit of colour. When I finally made the connection I was mortified, especially as Ralph was such a courtly fellow.

On one occasion when I went down to interview Fred Chaney, he charged out of his office, picked me up, threw me over his shoulder — cave-man style — and carried me into his office. His press secretary, Keith Kessell, ran in after him, aghast at what he had done. I pressed on with the interview.

A while later, on an assignment when we cadged a lift in a car with some politicians, Michelle Grattan had to sit on Gareth Evans' lap, so I didn't feel so bad.

There was a water cooler near the press-gallery boxes. The water had a suspiciously yellow hue. My colleagues warned me never to drink from it, hinting that some of the men might have made deposits and not withdrawals. I followed their advice.

Gay Davidson was the first woman to head a political bureau. The *Canberra Times* office was diagonally opposite the gents, and when Gay didn't have enough time to run round to the ladies, which was some distance away, she popped in there. Gay was pretty fearless.

For a few years we ran the egg-beater award. Don Baker bought the kitchen gizmo from the supermarket, and it was presented every week to the author of the biggest beat-up. It was hotly contested.

We had a fridge that was stocked with beer and sold at a profit to everyone in the gallery. If Don ever found any milk in the fridge he would throw it out the window and into the courtyard, where it would land somewhere between the opposition leader's office and the non-members' bar. He called it throwing milk. You can't even open the windows in the 'new' building.

Mungo MacCallum wandered round the offices, incessantly dispensing advice with a beer in one hand and a cigarette in the other. I wondered how he managed to stay so thin with all the drinking he did. He reckoned it was because he threw up a lot.

The chief characteristic I shared with most of the journalists in the gallery was my politics: left of centre. The overwhelming majority of gallery journalists were Labor supporters. Not much has changed since. The Greens have peeled off some Labor sympathisers, but in the gallery itself conservatives are few, and often reluctant to out themselves. It can be a lonely place for anyone who functions outside the pack.

In the 1970s, the gallery was involved in a deep love affair with Gough. Richard Carleton confessed one night at dinner that he was not 'one of those who thinks the sun shines out of his arse'. If any others felt the same, they weren't game enough to say it.

On the day of the dismissal, 11 November 1975, I ran into Liberal Party staffer Vincent Woolcock at the press-gallery boxes. Reaching up, I grabbed him by his suit lapels and warned: 'You won't get away with this.' Years later, we married (after I conscripted my brother to help break the news to Andreas that I was going to marry a Pom who worked for the Liberals), and months later Malcolm Fraser scored the first of his landslide election victories.

The point was, no matter how much gallery journalists loved Gough, they couldn't save him. Well may we say 'God Save the Queen', because nothing could have saved that prime minister and his government from themselves.

THE GALLERY'S LOVE is never enough to save anybody. Good conservative politicians know this, or are taught by their staff to recognise it and to act accordingly. If they want to succeed, they have to pitch beyond the gallery.

John Howard learned this lesson well the second time around, largely thanks to his highly experienced and thick-skinned press secretary, Tony O'Leary. Howard paid due respect to the gallery, and wooed gallery journalists assiduously, as he had to; but if he wanted to send a message to the punters, he bypassed the gallery and went straight on to talk-back radio.

It didn't make the gallery irrelevant. It was just not pre-eminent.

The Libs had grown weary of its predictable news reporting and commentary. This generally ran along the lines that if, on a rare occasion, Labor displayed incompetence, it was nonetheless well-meaning; or that, if Labor was competent but had made cruel decisions or broken its promises, its actions were justified in the national interest. Alternatively, whatever the Libs did and whatever their motivations, they were just plain demonic.

Waning newspaper circulation and Howard's strategy effectively sidelined many correspondents and further reduced their influence. The correspondents hated it.

Already powerful, the radio talk-show hosts became compulsory listening for political writers and observers. Alan Jones was the most critical, the most exacting, and the most influential, especially in the key western suburbs of Sydney. You refused a request from Jones at your peril. But he was not the only one; Neil Mitchell in Melbourne was another. The broad and often contentious reach of the ABC could not be ignored, either.

Then there were the Sunday-morning TV talk shows. Each network had one, with Laurie Oakes leading the pack. Ministers would seed a story in the Sunday papers, drop the lot on the talk shows, and thereby set the agenda for the high-rating Sunday-night news. Major daily newspaper correspondents were left with the transcripts and follow-up. Every vacuum was filled.

Bypassing the gallery was refined as a deliberate strategy in prime minister Howard's office after the first two tumultuous years of his government, when ministers and staff were dropping like flies. This fulfilled three objectives: there was always a pool camera in on the interview to ensure that television had access to pictures as well as the words; the message was sent instantly and unfiltered to a target audience, usually of 200,000–300,000 viewers; and newspapers could work off the transcript of the interview.

The added bonus was that, well before the papers came out, the desired message had got through to millions.

Another technique was to feed a story to a selected newspaper — one that could be counted on to treat it in the right way — and then use radio in the morning to give it lift-off. The Internet, principally YouTube, swung into play later, but did not have the prominence it is destined to reach.

No one could ever accuse the prime minister of being inaccessible. Howard rarely knocked back an interview; he never hid when there was bad news; and he was well-briefed and well-disciplined. As were his media advisers: O'Leary, who remained with him until the end, along with David Luff and Ben Mitchell.

It worked a treat for a decade. There was always a message to deliver, the opposition was forced to respond, and Howard could skilfully handle the questions and stick to the message. He also relished the contests with the tougher interviewers.

But, like everything else, it reached a point where it stopped working. The messages ran out, even though the prime minister's addiction remained; the opposition, under a new leader who pretended to be a younger version of John Howard, wised up; and the media decided they had had more than enough of Howard, and started courting a new playmate.

It's not a contest for the faint hearted. Because the stakes are so high, there is no place for weaklings in politics and political journalism. It's a toss-up who is tougher, more devious, and more scarred — the reporters or their subjects.

Peggy Noonan, a former Reagan speechwriter, had a great take on political journalism. 'Modern political journalism is a protection racket,' she wrote. 'Robert Novak [a political columnist] once told one of his assistants: "In this town you're either a source — or a target." I always like his saying that because it was true. Talk or die.'

It's like that here. Charmers and bullies. Bribers and blackmailers. Blabbers and users.

First, a journalist will ask nicely; then, if that doesn't work, intimidation might. *Tell me what I want to know or I will get it from someone else;* or *If you don't give me your version, I'll print the one I've got* — which, of course, could be wrong or damaging to whoever is on the other end of the conversation.

If I rang a Labor backbencher seeking information and they told me they never gave briefings about caucus discussions or decisions, I never rang them again. And I never mentioned their name in a story either. Unless they had done something wrong, of course.

Generally, though, I couldn't believe how effortlessly politicians knifed each other, with the Libs invariably doing it better, and more often, than Labor did. Practice makes perfect, I guess.

Blabbers were pretty much guaranteed a run by everyone, everywhere, until they brought themselves undone. I would usually begin with a charm offensive to get what I wanted; if that didn't work, I would drop the charm bit. In my early days, I was told I was 'too nice' to be considered for a bureau chief's job: it was toughen up or get out. I learned to slice and dice anyone who deliberately fed out misleading information, or who spoke to others and not me.

It's not just print journalists who play rough. If politicians refuse to go on radio, shock-jocks write poisonous editorials and read them out on air, every day, until they get what they want. Television producers put an empty chair in the studio where the talent should be, and get the hosts to bag the hell out of them in their absence.

The politicians can tell the journalists to get stuffed, or comply, or go to the competition. They have to be careful, though. Camaraderie among journalists evaporates in the hunt for stories. No one likes getting scooped. No one likes getting a call at midnight from the editor, asking why they have missed a story.

Laurie Oakes' scoop in July 2002 on Cheryl Kernot's affair with Gareth Evans caused deep ructions in the gallery, as reporters took sides. Glenn Milne and Alan Ramsey were two who took Laurie to task.

They were wrong. No matter which way you look at it, the Kernot–Evans affair was a legitimate story.

This doesn't mean that all accounts of sexual peccadilloes are newsworthy. Once, a chief of staff to a cabinet minister, while seated next to me on a plane, proceeded to tell me, unprompted, about his minister's affairs. According to the staffer, it didn't affect his boss's marriage, because his wife was having them, too.

This staffer's minister had boasted to his mates that he loved being in government because power secured a better class of fuck.

I thought this was interesting, but it didn't rate as news.

However, if the leader of one party has an affair with the leader of another party, and then defects to that party, that is a story in anybody's language. And the affair is an integral part of the story. What's there to debate?

Milne hated being scooped by Oakes, and Ramsey was influenced by his affection for Cheryl (which, incidentally, had been ignited at a pre-Christmas lunch at our house more than a decade before), even though he and Oakes had been mates for almost 30 years.

Many journalists had known about the affair between Cheryl and Gareth, and had chosen not to reveal it — because they considered it irrelevant, or they were fond of the participants, or (and this would be the only legitimate reason for their failure to report that particular liaison) they didn't have enough evidence to prove it.

The rule that details of affairs were only to be published if they interfered with the politicians' day jobs has been applied flexibly for some time now, and has been ignored when it suits. It has always depended on who was with whom, where, when, and why. And its relevance usually derives from who wants to bring whom undone — whether it's media bloodlust in a hunt to get the politician, or the politicians' own colleagues blabbing to journos as payback.

Journalists and editors wave around one tiny figleaf or another to justify publication. Rival outlets tut-tut furiously when they get scooped, and in the process air all the salacious details. The time has come for everyone to stop pretending, admit that they love these kinds of stories, and acknowledge that they will use any excuse to publish, no matter how flimsy. That way, everybody knows the rules — there are none — and can behave accordingly. The handwringing doesn't fool anybody.

In spite of the legitimacy of the Kernot–Evans affair as a news story, the way journalists lined up either for Oakes or against him gave an insight into the power-plays in the gallery: it showed that they are just as intense and just as deadly as any in the backrooms of the major parties. Politicians and staffers who ignore them have to be prepared to pay a price.

Just as journalists use politicians to get what they want, politicians have to work out which journalist to use, how, and when — and whom they can afford to offend in the process. They have to walk a minefield and be prepared to cop the explosions. Or the revenge.

Try as they might to pretend otherwise, federal politicians are enthralled by the gallery. They mainline political news and commentary, and because gallery journalists write more about them than anybody else, it doesn't take much to get the politicians hooked.

A few make the mistake of thinking that if the gallery treats them kindly, good fortune will follow. Likewise, if the gallery hunts them like a pack of wild dogs, they fear they are doomed.

It's true up to a point. And it was certainly truer a decade ago than that it is now, thanks to the growing power of the media outside Canberra.

The gallery can still set the pace for others to follow. Senior members of the gallery can help build or destroy careers. They make judgements about who is good or bad, and report accordingly. Invariably, the benefit of the doubt goes to those on the left rather than the right.

How else could you explain Mark Latham's ascension? Latham self-destructed; he was not pushed into political suicide by the gallery.

Eventually, voters saw through him — as they inevitably would — despite even a respectable journalist like Paul Kelly once describing him as a 'populist genius' (*The Australian*, 4 September 2004).

Latham, a much better political writer than a political performer, was a ticking time-bomb, and everybody knew it. Few gallery journalists could bring themselves to write it, though. For some, he was a weapon with which to beat up on Howard; for others, a fascinating political study.

The Latham saga says much about the relationship between politicians and political writers. It is symbiotic, parasitic, narcissistic, and toxic.

The trick for journalists is to get close enough to their subjects to extract information from them, yet not so close that they cover up or overlook their flaws, or forget which side they're on. They will go a long way to protect their sources — or those they 'love' — but, eventually, if they are doing their job properly, they have to give them up.

Politicians have to exercise eternal vigilance. A friendly journalist is not necessarily a friend. As US president Harry Truman said: 'If you want a friend in Washington, get a dog.'

Substitute Canberra for Washington. There are alliances, there are dalliances, there are affairs, there are marriages of convenience. There are very few friends in politics.

That is as it should be. A good journalist's prime objective should be to get the story, get it first, and get it right (although that seems to be waning), without being swayed by likes or dislikes.

Of course, it's a lot easier to do someone in if you don't like them or don't like what they stand for. After the 1977 election, when Malcolm Fraser announced that he was going to make Glen Sheil his minister for veterans' affairs, I was told to interview this bloke, whom no one had ever heard of.

With a sinking heart, I asked our telex operator-cum-librarian for the file on Sheil. There were two yellowing clips in a tatty folder: one reported Sheil's support for apartheid, which I found repugnant; the other, that he had proposed a rabbit-breeding scheme to feed African tribespeople.

Hallelujah! What had seemed like a story destined to run as a brief suddenly had potential. I knew that, if I handled it the right way, I could cause a fair amount of grief for the little-known senator.

In my best saccharin-sweet voice, I got Senator Sheil on the phone and congratulated him profusely on his appointment, wishing him well and saying that he must be very excited about the challenges ahead. Yes, he said, he was. Then I asked him three questions.

Did he still support apartheid in South Africa? Yes, he did.

Did he think it would be a good idea for Australia to adopt a similar system with Aboriginals? Yes, he did.

Did he still think breeding rabbits was the answer to famine among the Bantus? Yes, he did.

Glen Sheil became the only minister to be appointed but never sworn in. He had hanged himself in three short sentences.

Malcolm Fraser dumped him, and for a long time afterwards new ministerial appointees were counselled against interviews until they were across their brief and had a clear idea of what they wanted to say. Or not.

Labor is much more ruthless in its dealings with the few journalists deemed to be unfriendly. Or even with its own when they fall out of favour.

For example, when Malcolm Fraser's former press secretary David Barnett was given a job in the Canberra bureau of Sydney's *Daily Telegraph* after Bob Hawke was elected prime minister, the NSW Right went ballistic, and exerted pressure on the paper's Sydney executives to drop him. Every newly employed journalist is on three months' probation, so it was no surprise when David found himself without a job at the end of that period.

There was no outcry over this incident. Even now, former Labor prime ministerial press secretaries or ministerial advisers are able to slide into high-profile media jobs, seemingly at will. There is a two-way street between Labor governments and television, radio, or newspaper offices. This is not necessarily a bad thing, so long as there is room across the spectrum for talented people.

But there isn't. People who have worked for conservative politicians find that there are either few media jobs available — the conservative quota has been filled — or they are told that they have to wait out a 'cleansing' period first.

Greg Turnbull, who had also worked for Paul Keating, finished up as Kim Beazley's press secretary, and a few weeks later turned up as political correspondent on Network Ten. There were grumbles in the Howard government, but to my knowledge no one complained to head office about his appointment or sought to have him removed. No one would have dared.

When Turnbull left, Ten replaced him with Stephen Spencer, who had been Simon Crean's press secretary.

The rare exceptions, like David Turnbull, who was taken on by Nine after he left Peter Reith, only serve to prove the rule. Coincidentally, Turnbull was deemed surplus to requirements not long after the election of Rudd Labor.

KNEECAPPING IS A LABOR RIGHT SPECIALTY, and Graham Richardson revelled in his reputation as an enforcer for the NSW Right during Bob Hawke's prime ministership. So, when I reported in *The Australian* that he had stood for the chairmanship of a caucus sub-committee and had failed to get elected, he wasn't impressed.

Richo especially did not think my gags were funny. They were of the 'PM's numbers man down for the count' variety, which made him look weak and inept instead of strong and scary.

He rang to tell me I was either stupid or a dupe of the Left; by the time our conversation finished, he decided I was both. Strangely enough, I never took kindly to people ringing me up to abuse me, and wondered aloud to my mates if I was going to get a visit from Tommy Domican.

My remarks were reported back. Richo first tried to put the skids under me at head office in Sydney. Fortunately, I was in good favour in those days, and he didn't get very far, so he put me on a black list and instructed his right-wing factional colleagues not to talk to me.

Labor's good at running black lists, too — not just against journalists, but lobby groups and business people who stray too far from an acceptable line.

Later, as a press secretary, I couldn't have got away with a black list even if I'd wanted to. There were times I wanted to, but trying to get Liberal politicians to stop talking to journalists — even ones you knew were trying to do them in — was impossible.

There are politicians who don't have to be bullied or charmed to blab. They just blab.

Blabbers and users.

They will talk to journalists because they think the journalists are well-disposed to them; or they want to buy them off by trading one good story for one bad story; or they want to advance their own career by damaging either an opponent or a colleague; or they just want to get their name in lights. Or everything at once.

The really wily ones bypass journalists completely and go straight to the editor. Or the owner.

In 1985, the Labor government was being torn apart by the MX missile crisis after the prime minister, Bob Hawke, had agreed to help the United States monitor MX intercontinental ballistic-missile tests.

The party's Left did a passable simulation of an MX, and Hawke was forced to back down, triggering a massive nosedive in the value of the dollar.

In the story of who stood where, I reported that the treasurer, Paul Keating, had told Hawke to hold firm and not give in to the Left.

After I filed, the editor, Les Hollings, rang to say he was intrigued to see this fact in my story because he had been told by 'someone' that Keating had told that someone that he had told Hawke not to back down. I was working with Kelly at the time, and we figured from what Hollings had said that Keating had rung Rupert Murdoch and told him what he had told Hawke. Keating always made sure he kept Rupert on side.

Rupert always knew more about what was going on than any of his reporters did. Just before the 1990 recession we had to have was revealed in all its gory glory, Murdoch hosted a cocktail party at his sprawling Canberra residence for all the most senior politicians and his correspondents.

Rupert invited the journos to stay on and, as we stood in a semi-circle around him, he rattled off a few questions. Laura Tingle was then *The Australian's* economics correspondent, and Rupert asked her what she thought would happen to the economy. Laura volunteered that it was going to be a soft landing, that the economy would skip along the bottom a bit, and then pick up pretty quickly.

Rupert bet her it would not be soft, that the economy was in effect heading for a crash landing, and — if my memory is right — predicted that unemployment would hit double digits. Rupert won that one, too.

Occasionally, it's not a case of talk or die, but talk and die. Motormouth politicians can talk themselves all the way to oblivion. Stick a microphone under their noses, or a camera in front of them, and it's like a fakir with a flute. They begin swaying to that music, get carried away by the rhythm of it, and just keep going. And if they get into trouble, they think they can fix it with just one more interview.

I told Peter Reith once that sometimes it was best to quit while you were ahead and not to agree to every interview request. He looked at me as if I was speaking Greek.

As a journalist, I had written that the most dangerous place to be was between Reith and a camera, so it was predestined that when he got into trouble with Telecard, he would talk himself all the way out of politics.

Journalists do whatever they can to keep politicians talking, including plying them with expensive meals and drink. Once I got the hang of it, I never left a table with a politician without getting a story. And most of them knew that their supper came at a price. Malcolm Fraser got it right when he said there was no such thing as a free lunch.

I refined my techniques by observing Laurie Oakes. Years before, I'd expressed my displeasure to him when, as a junior in the *Sun-Pic* office, I'd watched him turning his considerable charm on a particularly unsavoury character.

Laurie can be terrifying — as scores of other journalists, staffers, or politicians quickly learn — if he is crossed. But he's a charmer, too, and this time he was like a Venus flytrap drawing in its prey.

'How can you even bear to talk to him?' I asked.

Laurie was unapologetic: 'I would talk to the devil himself to get a story.'

The combination of Old Parliament House and a government that was out of control made life especially easy for journalists. The politicians, and their staff, couldn't escape, even if they wanted to — and most of them didn't want to.

Sooner, rather than later, you would come across someone who would tell you something. It was always for a reason, of course, even if you couldn't tell straight away what that might be.

Oakes, who got more than his fair share of scoops, remembers he had heard whispers in 1973 that Labor was considering cutting tariffs. He asked a Labor staffer, who told him to hang on a bit. The staffer went away, came back a few minutes later, and stood at Laurie's office door. He didn't say a word, just held up both hands twice, and one hand once — twenty-five. Labor had decided to cut tariffs by 25 per cent.

In the middle of the constitutional crisis in 1975, after Malcolm Fraser had blocked the budget, Clyde Cameron rang to tell me that he and other senior ministers had been to see Gough. They had told Gough not to buckle to Fraser and call an election, but to hold out.

Paul Kelly and I shared a broom cupboard, so I told him what had happened. Kelly rang down to Whitlam's office, and his senior adviser Michael Delaney charged upstairs lickety-split. Delaney didn't exactly deny the story, but pooh-poohed it enough to make us hold off. Next day, Brian Toohey had it all over the front of *The Australian Financial Review*.

Clyde wanted the story out to make sure that Gough was locked in, and of course to highlight his own influence.

Then there was John Wheeldon. A left-winger, he was the minister for repatriation and compensation, and fancied himself as the intellectual powerhouse of the Whitlam government. He was intelligent and highly amusing, and extremely ambitious, and had dinner with people as fascinating as Gore Vidal and Princess Margaret. He invited me out for dinner a few times, so I went.

My only interest was getting stories, and I was doing pretty well, thanks partly to him and partly to his new chief of staff, a charismatic Indian Fijian called Jim Anthony, and a few other blabbers as well. The Whitlam government was full of them. And I say that affectionately.

Wheeldon had other motives, as I soon discovered. One Sunday in February 1975, walking through Kings Hall, I came across Jim. He showed me a note that had come out of the cabinet room. It had one line scrawled on it: 'Lionel Murphy to the High Court.'

Mimicking the old attendant with the handlebar moustache who would waltz around the empty hall late at night, I pirouetted on the polished floorboards, thanked Jim, and raced back up to the office.

Mike Steketee was the senior correspondent that day, so I told him, and he began working on the story. Whitlam was forced to announce it by the end of the day, but the few hours' break was invaluable to us.

A couple of days later, while driving to Melbourne, I ran off the road on the Hume Highway at Tarcutta and totalled my car. After I threw up from the shock of it all, the nurses at Wagga Wagga base hospital wanted to know what I had been eating. The answer was, Doris Cameron's home-grown peaches, specially brought over by Clyde to thank me for some flowers I had sent him.

The police had found a hypodermic syringe in my car and, not surprisingly, wanted to know what it was doing there. Peter Gurrie, who worked for the health minister, had got it for me. I had volunteered to take oranges to the press-gallery cricket matches, and I was going to inject them with vodka as a prank. Oh, God. Just silly, officer — not high.

Two weeks later, punctured lung and broken ribs repaired, I went back to work and visited Wheeldon in his office. He was pleased to see me. That was nice. No, he was very pleased to see me. Uh-oh.

Extremely pleased in fact, because he had been worried, he said, that I was going to die before he had succeeded in seducing me. This was ridiculous. He flung his arms across his door to prevent me leaving. It was so ridiculous that all I could do was laugh at him. He put his arms down and let me leave.

The time had come to scrub him as a source.

Soon after, Jim approached me to write a story about Wheeldon. Jim was getting increasingly frustrated with him because he wasn't concentrating on his ministerial duties. Jim wanted to give him a prod. I wrote a story quoting unnamed sources concerned about the rising pile of correspondence that Wheeldon was neglecting.

It had little or no effect. In mid-July 1975, Jim was scheduled to speak at the annual meeting of the Australasian Political Science Association at the Australian National University. He was determined to give Wheeldon an even bigger touch-up, and drove me with him to the conference so I could report his remarks.

That night, Jim invited me and a couple of other friends to his house for dinner. He was making pancakes and he wanted to see the story I'd filed, so I showed him. It quoted Jim's speech to the seminar, in which he'd said that Wheeldon spent 95 per cent of his time in Perth, his home state, looking after party-political matters, and only 5 per cent of his time administering his two departments.

Jim's tenure was already under threat. He went ashen and realised he had gone too far, but it was too late. The story was on the front page of *The Australian* next morning, and he was sacked immediately. This was another nail in Whitlam's coffin and, as was so often the case back then, it was hammered in by one of his own.

After he left Australia, Jim corresponded with a mutual friend, and wrote asking if I was still crawling over bodies to get to the top. If only I was that focused.

I had now burned two excellent contacts in a short space of time. Barry Cohen said that he admired what I'd done, even though it had damaged Wheeldon, who was a friend of his, and someone he thought was a friend of mine. I doubt he would have felt the same way if it had been him.

The last thing on my mind was what consequences might flow from that story. Every now and again in later years, I would pause to wonder what impact damaging stories might have on peoples' lives and careers; but I knew that, if I thought too long about it, there was the danger I would freeze and talk myself out of writing it, or I would write it softer than I should. I thought then, and still do, that it's best not to overanalyse and to just get the job done.

In any case, often there is little time to think of consequences (even less so now, with the pressure to supply news online), much less to agonise about how to write a story or what it means. The pace is so fast and the deadlines so relentless that there is not much time to reflect.

That's how it was with Mick Young, too. Mick was another of those engaging characters who was treated kindly by most journalists, including me. He was the one who had told me about Keating's position on the MX missiles. Unfortunately, Mick got into trouble once too often. None of us could save him, even if we had wanted to.

His handling of a donation to Labor from a woodchip company

came under scrutiny. It was about the third time Mick had got himself into serious strife. Along with three other journalists, I took him to task for his latest imbroglio. He desperately wanted to be Bob Hawke's deputy, but since the deputy's job was to keep the boss out of trouble — not create it — the four of us, all senior reporters from separate publications, declared him unsuitable for the job. When a badly wounded Mick announced that he was resigning from the ministry and leaving the Parliament, too, Hawke's office spun the story that a 'gang of four', including me, had been responsible for destroying Mick's career and driving him out of politics.

Occasionally, after this, I would see Mick around, but he never spoke to me again. When we passed in the corridors of the new building — which was a rarity — he would pretend that he couldn't see me, even if it was just the two of us.

I felt sorry for Mick, sorry that his career had ended this way, and sorry that he held me partly responsible. Although I stand by what I wrote at the time, I might have been tempted to pull my punches if I could have foreseen the outcome, simply because a parliament with Mick Young in it was better than a parliament without him. But, like I said, it is not always feasible, or sensible, to allow the possible consequences of publication to influence the reporting of an event.

Mick's disasters were self-inflicted — they were not brought about by me or other journalists, and we would not have been doing our jobs if we had overlooked them. Politicians walk tightropes without safety nets every day, and he fell off once too often. His bright personality, with its attendant risky behaviour, made him interesting and attractive, but it also helped to bring about his downfall.

We moved to the new Parliament House a few months after Mick's demise. If we had still been in the old building —where people were thrown together more often, either in the non-members' bar or elsewhere — there might have been an opportunity to have it out during one of his visits. He could have yelled and cursed at me, and maybe felt better as a result of getting it off his chest. Who knows? I would have told him that he'd been a silly bugger and would have apologised for the way that things had turned out — although not for what I had written.

In the old building, Mick would often sit in his office with the door open and, if I walked past and saw him, I would wander in for a chat and a joke. It was the same with other ministers.

The vast, impersonal new building, with corridors more clinical and more forbidding than those in modern psychiatric wards, put up many barriers between the inhabitants. Opportunities for spontaneous meetings would be few and far between.

The magic of the old building lay in its intimacy. Not only did journalists get to know the politicians, but the politicians got to know one another, too — even if they were from opposing sides. Familiarity might breed contempt, but it can also build affection and respect where it is deserved.

When we moved out in 1988, we knew it would never be the same, or as good. And it never was.

CHAPTER FIVE

The good, the bad, and the ugly

Paul Keating has polarised Australians for more than three decades: he has either been hugely admired or deeply loathed. And he has never been reluctant to tell you — good or bad — how he feels about you, too.

My relationship with him, like the rest of the country's, can best be described as love/hate/love/hate. When it was love, he called me 'luv' or 'darling', and when it was hate I was a 'tightarse', 'venal', or 'a Tory bitch'. Eventually, it went the same way as Mick, and I became a non-person.

One Friday in September 1990, I had arranged to visit the administrative services minister, Nick Bolkus, in his office, in the forlorn hope that he might give me something for my Saturday column. Labor was being ripped apart by the debate on privatisation. I had known Nick from his days as a humble staffer, and our shared Greek heritage had created a bond, but the bugger hardly ever leaked me anything worthwhile, so I had little hope it would be different this day.

We had just finished the pleasantries when the door to his office swung open and in walked another good mate and Nick's left-wing factional ally, the immigration minister, Gerry Hand. 'Are you telling her what happened last night?' Gerry asked.

And before Nick could say no, he wasn't, Gerry launched into his version of the drama that had engulfed the previous night's cabinet meeting as they struggled to reach agreement on the privatisation of the airlines and Telecom.

It was sensational. Keating, pitted against Kim Beazley, had lost his temper, thrown his pencil down on the cabinet table, sworn at them as only Keating could, told them he was 'fed up' and that they were hopeless, and stalked out of the room. As he was leaving, Robert Ray yelled at him: 'Go on, have a dummy spit.'

I knew if I started ringing around on this cabinet story, the people I spoke to would find a way to spike it or spite me. This had happened before. It was a standard operating technique for minders to wreck a damaging story or punish a journalist they didn't like: they would put out an alternative version, or brief a whole new scoop to a competitor.

The trick was (and still is) to ring the main players late enough so they couldn't alert anyone else, but not too late for them to say they weren't given a chance to respond, even though it really was.

Newspapers are put to bed early on Fridays because the Saturday editions are so big, so I waited almost until lock-up time and then rang Mark Ryan, Keating's press secretary. Ryan sprinted up to my office.

'So this story is being spread around, is it?'

'Hope not.'

That was it. The story, 'Paul Lets Fly', ran all over the front page of the biggest-selling daily newspaper in the country. The episode exposed deep fissures in the government. Keating had little respect for Beazley and he loathed Ray, whom he described privately as 'the Fat Indian'.

But Ray was every bit as tough as Keating. Back in the mid-1980s, while Bill Hayden was still foreign minister, Bill had called me to say he had just spoken with two of his Centre Left factional colleagues, Rosemary Crowley and Peter Cook. They had been in a meeting with Ray, who had relayed to them rumours that Bill was leaking stories to me because we were having an affair.

Trying to make light of it, Bill said he had told his wife, Dallas, what Crowley and Cook had told him, and had assured her it was untrue because, apart from anything else, I was too old for him!

Glenn Milne had already told me that Bill was being blamed by his colleagues for leaking to me. I told Glenn that it didn't happen as often as they thought or as much as I would have liked.

This was an especially hurtful accusation, however, because of what it implied about me as a journalist: first, that I had only one source; and, second, that I had him as a source because I had had him, so to speak.

Steeling myself, I called Ray.

'Have you been telling people that Bill Hayden is leaking stories to me because he and I are having an affair?' I asked.

He denied it. 'No, it wasn't me who made the accusations', he said. 'I simply told them that this was a rumour going around. I think it came out of the ABC.'

'Well, I'm glad to hear it wasn't you, because if I find out who it is, I'll slap a writ on them so fast it will make their head spin.'

Ray, more Machiavellian than the original, told Bill later that he had relayed the rumour to Crowley and Cook to see how long it would take them to report it. And presumably how long it would take Bill to tell me.

Ray and I got along okay after that, but it wasn't what you would call a close working relationship.

Keating and I were in our 'love' phase in April 1989 when I flew with him to Queensland on a VIP jet so I could do an extended colour piece on 'Keating the man'. We went to an art gallery, had a private meeting with the premier, Wayne Goss, and then attended a lunch. On the flight there and back we chatted, and I asked him about his image.

His enemies in the party were saying that the punters hated him — that he was out of touch and too verbally violent. I referred to the problems that his style was creating, and mentioned that his Labor colleagues were now talking about lining up Simon Crean or Kim Beazley to supplant him as Hawke's heir-apparent.

'Simon couldn't lead a horse to water, and as for Kim …' He dismissed them with a wave of his hand.

Keating was brilliant at characterising other peoples' flaws, but what about his own shortcomings?

'Don't worry about that, love. I can just flick the switch and go to vaudeville.'

That line has since become part of the political lexicon, because anyone who watched old Hollywood movies — and Keating, who was mad about Fred Astaire, had watched them all — knew exactly what he meant.

Keating loved the resulting article. He came up to my office to see me, but I was out, so he scrawled on the back of an old press release: 'Thank you darling X X X PJK.'

Keating also loved the giant cartoons of him that *The Sun* ran on the front page on budget days. In May 1987, after his Banana Republic pronouncement, we drew him as the Grim Reaper. In May 1988, I suggested we do him as Scrooge, taking a punt that there would be not much in the way of giveaways that year. He came into our office just as the fax of the front page was rolling off the machine, so he wanted to see it. Holding my breath, I showed him. He grinned and then signed it: 'You bet Paul Keating $$$.'

'They want to know there's someone here looking after their money,' he said.

After another budget, Keating felt obliged to explain to me the importance of a family-benefit initiative that it contained. 'It's a pro-fucking measure', he said. 'You know, we Catholics, we just love fucking.' It wasn't your usual post-budget sales technique.

As always, the love phase was destined not to last. As Keating's relationship with Hawke deteriorated, so did mine with Keating, even though I believed that Hawke should have left the leadership and handed over to him. I did not then — before the recession, that is — believe that Keating was the electoral poison many thought him to be.

I wrote a piece about Keating and Hawke being locked in a loveless marriage, predicting that Hawke would never willingly move to make way for Keating, because he thought that Keating was unelectable.

It's a familiar refrain, but that's what happens. Leaders of all political colours always manage to convince themselves that, no matter how badly they are travelling, they will always do better than the bloke trying to knock them off.

Keating was outraged, and called the article venal.

I was not saying what I thought should happen. I thought I was stating the bleeding obvious; and Rupert, who was in town for the birth of the newly created *Herald Sun*, thought it was so boring that he wondered why it was in the paper at all. So I managed to please nobody. In fact, it had appeared because it was the first edition of the new paper, and the editor had insisted I had to have a piece in it. See, it's not always a conspiracy.

They sat Keating and me next to one another at the Press Gallery's annual end-of-year dinner that year, just before I left to take up a posting in Washington as News Ltd's correspondent, so we could make up. These dinners were supposed to be off the record — which was a huge joke, given that any time anything was said that was worth reporting, it got reported.

This was the night that Keating gave his Placido Domingo speech, making his pitch for the Labor leadership. We talked a bit during dinner about his favourite television shows, like *The Honeymooners* (how sweet it is, or was), but he was clearly unhappy. He was a bit 'miz', he said. One of his friends in Treasury, Chris Higgins, aged only 47, had collapsed and died the day before, and Keating was deeply affected by it. That's what his speech was really all about. He was worried he would run out of time.

The good, the bad, and the ugly

Before the night was over, reporters at the dinner had briefed his speech to the Sunday papers or to colleagues who were not there so they could write it. This was exactly what Keating wanted.

Even two years later, when I came back from my stint in Washington, Keating was still not pleased to see me. I had been brought back in time to cover the 1993 election, which Keating managed to win. Keating was bitter about the media's treatment of him during the campaign, and always believed that he had won despite the best efforts of journalists, including me, to tip him out. That wasn't true. I thought John Hewson was a zealot and deserved to lose. Afterwards, even Robert Ray described my coverage as reasonable, or at least not as bad as some of the others.

Nevertheless, Keating figured he didn't owe anybody anything, not even the voters, and behaved accordingly. Big mistake.

Prime minister Keating attended the Seattle meeting of APEC in November 1993. The meeting went well enough, and the next day Keating was scheduled to visit the Boeing aircraft factory.

It was a cold day, and we journalists were first ushered inside the building and then quickly ushered out again, even though there were snow flurries.

With our noses pressed up against the windows like so many Orphan Annies, we could see trolleys of pastries and hot coffee wheeled past for the dignitaries. We were kept outside in the freezing cold, and offered nothing.

When we finally made it in, we followed Keating around for a bit, then assembled under the wing of a jet for a press conference.

Paul Bongiorno asked Keating his thoughts on the absence of the Malaysian prime minister, the prickly Dr Mahathir, who had boycotted the meeting. Keating first dismissed the question; then, when Bongiorno put it to him again, pleaded with him not to ask him questions about Dr Mahathir, protesting that he 'couldn't care less' whether Dr Mahathir came or not.

'APEC is bigger than all of us — Australia, the US, and Malaysia, and Dr Mahathir and any other recalcitrants,' he added.

With the press conference over, we got back on the press bus for the ride into the city. *The Herald Sun* had an afternoon edition in those days, and I knew if I waited until we got back to the hotel I would miss the deadline, and would be beaten to the story by the television news. None of us had mobile phones then. There was a phone beside the bus driver, and after getting his permission I dialled up the news desk in Melbourne.

I filed the old-fashioned way, dictating off the top of my head, to a copytaker, saying that Keating had slammed Mahathir, calling him a recalcitrant, and I added some flourishes about this being a blow to relations between the two countries. It ran on the front page with banner headlines: 'PM HITS OUT AT MALAYSIA'.

Everyone on the bus heard the story, including the girl from Keating's press office assigned to look after us, who obviously reported back the proceedings.

Mick Millett, then on *The Sydney Morning Herald*, told me that the Keating office blamed me for the ensuing ruckus because the other journos felt obliged to follow the line I had dictated over the phone.

Mick, a first-class reporter, was a bit miffed by the insinuation. Neither he, nor Oakes, nor the others on that trip needed me to point them in the direction of a good yarn. By then, I was well on the way to becoming public enemy number one.

When Alexander Downer became opposition leader, Keating waged class war against him, so I wrote a piece pointing out this was a tad hypocritical from the man who pretended to be Collingwood's number-one fan but who never knew when they were playing, and had once bragged about beating the Queen in a game to guess the maker and date of a piece of antique silver.

It tipped Keating over the edge. On radio the next day, he denied the silver story, and claimed that I was an apologist for the Liberal Party: 'Niki's husband is a key member of the Liberal Party, so Niki writes what comes from the federal secretariat or her husband.'

The guts of the story on the silver-dating contest had actually come from Keating himself, boasting about it to journalists. However, I concede I was wrong in saying it was the Queen. I think it was Princess Di.

The fact was, my scribblings caused my husband a lot of grief in the Liberal Party, and Keating's outburst prompted a *Bulletin* column from Oakes on 7 June 1994, defending me and pointing out that I was every bit as tough in my reporting on the Liberals as I was on the government.

'There has been no love lost between Savva and a series of Liberal leaders,' Oakes wrote, and he criticised Keating, who by then was calling me 'the Tory bitch'.

For a time, he called Laura Tingle the 'fat-arsed bitch', but she and Keating soon made up. Laura never could resist his charms.

Keating and I never made up. For me, his charms grew ever more resistible, especially when the recession we had to have put a million people out of work, and Labor started selling off assets like Qantas and the Commonwealth Bank, after ranting for years about the Liberals' evil privatisation policies.

At almost every press conference that Keating held when interest rates went up, I would ask him what would happen to jobs as a result. He would assure us that everything was under control, and would insist that they knew what they were doing.

My stronger leftie sentiments, and my confidence in Keating, began disappearing at the same time the jobs did. When *The Sun* had drawn him as the Grim Reaper for its May 1987 budget front page, the news editors had already decided on the headline to go with it, which had Keating as not only grim but cruel as well. I thought this was way too harsh, and talked them into changing the headline to 'Grim but Fair', believing the pain was being spread around and that Keating was trying to do the right thing. In those first few years of the Hawke government, there is no doubt that most us were in the

Keating cart, and our reporting reflected it.

When the economy started to improve, Keating couldn't work out why people were not suitably grateful. During an interview with John Laws, where he had first berated TV crews trying to film the interview, he turned on the punters: 'I mean, what are people going on about?'

In a comment piece on that performance, I quoted the crews' private nickname for him: Captain Cranky. The ALP's national secretary, Gary Gray, liked it so much that he pinched it and turned it into Captain Wacky. Their relationship was poisonous.

It came as no surprise recently when a friend, former NSW cop Grahame Mackenzie, who had gone to school with Keating, said he had beaten him up in the playground. A nun caught Grahame and gave him a clip over the ear, but when he told her he had punched Keating because he had ripped out another boy's hearing aid and thrown it in the bowl of a bubble tap, making the boy cry, she gave Keating a few whacks herself.

Keating did have, as he boasted, his 'rusted-on' supporters. After John Howard won the 1996 election, Trevor Kennedy and I were fellow dinner guests at David McNicholl's south-coast holiday home. Kennedy had seen Keating, and said the former prime minister was feeling especially morose. It wasn't just that he had lost — it was the fact that he had lost to *John Howard* that made it hurt so much.

After all, Kennedy observed, it wasn't as if Keating had done anything really wrong.

This was too much for me. 'You mean, apart from giving us the recession we had to have and putting a million people out of work,' I said. Ever so sweetly, of course.

Kennedy turned his back on me, and we did not exchange another word.

The good, the bad, and the ugly

HARD AS IT MIGHT BE TO BELIEVE NOW, the politician I was toughest on was John Howard.

We were watching the news in the press-gallery office one night when a member of Andrew Peacock's staff walked in and saw Howard on the box. 'He's got new teeth,' he said. His name was John Harvey and he was a dentist, so he knew what he was talking about.

Howard was in trouble then, as he was for a good part of the 1980s. My story the next day was both cruel and apt: John Howard was hanging on to the leadership of the Liberal Party by the skin of his new teeth.

Not content with that, I followed up with a column, putting it together with the more modern glasses he had acquired, and gleefully pointed out that he had had his eyebrows freshly clipped — an attempt, I wrote, to tame the old ones, which I said resembled wayward caterpillars.

It provided fodder for Keating and other comedians to ridicule Howard for years. Howard didn't complain. He didn't ring journalists and swear at them. In fact, he hardly ever swore.

During the 1987 election campaign, Keating rang to tell me personally, as he did other journos, that the Liberals had got their tax policy wrong because of a double-counting error. When Howard held a press conference to explain the mistake (which Jim Carlton, the shadow minister, had made), I asked Howard three times whether, as leader, he accepted responsibility for the error. I finally got the answer I wanted: Yes, he did take responsibility for it. I needed that admission to justify the headline I envisioned in *The Sun* and suggested for the next morning, 22 June 1987: 'Howard: My Sums Wrong'. It was a killer. They hung the posters of that front page at ALP campaign headquarters.

Perhaps it was my working-class roots — the same ones that made me worry about jobs in the lead-up to the recession — but I was wary of Howard's position on industrial-relations reform. An article of mine that attacked the so-called 'New Right', which was pushing reforms that were then considered way too radical, had been copied and sent out to people by the Labor Party, seeking donations to fight the nasty right-wing extremists.

The lead-up to the 1987 campaign had been disastrous for Howard as a result of the 'Joh for Canberra' push, which split the coalition. He copped a pounding every day, not just from me but from the gallery generally. The unflappable, consummate political operator Tony Eggleton, the Liberals' then federal director, who had handled everything from Harold Holt's drowning to Malcolm Fraser during the dismissal, told me after a particularly vicious time for Howard that he didn't know how the then opposition leader managed to drag himself out of bed some mornings. In spite of everything, Howard hung in and fought back every single day. He did much better in the campaign than everybody expected. There was a lesson in there about not quitting when you're behind — and it could be that he learned it too well.

Only twice did Howard try to counsel me directly: once, when he called a group of us to Sydney to try to explain his Asian immigration remarks — another issue on which I pounded him relentlessly; and again at the start of 1989, when I began the year by reporting on another bout of leadership speculation.

Within a matter of months, he had been replaced by Andrew Peacock.

There is little profit for politicians in attacking journalists directly or by complaining to their editors. Journalists hate admitting they are wrong, and will seldom retreat, and editors usually stand by their reporters.

I don't know of a single journalist who hasn't made a mistake, big or small. The errors are not always driven by malice; more often than not, they are caused by carelessness, or by being fed inaccurate information, or as a result of pressure from head office to produce a story. I made a few beauties myself — some of which I have deleted from my memory bank, and others that I can't forget.

One of my best efforts involved senator John Button. I was walking through the airport terminal at Tullamarine in Melbourne when I heard Button calling out to me. He had one of his boys with him. 'Son, this is Niki Savva from the Melbourne *Sun*. Remember, I told you about her.'

Thinking the lad had been eager to meet me, my head began to swell, fit to fill the terminal.

'Yeah, remember she wrote that I barracked for South Melbourne [the Sydney Swans]? See, son, I told you, you just can't believe anything you read about me in the papers.' And off they went, while I dissolved into a puddle. Button was a Geelong supporter to his marrow. In his eyes, that was the worst crime I could have committed, but it also gave him a wonderful free pass: from then on, he could, at least to his family, deny every bad word that was ever written about him.

NO MATTER HOW DIFFICULT journalists are at home, it is nothing compared to the way they behave when they are away.

Years ago, journalists who covered the National Party leader on the campaign trail began calling themselves the Wombats. It came from a postcard they had found of the furry bush animal with the caption: 'Wombat — eats roots and leaves.' Geoff Walsh, then on *The Sun-Pic*, later Hawke's press secretary and ALP national secretary, was a foundation member.

There used to be a rule among journos that everything which happened on the road stayed on the road. Any event outside a 200km limit was not to be discussed back home. Wives, husbands, loved ones, and those not initiated into the sacred rites of news-gathering had to be protected. Obviously, the reporters needed to be protected, too.

The rule has broken down a bit, as has the rule about not reporting on the private lives of politicians; but if you think that managing the media is difficult at home, the problems away are compounded.

Everybody gets cranky and disoriented. There are too many technical problems encountered in trying to file; too many lost buses; too much weird food; too much drinking; too many late nights; too many airports; too much jet lag; and too too much of everything except genuine news stories.

And it's not only the journalists who muck up. Australian prime ministers love prancing about on the world stage, but their statesmanlike poses are soon brought undone by whatever drama happens to be running back home. The result is sometimes hilarious.

On one extended overseas trip in 1989, Bob Hawke got into so much trouble that he introduced the so-called London Convention: he would answer no more questions on domestic issues while he was overseas. This was after he had allowed speculation to run on a possible half-Senate election; had canvassed the prospect of a luxury goods tax after the release of the worst balance-of-payment figures on record, and — worse — did it while standing in the middle of the uber-luxurious foyer of the Hotel Meurice in Paris; and had, three times at a press conference in London, after a meeting with the British prime minister, called Margaret Thatcher 'Mrs Fraser'.

We exacted some sweet revenge in Budapest. After dinner, I suggested to Glenn Milne and Michelle Grattan that we should suss out the one-and-only casino in the city. I knew Hawke would go there: 'Let's spoil his night.' We all turned up at the same time. While we couldn't stop grinning, he looked as if he wanted to throttle us or get his security detail to do it for him.

On another trip, we were passing through beautiful but boring Switzerland. We attended a cocktail party with Hawke, and afterwards went off to dinner thinking that Hawke was safely tucked up in bed. Instead, he slipped over to France to another casino, and gambled the night away. Talk about keen. It took his entourage two hours to drive there and two hours to drive back. I only found out about that expedition from Barrie Cassidy much later. If we had known at the time, we would have followed him there, too.

In October 1985, we accompanied Hawke to the Bahamas to cover the Commonwealth heads of government meeting. Oakes and I had dinner at the casino, as you do if you are in a James Bond playground, and then, after he retired, I went searching for playmates. About 4.00 a.m. we decided it was time for a swim to wake us all up. John Lombard stripped off, made a run for the pool and, as he dived in, stubbed his big toe on the concrete surround.

John could feel no pain, but his toe was bleeding badly. Around sunrise, when it hadn't stopped, I thought we should consult a doctor. The only one we knew who was available was Hawke's physician Joe Feldman, who had accompanied him on the trip. He was staying down the road at Hawke's hotel.

John got dressed, we showed his big toe to security to get access to Hawke's hotel, and rang Joe. The trouble was, we couldn't stop laughing. Joe took one look at us, rolled his eyes, and sewed up the toe with a few stitches, sans anaesthetic. No point wasting it. If we had been allowed to tell people, I'm sure I would have been awarded a medal for saving John's life.

That day was the leaders' retreat, and only a pool crew was allowed to attend to watch the great men tee off at the golf course. Hawke's first shot veered off to the side and plopped along the green a short distance away. The reporter assigned to cover the day, Janine Perrett, happened to be lying down on the grass, resting up a bit.

The foreign press ran footage of the prostrate Perrett as if she had collapsed in embarrassment at her prime minister's performance. If only. Then and there was born a new phrase in the journo's lexicon, thanks to the dry wit of Bruce Jones: 'Pissed as a Perrett'.

The good thing about Hawke was that he didn't hold grudges. On the trip home he would be down the back of the plane with the journos, catching up on all the gossip, or joining in the group sing-along. Or he would invite selected male reporters up the front for a game of poker.

He would rope staff in, too. Male journos couldn't stop laughing when they told us about Craig Emerson's fate. Emerson, once Hawke's economics adviser, made the mistake of going to the toilet when he had a big stash of money assembled in front of him. Hawke mischievously swept up a big handful of Emerson's winnings and put them on his pile. Emerson saw what had happened when he got back, said nothing to his boss, and meekly resumed playing.

Keating used to come down the back of the plane, too, but not for anything as frivolous as a sing-along. Before he became prime minister, Keating said he would never travel with a plane full of monkeys down the back, but he did. They all did, except Howard, who had the media on a separate plane.

Keating the crazy-brave loved courting conflict, and liked to brag that he didn't get grief — he gave grief. In 1995 he was flying to Germany for a technology conference, with a stopover on the way in Singapore and a meeting with the prime minister Goh Chok Tong. He wandered down the back of the plane in his tracksuit bottoms and shirt — he wasn't always done out top to toe in Zegna — and pretty soon launched into a tirade against Kerry Packer, with whom he had been feuding over media-ownership laws and plenty of other things besides.

The gist of it was that Packer had done a deal with then opposition leader Howard to change the laws and allow him to buy Fairfax, that Packer was too busy playing polo to concentrate on his business, that he was hopeless because he couldn't grow his business outside Australia, and that Murdoch was smarter and better because he had built a world-wide organisation.

We wanted Keating on the record, so a group of us, including Jim Middleton and Michael Gordon, approached Keating's press secretary, Greg Turnbull, in Singapore the next day to see if we could get quotes.

Keating was scheduled to have a press conference with the Singaporean prime minister, and Turnbull suggested that the journos should ask him about it then. So we did. Keating said publicly what he had said privately, while prime minister Goh stood there, superfluous and bewildered by the whole thing.

We had no need for egg-beaters. The story ran for days across whole continents, and completely wrecked Keating's trip.

You might have thought that the feud between Packer and Keating would have ended with Packer's death, but it didn't. It will continue until Keating is laid to rest, too — and even then it might not be over.

THE GOOD, THE BAD, AND THE UGLY came together for a group of us travelling on a VIP aircraft with Andrew Peacock on a swing through ASEAN countries, India, and Pakistan in late January and early February 1980. Peacock was trying to drum up support for a boycott of the Moscow Olympics because Malcolm Fraser wanted to punish the Soviet Union for invading Afghanistan.

It was one of my first overseas excursions as a reporter. I was congratulating myself for having been sent, thinking it was because I'd got the scoop on the planned boycott. In fact, I'd been sent because Peacock had exerted pressure on *The Sun* to cover it. He had been provided with a VIP aircraft, which had been fitted out as a troop carrier. We would stretch out on the floor and sleep during flights, because we certainly weren't getting any at night. By our last night in Jakarta, I had run out of money — *The Sun* had given me a pittance in expenses for a ten-day tour, and I had no credit card — and two RAAF crew bunked together so I could have a room in the hotel. Alan Griffiths, an eccentric but extremely talented senior bureaucrat in the Department of Prime Minister and Cabinet, took pity on me and slung my oversized handbag around his shoulder as we trudged around, including in refugee camps in Thailand, where lunch for us visitors came in a cardboard box full of goodies from the opulent Oriental Hotel. We could barely swallow from the embarrassment.

That trip brought together the best and worst of everything. Good stories and reprehensible behaviour. By us.

The incredibly suave Andrew met up with the equally suave governor of the north-west province of Pakistan, and we were flown by helicopter from Peshawar to the Khyber Pass for a meeting with the Afghan freedom fighters, as they were then called — almost certainly now, the Taliban.

It took some time for the meeting to get underway. I was the only female reporter on the trip, and the Afghanis were refusing to discuss any kind of business in front of a woman. They finally agreed to allow me to sit in on the meeting, but all the men blotted me out. No one would make eye-contact or acknowledge my presence. I was deemed not to exist. It was not the last time that something like this would happen, although this was cultural, not political.

No matter. We all got what we desired most: a Khyber Pass by-line.

Barrie Cassidy did two pieces to camera from there for the ABC. In one of them, he signed off, 'Barrie Cassidy, up the Khyber Pass for ABC news.' The ABC mistakenly ran that one — or so they told Barrie later.

The next day, we were granted an audience in Islamabad with the president of Pakistan, General Zia-ul-Haq, who the previous year had hanged the prime minister, Zulfiqar Ali Bhutto, Benazir's father.

The general had a dark complexion, black hair, and startling pale-blue eyes that accentuated a certain madness about him. He was trying to persuade the United States, and Peacock, to arm Pakistan and the Afghani *mujahideen* to fight against the Soviets in Afghanistan. He was painting such a dire scenario that journalist Bruce Jones agreed that it did sound very dangerous, and suggested that perhaps Australia should reconsider its forthcoming cricket tour.

The general hesitated a moment and then said: 'I think I have been exaggerating the situation.' Everybody burst out laughing.

Peacock had also met with India's prime minister, Indira Gandhi, in New Delhi. The Australian TV cameraman jumped on to her coffee table to get a better shot, lost his balance, and fell over, badly scratching the table and creating general mayhem.

If only that was the most embarrassing incident on the trip.

On one of our night stops, the guys decided to go to a live sex-show. I had not piked on any of the evening outings, and decided I would not do so then. I was imagining a dimly lit stage with a bed surrounded by pink tulle curtains, candlelit tables, and comfortable chairs set well back from the action.

Embassy staff told us to go to a certain laneway, ask for Junior, and tell him what we wanted. Gary O'Neill handled most of the arrangements. Junior took us to a small house and lined up a few people, men and women. The blokes selected three, a man and two women, and we were taken to a room no bigger than a small bedroom.

There was a red, vinyl-covered double bed in the middle, and benches either side for the 'audience'.

No tulle and no distance. I kept my eyes covered the whole time, too mortified to look, and wishing I had earplugs as well. A couple of the males also could not bear to watch. I should have had the courage to leave, but didn't. I did some pretty shabby things as a journo, but that was the worst.

CHAPTER SIX

Nothing lasts forever

In 1991, Marlin Fitzwater, official spokesman for George Bush the First, also known as 'the mouth from the south', was preparing to visit Australia for the first time with his boss. So what was he expecting? 'All the women are beautiful and all the men are like Crocodile Dundee,' he told me.

When I tried to tell him it wasn't really like that, he didn't want to know. 'Yes it is.'

Nowadays, substitute Hugh Jackman for Crocodile Dundee. That's the thing about Americans: they like to kid themselves as much as we do.

Every prime minister since Bob Menzies has hyped up Australia's 'special relationship' with the United States. The media drools over every mention by every president or secretary of state, no matter how banal or pro forma they are. The truth is, Australia ranks pretty low in the minds of American politicians and policy-makers. If Americans think about us at all, it's in a romanticised kind of way, as the place America used to be — pioneering, rugged, unspoiled, frank, and fearless.

They see us as a nation of Steve Irwins wrestling crocodiles, and Elle Macphersons with perfect bodies, walking down perfect beaches. These are fantastic images, but fantasy just the same. We are well-liked, but neither well-known nor well-understood.

On my first visit to the States for a three-month holiday in the late 1970s, I was repeatedly complimented on my English. One thing they knew and approved of, especially in the south, was the White Australia Policy.

My tall, redheaded girlfriend, Lissa, and I (a pairing which prompted one African–American man to call out as we walked past him in the Capitol, 'Ah like 'em tall an' ah like 'em small') stayed a few days with a highway patrolman and a deputy sheriff at their apartment above a mansion outside San Francisco.

They held a party in our honour that ended in farce and could have ended in tragedy when the highway patrolman, drunk and frustrated, threatened to shoot a fellow cop who was having more success with women than he was.

He had a huge collection of handguns and rifles in different cabinets. It didn't sound like an idle threat — so Lissa, I, and the cop whose head was going to be blown off raced around, gathered up all his weapons, and hid them. Next morning, our host had no memory of his foul temper, and wondered why a couple of his pistols were in the shower recess, and others under the bed, or in the wardrobe.

Apart from the guns, there were the drugs.

After dinner one night at his home in Honolulu, my date produced one of those wooden pineapples that were in vogue at the time for serving up savouries, and instead of cubes of cheese with pickles, there were dozens of joints splaying from every cavity. I politely declined.

At the Seattle Greyhound bus station where I was waiting to catch a bus to San Francisco, a stranger sat down opposite and struck up a conversation. When it came time to leave, he gave me a present. A cigarette pack, it was stuffed full of joints. I thanked him, and as he walked away I threw them in the bin.

Back then in Canberra, sharing a joint after dinner was considered adventurous.

My fascination with the US never dimmed. It just grew, and after

16 years reporting in the gallery, six of them as a bureau chief, it was time for me to drink up another cultural cocktail.

Colin Duck, then editor of the Melbourne *Sun*, reluctantly arranged a Washington posting for me. Having read *Boys on the Bus* by Timothy Crouse, about American journalists covering a US presidential campaign, I couldn't wait to do the same.

Unfortunately, there are very few places in the world where Australian foreign correspondents — like our diplomats — really matter. One is Papua New Guinea; the other is New Zealand.

In Washington we were then, and still are now, very much on the periphery. To make it even more difficult, the White House press corps ran a caste system. There was a select pool of reporters and camera crew on board Air Force One with the president, and access was strictly controlled.

The pool rotated among the most senior correspondents from the most prestigious outlets — *The Washington Post*, *The New York Times*, and all the networks and the top wire agencies. Everyone else travelled on a separate White House press charter, and Australian journalists were usually seated in the rear in the Asia–Pacific section.

At every stop that the president made on his travels, there was a specially dedicated press room. The pool reporters on Air Force One provided written accounts, irreverent and hilarious, of the president's every move and wheeze for all the other media. Transcripts were also provided.

Or we could just stay home and watch everything on CNN. We were the journalistic equivalents of battery hens.

When I finally got on a bus, it was to cover part of the 1992 Clinton campaign in Florida. It was no fun — especially when Al Gore gave the same speech, the same way, at every stop. Gore asked people to think what it was like with Bush in office: grey skies, overcast, and miserable. He told them to imagine what it would be like if Clinton was elected: sunny, blue skies, birds singing.

At one stop in a huge tin shed, just as he said the bit about the birds singing, a bird flew in front of him and circled above his head. He stopped dead in the middle of his speech. Instead of saying, 'See, they're singing already', he was completely thrown. He lost his place in his carefully scripted speech for several seconds, made fish movements with his mouth, and then resumed as if nothing had happened.

I was sure that if half his audience had suddenly dropped dead — say, from boredom — in the middle of his speech, he would have paused for a moment before resuming at the same point, as if nothing had happened, and with every lacquered hair in place.

Cartoonists drew him as a lump of wood, and there was good reason for this. Even so, he would later have a profound impact on Australian politics.

I had arrived in Washington in January 1991. The first Gulf War was about to begin, so my editors back home were insisting I get into the bowels of the Pentagon to report on the behind-the-scenes war plans. At that stage, I didn't even have a pass to get in through the front door, but I managed to file all day, every day, for the duration, for both morning and afternoon editions, never missing a deadline. Thank God the first Gulf War was a short one.

At the end of it, even Piers Akerman, then waging his own war against the Kirner government in Victoria, rang to congratulate me on my coverage. I did not stay in his good books for long.

We flew to Moscow to cover the final US–Soviet summit between George Bush and Mikhail Gorbachev in 1991, and I made the mistake before filing of going off with Greg Hywood, *The Australian Financial Review*'s correspondent in Washington, to the home of journalist extraordinaire and bon vivant Robert Haupt, then the Fairfax Moscow correspondent.

Haupt had no food in his house except caviar, so we ate that, and drank a couple of buckets of Russian vodka. We were there for some hours. Eventually, when it came time to leave, instead of calling a cab to take us back to the hotel — there were none — Haupt walked out into the middle of the road and flagged down a truck. It was around 3.00 or 4.00 a.m.

'They're always out at this hour making deliveries for the mafia,' Haupt explained.

After we climbed into the cabin with the driver, I felt it my duty to make conversation with him. I wanted to know who he liked best, Gorby or Yeltsin. 'Gorbachev da, Yeltsin nyet,' I kept saying over and over, declaring my preference with my full complement of Russian, until the driver finally relented. 'Yeltsin da.' Thankfully, we had arrived at the hotel and there was no time to slug it out with him, so we begged him for some cigarettes and away we went.

Needless to say, I was incapable of writing anything. Nothing much happened, I think. In all the years of reporting, it was the only time I failed to file.

Piers, whose particular specialty in bars was limp falls, was outraged, and vented his outrage to the newsroom about journalists on expensive overseas trips who didn't produce stories.

Piers and I get along well, except when he is in a position of authority. He congratulated me once on getting a story by describing me as a rare combination of boobs and brains. It was always best to ignore those kind of provocations in newsrooms, as it only encouraged them.

During the 1992 US presidential campaign, Pilita Clark and I flew from Washington to the West Coast, ostensibly to cover Bill Clinton and the California primary. We spent the night in San Francisco, then hired a car and drove from there to Los Angeles along the Big Sur highway.

As a journalist I had been everywhere, from El Salvador to St Petersburg, Honduras to Hanoi, New York, Paris, Amsterdam, Moscow, and Martinique.

The most moving experience was the dawn service at Anzac Cove at Gallipoli with the surviving diggers to commemorate the 75th anniversary of the landing. Tim Fischer stunned us all by striding out of the sea in his trunks. We didn't even know he was there. Tim, a genuine eccentric, had gone for a swim because he wanted to know how the diggers had felt when they jumped into the waters to bathe.

The weirdest moment was when Winston Churchill's grandson told me and a couple of others that, if it were not for his grandfather, 'We wouldn't be here today.' Perhaps we should have been grateful.

We went to France for D-Day celebrations with Paul Keating, who always had a much more relaxed travel schedule. Laura Tingle and I hired a car, and drove to Giverny to see Monet's restored house and garden. Most of the male journos went to the palace at Versailles. The camera crews caught Keating touring the Paris antique shops.

Yet it only really hit me as Pilita and I drove along that magnificent highway with the Pacific on one side and the castle of San Simeon on the other. Someone else was paying for us to do this. Rupert was paying my bills, and Fairfax was paying Pilita's. Did it get any better than this?

We did see Clinton — pudgy, man-boobied, and red-faced — at a Democrat rally, and we did write about the primary, and lots more besides during that campaign. So it wasn't a complete junket, but what other job could deliver such fringe benefits?

All of which meant, of course, that it was bound to end.

AFTER AN ESPECIALLY HAPPY OCCASION, Elpiniki will pull up at some point and recite an old Cypriot saying that she believes in as much as the evil eye: 'We have laughed too much today. We will pay for it tomorrow in tears.'

There was nothing else I wanted to be, other than a journalist, and I thought I would be one forever.

There had been offers over the years to go and work for politicians — mainly Labor politicians, because more often than not they were my 'mates' — but I wasn't interested. I didn't think

I could stand the secrecy, and I was worried about the duplicity and compromise that would be involved. Not to mention the disappointments and the separation from friends.

Plus, could I really bear to put up with people like me?

The old saying that all political careers end in tears is true. At the same time, I had always thought that journalists came out on top, no matter what the outcome. Not any more.

We all seem to be caught up in a whirlpool heading down a sinkhole which ensures that everybody will lose — politicians, the media, good government, and people.

The more licence that journalists take in their reporting — the more they beat up stories, the less attention they pay to accuracy, the more bias they display — the more politicians feel the need to control information.

The more robotic and scripted the politicians become to avoid gotcha journalism, the more Stepford husbands and wives we end up with.

The less information that gets out, the more likely it is to be mistreated when it surfaces.

The more this happens, the more governments try to hide the truth, or the more politicians and staffers feel compelled to lie Everyone loses credibility, and the public grows ever more cynical about their politicians and those who report on them.

As a journalist I lied often, usually about my sources, but about other things, too.

For example, in 1981 I was rung and told that Bob Hawke, then an opposition frontbencher, had recited a joke about Indira Gandhi at a special ALP national conference in Melbourne. The joke was crude, and not very funny and, although media were present when it was told, it had not been reported.

My source told me that the Indians were mightily offended by the joke, so I rang Hawke and told him I was writing a story that the Indians' concerns had filtered through to the Foreign Affairs department, and the Indian high commissioner had complained to the then opposition leader, Bill Hayden. Hawke wanted to know where the story had come from, and I told him it was departmental sources.

Hawke was sceptical, but in any case he got off the hook because *The Sun News-Pictorial* buried the story the next day and it got little follow-up.

The person who had tipped me off to the yarn was Alan Ramsey, who was then Bill Hayden's press secretary. Ramsey threatened a number of times over the years to write the real story, but I wouldn't let him. Now that we're both out of it …

Journalists can, and do, get away with lying; politicians and staff can't. Nor should they.

In my later life as a press secretary, I never (knowingly) lied. But I didn't always tell the complete truth. Both courses would inevitably land you or your boss in trouble. Lies are eventually found out, and the whole truth is either misunderstood or misreported.

In April 1998, Sean Aylmer of *The Sydney Morning Herald* had been told by 'banking sources' that the treasurer had dropped his opposition to the so-called Four Pillars policy, which prevented mergers between the big four banks.

This is a hardy perennial, trotted out regularly by one banker or another as they try to pressure the government to allow mergers to proceed, and I had to deal with it a number of times as Costello's press secretary. When Aylmer rang me to relay the latest rumours, and to confirm whether it had happened, I checked with the treasurer and relevant adviser, was satisfied that he hadn't dropped his opposition at all, and told Aylmer so.

Aylmer found it difficult to accept the denial. He told me straight out that I was 'paid to lie', and that politicians didn't always tell the truth.

Incidentally, more than a decade later, the Four Pillars policy remains intact, a bipartisan article of faith.

Journalists complain bitterly about identikit politicians, yet the media tend to pick on politicians who are even a little bit different. There is more pressure on politicians to conform, thereby guaranteeing more complaints from the media about the deadening dullness of the Parliament and the people in it, and making it harder to get talented people to run for office.

The more the media condemns politicians who dare to offer an alternative viewpoint, the less real debate there is, and the more public-policy formulation suffers.

Having been complicit from both ends, I know which is easier, which is more fun, which is more destructive, which is more dishonest, and which is more rewarding.

Political pygmies will dominate the system even more than they do now, and the media will increasingly latch on to celebrity candidates desperate for a power hit without either the passion or the commitment to do anything meaningful with it, but with the right name, the right looks, and the right lines to get there — the political equivalents of Paris Hilton.

Alexander Downer complained to me once about the effect that a certain style of reporting would have on politicians' behaviour. I was on *The Age*, and had been tipped off that he had posed in a fishnet stocking for a promotion for a charity production of *The Rocky Horror Show*.

This was too good to be true. I hunted down the photographer, who freelanced for the Adelaide *Advertiser*, from arch-rivals News Ltd. Much as I pleaded, he would not give me the photo.

I had the story, but it was the picture that was worth a million words. The photographer gave it to the News Ltd papers instead. *The Daily Telegraph* ran it on the front page, and cartoonists forever after drew Downer in fishnet tights and high heels.

When Downer's office found out that I had the story, they went into a blind panic. First his press secretary rang, asking me politely not to print it. Sorry, but no.

Then his chief of staff rang, threatening dire consequences if I did print it. Too bad.

Finally, Downer himself rang. He had posed in the stocking to help out charity, and my story would mean that politicians would be ever more reluctant to help out, and they would, as a breed, become greyer and greyer. He was exasperated. 'For God's sake.'

He was right, in a way. He paid a price, but so has the media. The only colour so far in the Rudd ministry comes courtesy of the redhead — although I suspect now that Julia Gillard has started toning down her hair colour, she'll be toning down a few other things, too.

Crossing over, then standing back, gives you a much clearer picture of the demands and the pressures on politicians and journalists. It pains me to say, as a result, that my opinion of reporters generally has fallen much lower than my opinion of politicians.

When it comes to scheming and lying, plain old hypocrisy, and dishonesty, journalists — apart from a few honourable exceptions — win hands down. If you can call it winning.

Having said that, I would have happily stayed a journalist, and possibly would still be reporting, if not for a stupid decision I made to leave *The Herald Sun*.

When Laurie Oakes hired me to work on *The Sun-Pic* after the dismissal, I became the first woman to be employed in the paper's Canberra bureau. Later, I was the first woman to become bureau chief and political editor of *The Sun*, and then the merged entity, *The Herald Sun*. My appointment in 1985 came with only two words of advice from two of the great editors of our time, Harry Gordon and Bob Cronin, who had hired me back from *The Australian*: 'Be tough.' Plus, Bob insisted I not use bad language in print.

In all the years I was there, and even through my absence in Washington, the gallery had not changed much. There were a lot more women but, as I looked around, more often than not I was the darkest person in the room — except when *The Sydney Morning Herald* photographer Palani Mohan was there, and he soon left.

By 1993, the long love affair between Keating and journalists was pretty much over. John Hewson had not been embraced — there was nothing cuddly about him — but even left-leaning journalists had found it difficult to stomach a recession that had put a million people out of work, and a privatisation regime that had turned conservative Liberals green with envy. There was so much political cross-dressing that it was becoming almost impossible to spot the differences between the two sides. In my mind, if a Labor government could, without regret, put so many people out of work, what exactly was the point of the party?

John Howard regained the Liberal leadership in early 1995, and moved closer to the centre. His years in leadership exile had taught him that, if he wanted to win, that's where he had to be.

I was still as happy as the proverbial in journalism, bragging to people that I had the best job in the gallery as national political editor of the biggest-selling daily newspaper in Australia. My editor and editor-in-chief supported me to the hilt, and I had a good team of young reporters, such as Cheryl Critchley, Phillip Hudson, and Michael Harvey. Janet Calvert-Jones, Rupert's sister, would drop me the occasional note telling me how much she liked my work.

It takes a special talent to wreck all this in a matter of hours, but I somehow managed to do it. It's that ethnic thing. Hubris — a fit of Greek, or pique, and your whole life changes.

The 1996 election campaign was over, Keating was gone — after telling us that he was sicker of us than we were of him, although that was a toss-up — and John Howard was prime minister. I was a bit strung out from the long days and nights of covering the campaign, and in no mood, if I ever had been, to be told what I should or shouldn't be doing by my superiors in Melbourne.

When they countermanded arrangements I had made for staff to travel interstate to cover stories, I took umbrage and overreacted. I grabbed a knife and hacked off my nose.

After 11 years on the paper this time around, I quit by fax, packed up my office, and left. There was an attempted reconciliation, which failed. The whole thing was too stupid and petty for words — without doubt, it turned out to be my worst-ever career move. I have never left or gone to any job for money; for me there were always other considerations. This time it was pride, and that always carries a much higher price.

One of my last pieces for *The Herald Sun* chastised John Howard for choosing to live at Kirribilli rather than the Lodge.

For the first time in my adult life I was unemployed, until the editor of *The Age*, Bruce Guthrie, rang to offer me the chief political correspondent's job in the Canberra bureau to work with Michelle Grattan.

Michelle was flat-out opposed, even though I told her that I wasn't interested in being the bureau chief, I was tired of running an office and staff, and I was more than happy to work under her.

It didn't sway her, and she asked me not to take it up. I took it anyway; not long after, Michelle left *The Age* for *The Australian Financial Review*, and I became political editor.

It was destined not to last. The phone call I had spent most of my life dreading came the night after the 1997 budget. It was much, much worse than anything I had expected or had tried over the years to prepare myself for.

One day, I had thought, I would get a call to say that Christina had died suddenly of a heart attack — as had happened to many of her friends with the same illness, all of them much younger than her. I wish that was what happened. It was the wish of a coward. Not surprisingly, Christina had a much braver way of looking at her fate.

She and my mother had visited Cyprus, and in the last few days of their holiday she felt unwell. I flew down to Melbourne for the weekend to see them when they got back.

Although they had only been gone a couple of months, I had really missed them.

Christina had arranged an ultrasound at Monash Hospital, thinking that her pain had been caused by recurring gallstones. I went with her, and we chatted while the medical staff ran a wand over her stomach. There was a poster on the wall of Lizard Island, and we mused about going there for a holiday.

The staff were unusually quiet. I should have suspected something from their silence, but just assumed they were being polite.

Christina went off to sign up as a member at the new casino, and I flew back to cover the 1997 budget for *The Age*. Costello's second budget turned out to be a bit of a letdown after the 1996 one. Howard had infuriated Costello by giving his first budget a seven out of ten, then compounded it by saying he would not accept the savings rebate, which was a key component of his second budget. Peter thought all his budgets were worth a ten. Naturally.

The night after the budget, Christina called. She was in hospital. The ultrasound had found three growths on her liver: all of them were malignant.

The years of blood transfusions had resulted in an iron overload. She probably had not been as diligent as she should have with her nightly injections to remove the iron, and the excess was being stored in her vital organs. Her liver had turned cirrhotic, and had created the conditions for the cancer.

Shocked, frightened, and desperately looking for some way to reassure her, but fearing in my bones that this was probably unfixable, I said: 'Okay, how about dialysis?'

'That's for kidneys, not livers,' she said patiently. Right. I knew that. I told her I would be down on the first flight down in the morning.

Not very helpfully, I finished up by telling her not to drop her bundle. Not for the last time, I wished I could have bitten off my tongue.

What I wanted to say was, *Don't worry, hang in there, we will get through this together and I love you,* but I knew my own bundle would then be all over the floor. All I did was get her back up. 'I haven't dropped my bundle. I'm ringing you, aren't I?'

She had been told so many times by so many doctors over so many years that she was about to die that she no longer believed what they said. She had defied them all, and she was determined she would do it again.

She wanted to fight and, while ever she wanted to, I would help her. The first challenge was to find a doctor prepared to treat her. The doctor who had diagnosed her was brutal, and a first-class bastard. He told her she had only a few months to live: he could recommend little in the way of treatment, given her other medical problems; indeed, he was not interested in offering any kind of treatment. She should, according to him, accept the fact that she was going to die and, if there was anything she wanted to do, she should go away and do it.

She didn't want to at all. She had heard it all before, and from better doctors than him. I asked him who was the best liver man in the state, and when he nominated Bob Jones at the Austin Hospital, I asked him for a referral.

His referral, in effect, told Jones not to bother treating her because she was overweight and had a terminal illness — well, two, actually — and that her best option was palliative care. His letter rekindled all her suspicions about some members of the medical profession. I had previously joked in a column that by the time the baby boomers reached pension age, there would be nothing voluntary about euthanasia.

Christina did not see the humour in it, because she had seen first hand that, for a percentage of doctors and nurses, treating difficult patients was more trouble than it was worth. She feared that any legislation which legalised euthanasia would only increase the pressure on chronically ill people to do away with themselves or have others do it. Luckily, we got an appointment with Jones the following week. We were talking to him when the door slid open and another doctor peered in.

That morning in Canberra, my husband, Vincent, had run into Michael Wooldridge, the health minister, who had asked after me. When Vincent told him where we were, Wooldridge said his mother had been treated there, that he knew a doctor who worked with Jones, and that he would ring him. This was how he came to be peering round the door, and how they came to realise that I was the Canberra bureau chief for *The Age*.

What had given me confidence was that we were seeing Jones before he had any idea who I was or what I did. The news, though, was awful. The tumours were large, they were aggressive and, if nothing was done, Christina would die in a very short time. Jones couldn't operate because of the size and position of the tumours, and he ruled out a transplant because of the threat of the cancer recurring.

It felt like we were being hit over the head with a huge mallet; then, just as we were getting back on our feet, along would come someone with another mallet and give us another whack.

Jones called in Dr Jonathan Cebon, the head of oncology, and his assistant, Dr Peter Gibbs. It turned out that they were about to start a clinical trial with a new drug; if Christina passed a heart test, they would put her on it. Unbelievably, given the number of her friends with thalassemia who had died of heart attacks, she passed the test — she was in. Jones and the other two doctors were brilliant, and they quickly gained her trust and respect. All she wanted was hope, and they gave it to her.

All this took time. I had informed *The Age*'s editor, Bruce Guthrie, of my predicament. My sister was unmarried and lived with my mother, who could neither read nor write nor drive.

Andreas had died of a heart attack 12 years before, a month shy of his 61st birthday.

I was not about to abandon my sister.

The meetings with the doctors were serial sessions of extreme physical and mental torment. Even with our combined knowledge of medical routines and procedures, and our command of English, it was impossible to get across everything the doctors were saying. The combination of fear and trauma corrupted both hearing and logic.

I would return to work for a week, then fly back to Melbourne to provide whatever moral, physical, or financial support was necessary.

Then Guthrie was sacked and replaced by Michael Gawenda, and Steve Harris was brought in as editor-in-chief. Even though I knew both of them well, I also knew that my days were numbered. They had a job to do, and I was obviously struggling to do mine.

No matter how good a journalist you are, you are only as good as your last story, and new regimes are seldom as understanding as the regime that hired you in the first place. *The Age* placed a high premium on its political coverage, and its national political editor was now absent, sometimes, for weeks at a time. It looked bad for the paper, and it placed extra pressure on the other reporters in the bureau.

Peter Costello took me to lunch at the Bamboo House one day to cheer me up. I had made a point, in every new Parliament, of singling out a few of the newer MPs I thought would go places, and had kept in regular contact with them. Peter Costello was one; John Brumby was another. Costello and I had always got along well. He had a disarming frankness in private, a trait that would come to cost him dearly; and, as well as being smart, he was great company. He told hilarious stories, and was an excellent mimic.

Costello knew of my sister's illness and, over rubbery squid, did his best to give me some hope. His wife, Tanya, had been seriously ill a few years before, and it was feared she would die. She pulled through, and Costello, a deeply religious man, said two factors were responsible for her salvation: good doctors and faith.

Luckily, we had found good doctors. As for faith, I had none.

'I fear by the time my sister gets through this, I'll be looking for a new job,' I told him.

'If anything happens, make sure you ring me first,' he said.

Sure enough, a few months later I was on the way out. First, Steve Harris told me what I should really do was take leave of absence and come back when it was all over. I could not afford to do this. Christina would often ask about my job, worried that I was putting it at risk. I assured her it was okay, even though I knew it would not be — she had enough to worry about. As well, we needed my salary to help pay for things. She was no longer able to work, and had gone on a disability pension. Elpiniki was on the age pension. One MRI back then cost $500, and there was no Medicare rebate. So I told Harris I couldn't just go on leave.

I felt like I was drowning. My family was in crisis, but the paper's patience had run out. Maybe things would have been different at my old paper — they might have arranged it so I could work out of the Melbourne office part of the time, or tried to help me through it in some other way — but it was way too late for that.

Towards the end of the year, I was told I would be demoted from my job as national political editor. I could take a hint. I couldn't really blame them, given my long absences.

The Age is really good at delivering lectures on the humane treatment of people, and I applaud them for it, but forgive me if I occasionally become impatient with sermons from the bleeding-heart brigade on how we should all show more compassion.

I resigned, and then rang Costello to see if he had any jobs going. I had to have a job, and I didn't have a whole lot of options. I also had to have a Melbourne connection, so I could continue to help Christina. I had always regarded Costello as a person of value. It is rare for people of his calibre to go into politics and, given everything they have to put up with, that's understandable. I believed then, as I do now, that he was a decent bloke. I knew he was pretty conservative in his outlook, but he did not have a racist bone in his body, and possessed a fine social conscience. He was a good family man, tight but not mean, intelligent, and dedicated to political life. Religion was, and is, important in his life, but he did not parade or flaunt it for political gain, or try to induce others to imitate him.

I felt I could work for him, despite the fact that there were a number of coalition policies and positions that made me uncomfortable. I was a republican; I disagreed fervently with the approach on One Nation; I thought we should say sorry to the Aboriginals; I liked Americans, but didn't think we should blindly follow them down every path; I didn't give a hoot about same-sex relationships, except that I didn't believe they should be discriminated against; and I was to the left of even many Labor MPs on social issues generally. To balance that, I admired Howard's courage in tightening gun laws, and agreed with his overall economic approach.

In any case, I thought that, with a bit of luck, in the treasurer's office I would be cocooned from some of the policies I found unpalatable. The government was about to embark on the biggest tax reform in decades. It was important, and looked exciting. If I could be a part of this, and part of an operation that kept the economy ticking over and providing jobs for people, it would help make up for a few of the things I didn't like. It had taken a while, but I had finally realised that good people sat in different places, and that Labor had lost its right to moralise about righteous behaviour, either economic or social.

Before taking up my posting in the US, I had told Nick Bolkus that, after more than 16 years reporting in the gallery, I had only three 'friends' in politics: him, Gerry Hand, and Bill Hayden:

two lefties and one centre-leftie. Nick, battle-scarred from South Australian Labor's factional wars, thought that was pretty good. It was no accident that they were all on the Labor side.

Now, seven years later, the person I was 'friendliest' with in the Parliament was one of its most conservative members, Peter Costello. I thought that maybe I could get Costello to change a few things about himself and the government. I thought I could help, and I certainly needed it myself.

Costello had already made it plain that he was keen to have me on board. I was a high-profile member of the Press Gallery, and pigs flew in flocks when someone in a position like that volunteered to work for the conservatives. I told him that my sister would always come first. He understood and accepted this. Despite the family pressures, he trusted me to do the job professionally, and I was utterly determined that I would.

Tony Smith had been handling the media for Costello, so he was moved into a new position as political adviser, with special responsibility for the tax-reform process. I was slotted in to the press secretary's job left vacant by Tony.

Costello had arranged the slot, pay, and conditions in a matter of days. For me, used to journalism and private enterprise — where people were sacked or hired in minutes — this was no big deal, but Costello rang me at home to tell me, and to point out the speed with which it had all happened.

All government appointments had to be cleared through what was known colloquially as the Star Chamber, mainly run by the prime minister's office. While they were pleased that a high-profile member of the gallery was joining the government at a time when it was under siege, some were not so happy that I was going to Costello. Once they heard I had resigned from *The Age*, some staff in Howard's office were hoping I would join them, but at that stage it was a bit too much of a leap for me; others were apprehensive about what influence I would exert over Costello, and where it would lead. In short, would my presence increase any potential threat that Costello might pose to the leadership?

When Peter rang to tell me how successful he had been in running the gauntlet, I said, half-jokingly, 'Well, I'm proud of you.'

'I hope that will always be so,' he said, also half-jokingly, although it was a bit hard to tell.

CHAPTER SEVEN

1998: tragedies and triumph

When I told my sister that I was going to work for Peter Costello, she said she would love me no matter what I did. Hmmm. Ditto, of course.

We had become close with Sharon, the nurse at the Austin administering Christina's treatment. She didn't love me nearly as much, and she was far less subtle: 'But Niki, what about your soul?' I assured her that my soul would look after itself, although I knew that her spontaneous comment would have been echoed by many of my former colleagues and friends.

It was a crossing over to the dark side that would not be easily forgiven or understood. Only a very small number of senior journalists had left the gallery to work for the conservatives, and fewer still were ever welcomed back.

On my first day on the job, I realised it was not my soul that was under threat, but my body and brain. As I woke to a 4.30 a.m. alarm to catch the first flight to Sydney at 6.10 a.m., I wondered what the hell I had got myself into.

Costello was delivering a speech at lunchtime, and the consumer-price index inflation figures were being released.

Treasury had done a draft of the speech, and I had gone over it the previous day — the Australia Day public holiday — to sharpen it up and make sure it contained a few news grabs. Costello complained often, both before and after I went to work for him, about not having a speechwriter and having to do it all himself. But even if a perfect product was presented to him, he always insisted on adding his flourishes and thoughts. The process, as I soon discovered, never went smoothly. Copies of the speech were being spat out of the copier as we left for the lunch. The office manager, Susie Munson, was frantically stapling the pages together and, with an invaluable eagle-eye, was giving the speech a final proof.

This was a pattern that was to be followed, one way or another, for the next six years: early starts, late finishes, and a mountain of work in between, including dealing with journalists who, like me — even worse than me — dedicated themselves to creating mischief. There was no time to goof off, no room for errors, no time for long lunches, or all-night drinking sessions, or sitting around carping and insisting that somebody else should fix whatever was broken.

Costello had given me a brief lecture about my responsibilities, which were to start work at 8.00 a.m. (if only) and to never bag his colleagues (which I only ever did privately).

My biggest fear was of saying something stupid that would cause a run on the dollar. My second-biggest fear was of mucking up the travel-allowance forms. The ghosts of sacked ministers and staff the previous year haunted every office.

The most challenging aspect of the job was to try and reshape Costello a bit. He was brilliant at the Treasury side, and adroit at the politics. But he needed a bit of sharpening up in both presentation and appearance.

Liberal Party research at the time showed that, although people thought he was intelligent, competent, and had a good sense of humour, he was regarded as arrogant and self-satisfied. When senior party officials found out that I was going to work for Costello, one of them breathed a sigh of relief. 'Thank God. Now maybe there will be someone there who doesn't think the sun shines out of his arse.'

Bit harsh, I thought. None of us was blind to Peter's faults, but his incredibly loyal and hardworking staff believed that the good in him far outweighed any bad. We grumbled to one another about his shortcomings, and whatever crimes and misdemeanours he had committed that day, but not to anybody else. Our only safety valve was in unloading to one another.

The press secretary's job of satisfying the media and his or her master at all times is like juggling a tiger and a python, and I was to become the kind of press secretary I had always hated — the type who puts up barriers. I was running my own kind of protection racket, trying to save him from himself. All of this was made much easier by Phil Gaetjens, Mike Callaghan, Elizabeth McCabe, Nigel Bailey, Michael O'Brien, Mitch Fifield, Tony Smith, and many others.

In politics, you can really only trust the people you work with, and even then some caution is necessary. There is no such thing as a casual or off-the-record conversation with journalists, and even discussions with friends and family are invariably circumspect.

The one person I was always brutally frank with was Costello. I made a decision at the very outset to always tell him what I thought; otherwise there was no point being there. By the end, though, that wore out both of us.

It's easy to forget that politicians are human, and that if you want to get through to them you have to find the right way and the right words. And you have to be absolutely certain that your way is the right way.

Yelling at someone after they have stuffed up, even if it makes you feel better — and it always does — is not always the best way. It is usually obvious to them and the rest of the world that they have boobed big time. The point is how to fix it, and how to prevent it recurring.

Although he is frequently accused of having a mega-sized ego, Costello was acutely self-aware, knew when he had boobed — even if he couldn't bring himself to admit to it publicly — and knew there were things about himself that he had to fix. I had only been there a few days when he asked me to write something for him about what he should do to round out his image. I did it in a bit over a page, suggesting more newspaper profiles to show his human side, a few softer television interviews, and more visits to marginal electorates to help out his colleagues. I urged him to remember that tone was as important as content, and that paying the occasional tribute to an opponent would reflect well on himself as well as them.

Finally, I had to broach the thing that really, really turned everyone off: 'A broad smile is cute, but a smirk is irksome.' He had to get rid of it.

This was not rocket science, and not necessarily easy, either. The smirk had developed because Peter was sensitive about his teeth and tried to hide them when he smiled — not because he was always satisfied with himself. He recognised that it was a problem and that he had to stop it, but it took years of practice and a bit of dental work brought on by nocturnal tooth-grinding to straighten out that kink.

Other, more mechanical, things were easier to handle. Stunts have a pretty short shelf-life, so we avoided them wherever possible. People will tolerate a degree of flummery and arrogance — after all, if politicians don't believe in themselves, who else is going to? What electors want to know is whether their politicians can do the job.

We also did not try to hide bad news by dropping it late on a Friday or burying it when a disaster was breaking. That tactic only works for a time, and then the very act of trying to hide becomes a bigger and more negative story.

I always believed in fronting up and taking our lumps, although Peter would protest whenever he had to get out there if the Reserve Bank increased interest rates. After all, it was not as though he had asked the bank to raise rates. He never did.

Just how much was involved in being a minder was brought home to me very early. Tony Smith tried to warn me when he wished me luck on my first solo outing with Peter, but I brushed him aside with a breezy 'She'll be right.'

The Liberals had organised a love-in at Thredbo in early February, and a party meeting had been set for the Friday night. Peter was to give a PowerPoint presentation on the deficiencies of the existing tax system, and to run through the general direction of the proposed new tax system.

His presentations were always very good, and when the meeting was over I went to bed. It was my first wrong call.

Peter stayed up and played snooker with some young punters in the bar. Apart from forgetting his charts and presentation on the billiard table, he walked into the bar's glass doors.

Luckily, his papers were returned to him, but the next morning he had a big bump on his nose. We had arranged a live interview from Thredbo with Laurie Oakes on Nine's *Sunday* programme, and here was Peter looking as if he had come off second-best to a bikie.

'You know, Niki, Tony always used to carry around a makeup pad to do makeup for television,' he said.

This was rubbish, but I didn't know that at the time. Tony was not a makeup-pad kind of guy. After the Iraq invasion, when we worried privately about the political consequences if there were no weapons of mass destruction found, Tony said he would strap the weapons on his back and carry them into Baghdad himself if he had to.

I fretted about how to disguise Peter's injury. All I had was some foundation for an olive complexion, so he would have looked as if he was made up for a Bollywood movie. Fortunately, Nine cameraman Doug Ferguson, who was shooting the Thredbo end, had some pancake makeup, and we smothered Peter in it.

The lesson from this was not that I should carry around a TV makeup kit, but that Peter should never be left alone.

As my first budget with Peter approached, we embarked on

some serious repackaging.

Michael Gordon of *The Age* had been keen to do an in-depth piece on Peter for the *Good Weekend* magazine, which was scheduled to appear on the weekend before the budget. We agreed, knowing that Michael is a lovely writer. The piece turned out to be a knockout, giving an insight into Peter's humour and his family, including an account of the illness that had almost claimed Tanya's life.

I made Peter stop wearing coloured shirts and flash ties, and made sure his jacket was dusted down before each media appearance. If he had an early-morning television appearance or doorstop, I would put drops in his eyes to try to disguise the redness brought on by late nights or lack of sleep, and I checked to see that his hair was neatly combed and his nails clean and clipped. (Once, when someone asked my position in Costello's office, I blurted out 'Nanny' before I could stop myself.)

I filled in the blizzard of quizzes sent in by the media (asking him to list his favourite movies, favourite restaurants, favourite music, favourite food); most times, our choices coincided, except once when he wanted to nominate *The Blues Brothers*, I added *Dr Zhivago* to try to get a bit more chick-appeal going. It didn't work.

This was on top of ensuring that he had his briefing notes, the most relevant media clips, and a selection of grabs or gags with him at all times.

He is one of the most reluctant shoppers I have ever come across — his idea of lashing out is to browse in a bookstore — so it was no small feat, on a stopover in Los Angeles, after he'd attended the spring meetings of the International Monetary Fund in Washington in April 1998, to get him into a Gap shop and make him fork out for a dark-blue casual shirt and a pair of blue-denim jeans to replace his Liberal-issue cream chinos. I wanted him to wear the outfit for the ritual Sunday pre-budget pic-fac (picture facility), or pig fucks, as the snappers called them, in his Treasury Place office in May.

These were cosmetic changes, but they were designed to emphasise his youth and energy.

On a more substantial note, Peter had not yet faced any questions about John Howard's decision to put Pauline Hanson's One Nation ahead of Labor in Liberal Party preferences, and I was certain that Laurie Oakes would ask him about this in his *Sunday* interview — another pre-budget ritual.

There was some unease about the morality as well as the political wisdom of the preference decision — reservations that I shared. Pauline Hanson was an Australian character I knew very well, even though I had never met her.

We needed a way of handling the issue that would not too directly challenge the prime minister, while still articulating a clear difference in approach. As I was dropping off to sleep, I had a light-bulb moment: Peter should just say he would put One Nation last in his own seat of Higgins! I wrote it down on my bedside notepad, so I wouldn't forget, and told Tony about it the next morning when he came to pick me up.

We had a routine before those major weekend interviews of gathering in the electorate office to workshop our responses and check out the morning papers, so we discussed the formula with Peter before the programme. We all agreed it was the best way to handle the subject. So, in response to Oakes' inevitable question, Peter said that he would put One Nation last in Higgins, 'not because I have any love for the Labor Party, but because I want to make it entirely clear that is not the future for Australia'.

We thought the interview had gone pretty well, and drove to Peter's Treasury Place office so he could finish writing his budget speech and pose for the pic-fac in his new jeans.

Before either happened, the phone rang. Tony O'Leary, a longstanding pal of mine and the prime minister's hardest of hard-nosed press secretaries, came on the line, expressing displeasure at Peter's One Nation comments, implying that we were undermining the PM's strategy. I couldn't argue with that. Our conversation only lasted a couple of minutes.

No sooner had he hung up than the prime minister rang for Peter. Their conversation lasted 45 minutes. Obviously, the PM was upset, and he told Peter so. He complained that, as a result of the interview, people would now be asking him what he would do with his preferences in Bennelong. According to Peter's account, he told the PM: 'Why don't you just say you will put her last?' to which the PM replied: 'Because I don't want you setting my agenda.'

And the PM was worried about Queensland, where the Liberals thought they needed Hanson's preferences.

Peter was a bit unsettled by the conversation. He feared that his colleagues would think he was positioning for the leadership, and that he had gone too far.

It was my first insight into the tentative side of Peter's nature. Although at the time I didn't fully appreciate its significance, this reluctance to strike would manifest itself later at critical moments, and would eventually smother his political career.

Tony Smith and I assured him he had done the right thing, and he went back to finish his speech and prepare for the photo shoot that would end up the next day (11 May) on the front page of almost every newspaper.

Forget the figures. The biggest breakthrough was the treasurer in jeans! The 3AW presenter Neil Mitchell couldn't believe it.

But there were more repercussions over the One Nation preferences on the morning of the budget. At the party meeting, the prime minister had led MPs in a round of applause for Peter Reith for his handling of the wharves' dispute. Although the treasurer was wiping out billions of dollars of deficit and restoring the finances, he did not rate a similar accolade. Peter was put out. Even though it increased the tension in the relationship between Peter and the prime minister, many of Peter's colleagues were rapt in his performance.

He also had a more pressing task, though — a final read-through of his budget speech, which had come back from the printers. And, as Peter read it, he noticed there was a mistake in the section on superannuation. What now? The lock-up for hundreds of journalists and the opposition would start in a couple of hours. Suspicions would be aroused if there was no copy of the speech in their pile of documents.

We had no alternative: I told the Treasury officials to pulp the speech and that we would get the corrected copy to them as soon as possible, and asked them to organise an initial print-run of a couple of hundred copies of the corrected version for the lock-up — and to worry about the rest later. Journalists wondered why the papers were still warm when they were handed out as they walked into the committee rooms.

The headlines the next day were all in a similar vein, heralding a budget that was 'Back in the Black'. Peter's stocks soared. Surprisingly enough, not everyone thought we were geniuses.

A couple of months later, in July 1998, Peter and I went to dinner at Kerry Packer's sumptuous residence at Bellevue Hill. James Packer, who had become friendly with Peter, was instrumental in organising it, figuring that Peter and his father should get to know one another better.

Howard was friendly with both Kerry Packer and Rupert Murdoch; as for Peter, he tried to make sure he kept the fathers on side and was always — quite rightly — very keen to ensure that he had the support of Rupert's son Lachlan, and Kerry's son, James.

However, that night at Bellevue Hill turned out to be, as Zorba the Greek would say, the full catastrophe.

It was the kind of dinner party you look back on with fascination and horror — so much so that I can't even remember what was on the menu, apart from us.

As well as Kerry and James, there were a number of Nine heavies in attendance, including David Leckie, Peter Meakin, Laurie Oakes,

1998: tragedies and triumph

Paul Lyneham, and Ray Martin.

Contrary to popular belief about how supportive he was of the Howard government, Kerry Packer did not have a good word to say about anybody in the government or anything that the government had done.

He told us that Labor was going to 'shit it in' at the next election, thanks to the impending introduction of the Goods and Services Tax (GST) — which he thought was a disaster — and more generally because we couldn't do anything right.

We treated workers badly, he said, and it was almost criminal how little nurses were paid. He knew because he spoke to them (the implication being that we did not). He scoffed at the tighter gun laws and said that, if he wanted to, he could go out right then and there and buy a gun. Of course he could — he was Kerry Packer.

It was downhill all the way from there. Peter was trying to be amenable by asking for suggestions about what the government could or should be doing. I veered off with some criticism of television and programmes such as *A Current Affair* for ripping into everyone and everything for no good reason other than wanting cheap headlines and to cut down tall poppies. That kicked things along for a bit, until Packer called it quits: 'Well, can we all agree to have coffee?'

When we said yes, he got up from the table to move into the lounge, saying: 'Finally, we can agree on something.' There was no point in pointing out that he was the one who had started it.

As the evening was winding up, he broke off from bagging us to bag Paul Keating, whom he loathed passionately. Keating, of course, reciprocated. The war between them had raged for years, and the worst place to be was in the middle of it.

We were milling about, preparing to leave, when Packer turned to Oakes and asked him why he had not done a story on Keating's piggery. He knew that Oakes had been given certain documents — which came as a surprise to Oakes. Oakes did not know that Packer knew he had the documents, and was taken even further aback when Packer wanted to know why, exactly, he had not produced a piece based on them.

Oakes replied that he had checked out the documents, and had found that they didn't stand up. He had been waiting for a source to come through, but he had not delivered. James said he thought that was fair enough, but it was not good enough for Kerry. It was apparently the one and only time that Packer tried to heavy Oakes. Oakes didn't budge.

At this point, Lyneham stepped forward, literally, and volunteered his services. He said he would look at the documents himself, even though as of that night he did not have them. Lyneham later somehow came by another set of the same documents, and fronted the extraordinary special *60 Minutes* programme on Keating's investments, which aired in March the following year.

Peter and I stayed right out of the Keating conversation, glad that Packer's attention had shifted elsewhere. We were about to go when Kerry himself announced that he was leaving. He had arranged to fly secretly to New York that night for treatment for his heart.

James offered to go with him to the airport, but Kerry insisted he stay with the guests. In the only show of affection all evening, he and James kissed and hugged. Kerry left, and so did we, soon after.

BACK IN THE OUTSIDE WORLD, Packer's predictions of the coalition's imminent demise seemed to be well judged. Although Peter was travelling well, the government was not. The tax package had not yet been released, and the constant speculation about the GST and the number of people it would kill or maim was taking its toll.

The post-budget bounce, which had taken the coalition's primary vote to 46 per cent, according to Newspoll, had been whittled away. The government was now running well behind, and panic was starting to set in. At the end of July, Newspoll had Labor's primary vote back up to 41 per cent, while the coalition's had crashed to 35 per cent. A procession of nervous-nelly MPs began trooping into Costello's office, urging him to make a move against Howard.

His support for the republic, the formulation and selling of the budget, and his prescience on One Nation, which had won 11 seats in the Queensland state election and rocked the coalition to the core, had won him a solid, if small, bloc of support in the party, mainly among the moderates.

Brian Loughnane — then chief of staff to John Moore, later the federal director of the Liberal Party and who, days after the 2007 defeat, at a gathering of the outgoing prime minister and his staff, was to describe himself as a Howard Liberal — crashed Kramer-like into the office I shared with Tony Smith.

Loughnane closed the door and pleaded for Peter to make a run for the leadership. 'He's the one who's got the momentum,' he told us, and offered his services to help make it happen. We declined.

Yes, Brian had been drawn to the party by Howard, but he was the ultimate pragmatist: he believed that the government would not survive beyond its first term, and that the only person who could save it was Costello.

It was not on. First, Peter did not then, nor did he ever, have enough numbers to make a credible assault on Howard; and, second, more critically, the timing was all wrong. Any attempt to destabilise the leader, barely more than a year into the government's first term, and as it was working its way through one of the biggest tax overhauls in history, would have been destructive and futile.

Planning for the tax package had begun more than a year before. The first meeting to discuss the broad parameters for reform between the prime minister, the treasurer, and their advisers in a specially constituted tax task-force took place on 11 June 1997. From the outset, nobody was under any illusions about the degree of difficulty involved. Even at that first meeting, they prepared themselves for the possibility of a double-dissolution election.

Peter Reith had suggested that there should be a plebiscite, but Howard and Costello wanted the full package out in advance of the election, preferably with the legislation already drafted. They wanted a mandate for it.

Hanging over every meeting like an evil mist was *Fightback!*, John Hewson's 1993 political suicide-note. Howard insisted that a copy of the manifesto should be in the room whenever the task force met, to ensure that everyone remembered its lessons and that no one went beyond it.

All the way through, Costello's fixation was on the rate at which the GST would be struck. It had to be less than the 15 per cent set in *Fightback!*, but not so low that people would believe an increase was inevitable. His view was that anything less than 10 per cent was unbelievable, and that anything above 10 per cent was unsaleable.

Ted Evans, at that stage head of Treasury, who had also been through Labor's ill-fated consumption-tax exercise, sounded his own warning at that first meeting. He said the reason that the GST had failed in the past was on equity grounds. Considerable work would have to be done on compensation and on closing tax loopholes.

There was discussion at that meeting about corralling third parties, but this proved to be as difficult as herding brown snakes. Labor was practised at getting interest groups on side, either through bribery or blackmail, and its efforts were always lauded as clever politics.

Once the media sniffed that the coalition had threatened anyone, or offered them inducements to get on board, there were howls of outrage. How dare the Liberals close down dissent or muzzle critics, or try to buy them off!

Welfare and charity groups were highly suspicious of the planned reforms, and business lobbies were unreasonable about or deliberately blind to the political compromises that the government would have to make if it was to have any hope of success.

On 23 March 1998, Howard, Costello, and the task force met with the Business Coalition for Tax Reform. The business coalition wanted the GST to buy out other indirect taxes, including payroll tax, and wasn't fussed if this was at the expense of income-tax cuts.

Howard was not sympathetic. He told them that the government had to 'offer something to the punters'. 'We need sweeteners,' he said.

The Asian financial crisis was still playing out and, with all the heartache involved in getting the budget back into surplus, Howard said they wanted to keep it there. The business coalition suggested a staged approach, to first introduce part of the package with some of the concessions, and then the rest later, with the GST funding other indirect tax cuts.

Howard told them they could put up a proposal for a staged approach if they wanted to, but he didn't necessarily agree with it. Costello said he would think about it overnight and get back to them the next day.

That was code for 'Forget it.' Costello thought that a staged approach would arouse suspicions, with people figuring that it meant the GST rate would go up in the second round. There was to be one package, one hit, one shot at getting it through. There was no other way.

On 1 April, there was some desultory discussion about striking the GST at a 7.5 per cent rate.

'It's not a goer,' the PM said.

'The political weak point is that no one will believe the rate will stay that low,' Costello offered.

They fixed on 10 per cent, which still meant that payroll tax could not be abolished. This pretty much ensured that business support for the package would be lukewarm.

They then considered abolishing tax returns, which would also mean the abolition of work-related deductions. This drew an admission from the prime minister that he was 'terrified' at the prospect of protesting nurses and others on the campaign. That dropped off the agenda, too.

The prime minister was also the first to raise at the meeting on 1 April the proposal to give the states all the GST revenue as a means of getting their support and establishing a 'solid compact' between the Commonwealth and the states.

Max Moore-Wilton, head of the prime minister's department, whose nicknames 'Max the Axe' and 'Much Moore Wilton' were well earned, suggested giving the states a choice of either a share of the GST or increases in funding.

The complexity of the undertaking was mind-boggling — what to apply the GST to, and what to leave out. Costello and Treasury wanted it as broad as possible: partly for simplicity, and partly for revenue raising.

Meetings began early in the morning and finished late at night, and spread over weeks and months as they debated health insurance, dental services, pharmaceuticals, medical appliances, education, tourism, charities, and even play groups.

The two most difficult issues from the very beginning and all the way through were fuel and alcohol, and they ended up costing Howard, Costello, and the government dearly.

Whenever Tony Smith and Nigel Bailey from our office emerged from the task-force meetings and reported the discussions about suggested exemptions, I had one rejoinder: the government could not charge pensioners a 10 per cent GST on their milk and bread and exclude, for instance, golf-club fees.

On 27 May, Peter Worthington, who had been conducting focus groups, gave the task force a sobering presentation in the Explorers Room, a small conference room in the cabinet suite. The encouraging news was that people were convinced that reform was essential. The last thing they wanted from the government was band-aid solutions. Some of them were sophisticated enough to raise Commonwealth–state relations, and all of them were cynical enough not to believe much of what the government told them about the GST.

After all, they well remembered that both sides had ruled it out in the past. They recognised that a goods and services tax would give them more control over their own income, but they worried about the impact on necessities.

Then came a slide that Worthington had captioned 'The Hewson Debacle'.

'If I heard it once, I heard it a thousand times. The cake. With icing or without,' Worthington told them.

Who could ever forget the cake that killed John Hewson in 1993? Peter Reith was to later claim that the reason Hewson tripped up on how the GST would apply to a cake was that he was not familiar enough with his own policy.

Costello did not have that problem. He lived and breathed it every day, and knew it as well as the Treasury boffins who had helped design it.

More ministers were brought into the discussions in July, each one bringing their own set of concerns: Jocelyn Newman was worried about Fringe Benefits Tax and welfare; Darryl Williams was concerned about family mediation centres; and Peter Reith sounded a warning, which later would turn out to be correct, about its effect on horse racing.

For every loophole that was closed, another three would open up. There seemed no end to it, but the prime minister was keen at the 7 July meeting to wind up the discussions. He told them that cabinet would have to sign off on the package the following week, that it would go straight to a party meeting, and that it would then be released by the end of July.

Howard was exuberant. 'We could win in a very big fashion if we get this right,' he told his colleagues.

The package was released at a lock-up for the media on 13 August. The two offices had agreed that the prime minister would speak for about ten minutes, and then Peter would go through the detail in a PowerPoint presentation.

Despite this, the prime minister went for a solid half-hour, determinedly making his claim of ownership of the package. By the time Peter got to speak, it was starting to get late, and journalists were itching to go off and start writing their stories. His thunder had been well and truly stolen.

Walking behind Howard and his wife Janette as they left the room, I heard her chip him about his speech. 'You went for far too long,' she said. He turned around, saw me, and did not reply, except to say, 'Mmm'. Howard wasn't stupid. He knew exactly what he was doing.

Initially, the package was incredibly well-received in the media. It offered a 10 per cent GST, balanced with the abolition of ten state taxes, and $12 billion in tax cuts — then the largest ever to be delivered. And there was a clincher: all proceeds would be given to the states, and the tax could not be changed — either increased or decreased, or its application altered in any way — without the express approval of every state and territory government and both houses of federal Parliament.

For what it's worth, I always believed that giving the GST revenues to the states was a mistake — there would be no thanks from the premiers, nor could they be trusted to spend the money wisely. Although Costello essentially agreed with this argument, he also believed that it would have been harder to sell the GST without the revenue giveaway. And he harboured a hope that some of the premiers might actually come out in support of it. As if.

Two days after the package was released, on Saturday afternoon, Christina rang. I rang her every day, sometimes a couple of times a day, but I am ashamed to say that I dreaded her calls — only because I feared the bad news that they usually brought, and I was worried that my words of comfort or hope would be woefully inadequate. Sometimes she rang to tell me that the latest treatment was no longer working and that the tumours had grown, or to ask whether I could find out more about a story she had seen on the latest cancer-cure.

This call was about none of the above, but it was the worst possible kind of news.

That morning, my brother's wife, Nicki, had bent over to spray a stain on the carpet and had keeled over. She never got up. She was taken to Monash Hospital and put on life-support.

Several meetings followed with doctors. At first, they described the series of tests they had conducted to determine if she was in a coma and still alive, including a very simple one in which ice-cold water was poured into her ear. Normally, this would at least provoke a twitch. There was nothing — no response.

The family gathered the next day to hear the awful news from the doctors. They had been using the term 'brain dead'. What that really meant, they said, was that, as a result of a brain aneurism, she was dead.

Nicki's two boys — Andrew, a month shy of his 16th birthday, and Peter, 14 — her husband, and each of us said our goodbyes to her separately at her bedside. The doctors turned off her life-support.

Nicki was buried a few days later at the Springvale Cemetery. Christina and I, holding hands and crying, watched her coffin being lowered into the ground. Christina turned to me and said: 'I always wondered which was worse, to die suddenly, or to go like this. At least when you suffer you get to know how much people love you.' She had bought the plot next to Nicki.

Their fathers had been lifelong friends, and had travelled out to Australia together on the same boat. Their daughters had been born a month apart; through the marriage of son and daughter, they had become in-laws; and they had both died not knowing the fate of their children. It was just as well.

There was little time to sit and mourn. Work was an escape from the constant pain of grief and fear. Providing answers to questions from hundreds of journalists, most of them hell-bent on tripping us up, and working 20 hours a day, seven days a week, was nothing compared to death and terminal illness.

Obviously, care was needed to avoid stuff-ups. I had already lost one career; I could not afford to lose another. Apart from anything else, Christina was not working, and we needed the money. More importantly, any problem thrown up at work, unlike other things, could be fixed.

The first-blush response to the tax package was excellent. The coalition was back in front in the polls and, not wanting to lose the initiative, the prime minister called an election on 30 August for 3 October.

For Peter, each day was like sitting for a tax exam. But whereas others might consider 95 or 98 per cent accuracy worthy of honours, he had to be 100 per cent right, 100 per cent of the time.

There were three of us with him everywhere he went — me, Tony, and Nigel, who knows as much about tax as anyone in Australia. My objective at all times was to avoid the killer cake or anything resembling it.

Peter would insist that Nigel sit within his range of vision during all interviews and question–answer sessions so that, if he even looked like he was about to make a mistake, a shake of the head from Nigel would warn him off.

We all went slightly mad. Every time we boarded a flight we would put our headphones on, and sooner or later Nat King Cole's 'Lazy Hazy Crazy Days of Summer' would croon through the internal sound system. Nigel would start singing along to that or Bobby Vinson's 'The Night Has a Thousand Eyes'.

Bill Clinton was in trouble with Monica Lewinsky; as he combed through the inquiry transcripts whenever we broke for coffee, Peter would ask for a definition of telephone sex.

We all had to find our ways of escape.

As it turned out, Peter did not make any major mistakes, even though in the last week of the campaign, with his confidence ballooning, he agreed to do a special with Ray Martin for *A Current Affair*.

This was killer cake meets triffids meets Independence Day — a walk through the Myer department store in Bourke Street, Melbourne, with Ray and cameras in tow, to explain how the GST would affect all the goods that Myer had to offer.

We tried to plot a route through the store that would primarily take us through goods (such as electricals and flooring) which might end up being cheaper with the removal of wholesale sales tax and, secondly, that would avoid goods which would obviously go up, or would be too complicated to explain.

Put simply, we wanted to stay away from the food hall at all costs, and the clothing department, too.

Nigel did a trial run through Myer with Mary Wooldridge, a campaign advance expert, and then we did a separate run-through with Peter on our carefully plotted route. Just to spice things up, I invited Virginia Trioli from *The Age* to tag along and to witness the filming the next day.

When you're on a high wire, you might as well be riding a bicycle and juggling a baby elephant as well. We were starting to tank in the polling, and any slips at that late stage would have meant political death.

Naturally, Ray had his own ideas of how the Myer piece should go, and kept spearing off into dangerous territory. Surprise, surprise, we ended up in the food hall at a coffee shop chock-full of cakes.

Miracle of miracles, nothing went wrong. Predictably, the result was not much flow-on coverage. Who's interested in a story about a politician getting something right?

On election night, Peter was a panellist on Nine, and as soon as we arrived at the national tally room we headed for the caravan where the Liberals' federal director, Lynton Crosby, had set up his computers and phone network. We had an uneasy feeling, and

Lynton confirmed it by telling Peter that he was about to ring Howard and tell him it was all over. The early figures showed the coalition copping a pounding and heading for defeat.

Journalists were describing Costello as the man who couldn't lose. This was plain silly. Given the choice, which job would any sensible senior politician prefer — treasurer or opposition leader? I had no doubt which one Peter would rather be.

We all felt a bit sick after Lynton's briefing. Peter was anticipating questions about the leadership, but we agreed he should say nothing until all the votes were counted and the result clearer. I gave him a pat on the back and reassured him: 'It'll be OK. You're wearing your lucky tie.'

The next few hours, as he ducked and weaved and padded on Nine's panel, were excruciating — until it became clear that the coalition had just managed to flop over the line in enough seats to win the election.

The coalition had not only failed to get the convincing mandate that Howard and Costello had desperately sought, but they had almost lost the election. Still, a first-term government had been re-elected while promising to introduce a new tax. It was an extraordinary achievement.

Howard could not have got through it without Costello, and vice versa. The feat failed to impress Kim Beazley, however, who claimed a moral victory because Labor had won the popular vote — so he had no compunction in opposing the GST.

The hard slog of implementation began immediately. There was no time to waste.

NOTHING, BUT NOTHING, ever goes according to plan. My world was slowly disintegrating. For 18 months, Peter Gibbs and Jonathan Cebon had tried everything to help Christina. She never gave up, and they never gave up on her. Their efforts helped extend her life by more than a year. We got to spend more time with her, she was able to travel to Italy and Cyprus again, and fulfilled a wish to see the Great Barrier Reef. But the cancer was pitiless in its progession. Treatment would work for a time, then stop. First they had entered her in a clinical trial with a new drug, then another drug, and then they had tried radiotherapy.

The options were running out, but I pleaded with Gibbs to keep looking for new treatments, if she still wanted to fight. At that stage she did, so he did, too.

Just as we did when we were young, we went with her to all the treatments. We saw hundreds of others going through the same thing, sat waiting in terror for results, and dreaded what lay ahead.

On 24 November, I got another phone call, advising me that Christina had taken a turn for the worse, and that it would be best if I went to Melbourne. I flew down that afternoon. The next three weeks were a nightmare in excruciatingly slow motion. Nothing would stop the tumours growing, and she had been placed on a permanent morphine-drip for the pain.

Then I read a news story about Bob Jones performing partial liver transplants, and I rang him to ask if he could do it for Christina and me. He could not. At that stage, it was doubtful she would survive the surgery; in any case, when she found out, she would not agree to it.

The constant stress, the pain, and the cascading symptoms were sapping her resolve. Getting the morphine-dosage right was difficult. Too much caused incredible constipation; too little, and the pain was unbearable.

One night, her nose started bleeding and wouldn't stop. I drove her to emergency at Monash hospital and they took us into a cubicle. Only a curtain separated us from the next bed, and we could hear what was happening there.

A young woman had been abandoned by her boyfriend, and in her misery she had taken a drug overdose. The doctors had pumped her stomach and were trying to counsel her.

Christina and I were thinking the same thing. I felt like ripping the curtain aside and saying 'Look. Look at my sister. She has had to fight for life from the day she was born, and you are just throwing yours away. Can't you see how precious it is?'

For every act of kindness in that hospital, there was an act of cruelty — deliberate or intentional. I could have cut out the tongues of the two nurses who asked if she was my mother. I learned to pre-empt such talk by introducing myself as her sister. I also learned to leave her alone in the hospital as little as possible.

When she was crying out for more morphine from one of the nurses, the callous carer told Christina that she was not her only patient, and that she'd have to wait. I complained to her superiors.

The doctor in charge of palliative care came to speak to Christina, and told her there would be little point in calling an ambulance to take her to hospital if she had another bleeding episode. She maintained her composure beautifully, and informed him that that was exactly what she would do, and what did he suppose she should do — stay home and bleed to death? After he left I started sobbing, even though early on we promised one another we would not sit around crying together. She hugged me, and said: 'Don't worry about him — he doesn't know what he's talking about.'

I later wrote to him, pointing out how proud I was of her at that moment and how disappointed with him. I urged him to be more judicious in his future dealings with terminally ill patients. He had the decency to reply, and apologised.

Not once in her 43 years did I hear Christina express self-pity or complaints. There were no 'why me's' or 'what if's'.

Her skeleton was being slowly corroded by osteoporosis. A too-vigorous hug would crack her ribs, and bones in her toes broke from the pressure of the weight. She dealt with all adversity as she might a bad hand in poker. It might be rotten luck, but that's what you've been dealt, so now let's get on with the next round.

Actually, it is not quite true that she did not complain. She grew contemptuous of the health professionals who treated patients like cattle or suitable subjects for experiment, who jabbed and prodded without any care for the mental or physical hurt they caused.

But she never would admit to the pain or the suffering. A setback was something to be factored in, not succumbed to. Two terminal illnesses, two death sentences — first the thalassemia, and then the cancer — wrecked her body, but left no mark or taint on her spirit or her love for those around her.

My great friend and one of my mentors, the journalist Wally Brown, was diagnosed in 2004 with the wretched motor neurone disease.

Wally, another of those extraordinary people who filled his life with everything wonderful — family, friends, food, drink, travel, gardens, and work, in that order — was beyond stoical. 'We all have to die of something,' he said.

Yes, but why do such good people have to suffer so? Maybe it is, as Christina said at the cemetery that day, so that they know before they die how much they are cherished.

In those last couple of weeks of her life, Christina could not walk very well, so I would put her in a wheelchair and push her around the hospital corridors, or take her outside for some fresh air. She would stay quiet for long periods of time, and we would just sit there together. Sometimes I would read to her, or we would watch television.

'It doesn't matter if you're in a wheelchair if you have your friends and family around you,' she whispered to her very dear friend Cheryl Tinker.

Icy fingers wrapped around my heart when the nursing sister told Steve and me that she had been classified DNR: Do Not Resuscitate.

Christina did not want to go to a hospice, so I took her home. Time was clearly running out. She had spent so much of her life in hospitals that I didn't want her to die there. Mum and I would look after her.

She was lucid initially, then later feverish and couldn't sleep. She would roam around the house at night, and early one morning hopped into bed with me. 'If it keeps going on like this, I don't think I can go on,' she said. I asked her if she knew how much she meant to me and she nodded, yes.

She told me she had written us two letters, and showed me where they were in her filing cabinet.

To help her rest, I increased her morphine dose. I would slip a few drops in with her flavoured milk — which, apart from ice-cream, was about all she was eating.

She didn't want to see anyone. More importantly, she didn't want anyone to see her. 'You are beautiful on the inside as well as the outside,' I would say to her, but she wanted people to remember her as she used to be.

The extra morphine dulled the pain, but it dulled the rest of her as well, and she did little else but sleep. I would let people come to her bedroom door to see her and make their goodbyes, but no further.

Mum insisted I cut the dose so we could at least speak to her and she to us, so I did.

On the morning of 17 December, she woke up and she was back. She was alert and talkative. We helped her shower and dress. I rang Dr Don Bowden, the head of the thalassemia unit at Monash, who wanted to see her, and who had been tireless in his support of her. He came for a cup of coffee; almost childlike, she was staggered at how emotional he was when he left.

'My doctor is crying. Crying,' she said in disbelief.

I rang one of her best friends, Helen Yanner, also a thalassemia patient, and told her she could come, too.

By the time the palliative-care nurse came for her daily visit, my spirits were soaring at the transformation. 'Maybe it's a miracle.'

She was a very wise and very gentle woman. 'There are all kinds of miracles,' she said quietly.

I rang my brother to tell him to come for lunch. He picked up his boys, Andrew and Peter, from school, and brought them as well. It had been a while since they had seen Christina like her old self.

Mum roasted salmon in the oven, which was one of Christina's favourite meals, and we sat around the table talking about school days and playing guessing games about movies (such as, 'What was the name of the hunchback of Notre Dame?' She knew it was Quasimodo). I had made a Christmas cake and wanted to cut it, but she wouldn't let me. She asked me to make her favourites: mince pies. She would wait for those.

Steve and I put her to bed in the late afternoon. She was still alert, but tired. After Steve and the boys left, Mum and I got out the photo album from her 40th birthday and went through the pictures, and then found a copy of her speech. I read it out loud. When it came to the part where she paid tribute to Mum, she blew her two kisses. When it came to the bit about me, I skated over it. I knew I wouldn't be able to get through it.

'Who wants to hear that again?' I said.

'Yeah.'

We kissed her goodnight, and started getting ready for bed. We were exhausted but happy. Maybe she could make it to Christmas. As I slipped on my nightie, I heard her little bell tinkle, and I ran into her room. She was bolt upright in bed, with both her hands outstretched. Before I could reach her, she had fallen back on the bed, and her body began to seize up. It only lasted a few seconds, and then it stopped.

CHAPTER EIGHT

Killing dragons, getting stoned

Christina's death, and Nicki's, too — one, decades in the making, and the other having happened in an instant — put everything into perspective. It didn't make work less important. Everything became more important, while at the same time reinforcing another obvious fact of life: political setbacks fall a long way down on the misery index. You have the power to fix them, and they can be fixed by doing the right thing at the right time.

The surest way to Loserville is to panic, lash out, mope, or feel sorry for yourself, or to forget the other golden rule of politics: no matter how bad a situation is, it is always possible to make it worse.

Yet it happens so often that politicians, even the best of them, suffer brain snaps. One minute they're behaving like rational human beings, performing superbly; the next minute, their brain cells have collided with their egos or emotions — or if it's really, really bad, with some vital part of their anatomy (see Bill Clinton) — and off they go.

Instead of getting out the old billycart and getting on with it, they flap around till the wheels drop off.

We were not at that point when I returned to work in January 1999. The cracks would appear over the next few years — small ones at first and then, later, ones big enough to swallow you up whole, billycart and all.

In those early days, our conversations each morning would begin with Peter asking: 'What disasters have befallen us today?'

There were days when we could laugh about it. Other days, it was no laughing matter.

Delivering the bad news every morning is one of the lesser joys of being a press secretary, especially to someone who had become expert at avoiding television and radio news bulletins. To try to avoid being the office nag if there was an internal policy stuff-up, I would insist that the relevant adviser tell the treasurer first, then we would work out a plan to fix it, whether or not it reached the media.

Inventing jokes or word pictures to help tell the stories was another one of the requirements. Usually that was fun, even if things didn't always go as planned.

Peter had previously used the old nursery rhyme about the three little pigs — the first of which had built its house of straw; the second, sticks; and the third, bricks — to emphasise the importance to the economy of a solid foundation of tax reform. So, when the inflation figures for the June quarter came out in July 1999, I trotted out another animal analogy.

The figure had come in at a low 1.1 per cent, with the economy growing at more than 4 per cent. Keating would have called them a beautiful set of numbers, but I wasn't going to lead us into that trap, no sirree.

Instead, I suggested to Peter that he should say we had killed off the inflation dragon. I could picture the cartoons: St Peter slaying the dragon. He was taken with it, but was rightly cautious.

'Yeah, but I can't say inflation's dead. It might come back.'

Good point. 'Okay then, say that the inflation dragon has been put to sleep. It's dormant in its cave.' Much better.

Not even half an hour later, in his opening remarks at his doorstop welcoming the figures, he declared, 'There's no life in the inflation dragon.' Uh-oh.

Although he went on to say it was not stirring, that it was

dormant, it was too late. Peter Martin on ABC's 'PM' that night zeroed in on the dead dragon. Peter was furious, absolutely certain he had not said it. I had to produce his transcript to convince him that he had in fact killed the dragon.

The Reserve Bank governor, Ian Macfarlane, faced questions on it the next day, and refused to endorse the treasurer's remarks.

The inflation dragon remained part of the landscape until Kevin Rudd and Wayne Swan disposed of it and turned it into a genie to try to whip up outrage against Howard and Costello.

That was flawed as both an economic strategy and as a picture story. Inflation was the least of our problems, and the genie was too namby-pamby. Every time I hear 'inflation genie', all I can think of is Barbara Eden in her skimpy little bolero and harem pants.

Another word picture of mine, in July 2001, when Kim Beazley and Barry Jones released 'Knowledge Nation', Labor's blueprint for the future — notionally designed to improve the country's education, skills, and research sectors, and to create new industries and modernise old industries — had far greater success.

I had always got along well with Barry, and respected him. He was a teacher at Dandenong High School when my brother was there, and as kids we had watched him on *Pick A Box*. He knew something — usually lots — about everything, and he was always happy to tell everybody everything he knew.

When I was a member in the 1980s of the Hot Chocolate Club with Gerry Hand — a small group of lefties who would meet up in the Members' Dining Room in Old Parliament House at the end of sitting days, just to unwind — Barry would occasionally stop by for a chat, to tell us about the latest bionic-ear invention, the hole in the ozone layer or when, exactly, Halley's Comet was due.

Bob Hawke couldn't stand Barry. A few journos, including myself, were talking to Hawke at the back of his VIP aircraft once about his ministers, when one of my colleagues said to him: 'Take Barry Jones …' Hawke interrupted and said testily, 'No, you take him.'

When he was fighting off Gareth Evans for his seat of Lalor, Barry quoted Protestant reformer Martin Luther to declare his refusal to budge: 'Here I stand, I can do no other.' But in *The Herald Sun* the next day, the sub-editors had changed my copy to say that Jones had quoted Martin Luther King, the American civil-rights activist.

Barry thought that was funny. I was embarrassed, and roared at the news editor (it wasn't his fault technically, but they would never tell you which sub had changed your copy — it was like a secret society on the newspaper backbench). Didn't he know the difference between the two Martins? And, by the way, why did the subs feel they had the right to change my copy without even asking? I told him I was quite capable of making mistakes on my own, without having others make them for me.

Anyway, when the Knowledge Nation document landed on my desk, minutes after Barry and Kim released it, I didn't know whether to laugh or cry when I turned the page and found the incredible, indelible diagram of a complex tangle of cultural connections that Barry had devised to try and explain what it was all about. There was no need to go any further.

Peter was on holidays, and Nick Minchin and David Kemp, who were both in Melbourne, had been charged with responding. I rang Kemp's press secretary, Cathy Job, and told her that they should forget everything else, zero in on the diagram, and refer to it as 'spaghetti and meatballs'.

Just to be certain the message was not lost, I also rang Glenn Milne, who was Seven's political correspondent: 'Glenn, it's all about the diagram. Spaghetti and meatballs.' Mitch Fifield was also in Melbourne, so I called him, too. Mitch cleverly blew up the diagram to poster size, and gave it to Minchin and Kemp to wave about.

Knowledge Nation was dead within minutes. Deader than the inflation dragon.

I had a few pangs about that one. But, as the Mafia says, it was nothing personal — just business. Barry's idea might have been brilliant; but, in politics, being a genius doesn't count for very much if you can't sell your policies. While I felt for Barry, it was pretty silly of him to have included that diagram in the document; the opposition was just asking for trouble by using it. As it turned out, Beazley's office knew it, too: they had warned Barry, suggesting to him that he remove it, but he wouldn't listen. They should have insisted.

In the treasurer's office, we would spend hours going through every single one of our documents, policies, or press releases, to make sure there were no obvious hooks or mistakes that the opposition could latch onto and use to emasculate or ridicule a good policy or speech. I wasn't there to skate over, or excuse, Labor's mistakes, and this one was right up there with the best of them. There were plenty of others capable of doing that.

Part of my job (and it is the same for every political staffer, no matter where they sit) was to protect and promote my boss and the government's policies. Or, if I disagreed with them, I would shut up and try and find ways to change the things I didn't like. I didn't launch wilful attacks on Labor — and I gave credit where it was due when I was asked — but if the opposition did or said the wrong thing, I wasn't about to let it pass. And they returned the favour when they could, usually in a nastier fashion.

I felt no pangs, though, in launching strikes against Mark Latham. I had had minimal contact with him as a journalist. When I was at *The Age*, after I once gave him a passing flick in a piece that I wrote, he rang to — quite aggressively — have a go at me. I suggested we have coffee to get to know one another a bit better, but never got around to it. He held no appeal for me, either as a politician or a person.

When he was appointed shadow treasurer by Simon Crean, Latham went on *Lateline* and left open the possibility that Labor might reintroduce its disastrous, once briefly held policy of abolishing negative gearing. I worded up Oakes to make sure that

Elpiniki, Andreas, Steven, and me in Cyprus, shortly before Andreas departed for Australia in December 1951.

Christina, me, and Steven at Peter Leonidas' wedding, c. 1958.

At the coastline of Paphos, Cyprus. (Photo by Natalie Philippou.)

Christina, photographed during her first visit to Cyprus, c. 1976.

Steven and his four sons. From left: Peter, Thomas, Steven, Christian, and Andrew. Steve's partner, Dana Forte, is the mother of the twins, who were born in September 2009.

Christina and me.

My husband, Vincent Woolcock, and me. When Costello saw the photo he said we looked like Sonny and Cher.

Bob Hawke down the back of the plane, with Hazel, for a sing-a-long with the journos. In this photograph, Paul Lyneham leads the singing; I am behind him. The man in the fez was one of Hawke's coppers. It was after a visit to the Middle East in 1987.

Bob Hawke stripped down to his red speedos (they don't call them budgie smugglers for nothing) at one of the politicians-versus-press gallery cricket matches. (Photo by Julie Herd.)

Peter Conran, left, head of the Cabinet Policy Unit, and Arthur Sinodinos, Howard's former chief of staff, in the cabinet room for the staff farewell after the 2007 election defeat.

Before Julia it was Carmen. Female gallery reporters, plus Glenn Milne, surround Carmen Lawrence at the ALP's National Conference in Hobart in 1994. Back row, from left: Glenn Milne, Margot Kingston (with her arm on my shoulder), Lyndal Curtis, Annie White, Michelle Ainsworth, and Julie Flynn. Front row, from left: Brenda Conroy (who went on to become Lawrence's press secretary), me, Lawrence, and Fran Kelly.

Gough Whitlam with his arm around me. The photo was taken at Old Parliament House when a section of the press gallery was opened to tourists. There had been some reports of sexual harassment charges against a NSW Liberal minister, and Gough asked if it would be all right if he put his arm around my shoulder for the photo. Then just as Bowers took the pic, Gough said, sotto voce: 'Hold on a moment while I adjust my left testicle.' Of course he made sure he looked like a statesman. (Photo courtesy of Michael Bowers.)

Peter Costello standing under the sign 'Anything Is Possible' at Parklands High School in Burnie, Tasmania, at the end of July 1998, two weeks before the release of the massive tax reform package that included the 10 per cent GST. (Photo by Grant Wells, courtesy of *The Advocate* (Burnie).)

Peter Costello at the FDR Memorial in Washington, DC, April 1998. The memorial has sculptures of men standing in a dole queue. I told Peter to stand on the end of the queue so I could take the pic, telling him 'This will be us after the next election.' Even though they didn't know who we were, tourists standing around burst out laughing. Peter always worried that my sense of humour would get us into trouble. The battles were raging over the GST, and the coalition was about ten points behind in the polls.

Peter Costello with Christina and then captain of Essendon, James Hird, following Peter's address to the Essendon Football Club, a couple of days after he put the budget 'back in the black' in May 1998. (Photo courtesy of John Donegan.)

Crean was asked about it the next morning, whereupon Crean killed it off instantly. I came up with the line for Costello that Latham couldn't hold a policy position from *Lateline* to lunchtime.

Latham copped it on two fronts — first, his leader had repudiated him and, second, he was ridiculed by the treasurer. It should have helped sink him, but didn't. I suggested we call him Arthur *and* Martha, because there was clearly more than one person living in the Latham suit.

Everyone in the Labor Party and almost everyone in the Press Gallery was intimately acquainted with his character and his flaws, but they went ahead and made him leader anyway, and then pretended he was fit to be prime minister.

It showed how desperate some sections of the media had become by 2004 to get rid of Howard and the coalition.

OCCASIONALLY, AS A PRESS SECRETARY, I found that, whether I tried to 'help' journalists or not, there was no pleasing some of them. Michelle Grattan was a serial harasser. One day, she pleaded for something — anything — to help kickstart her column. Finally, against my better judgement, I relented. It was when Beazley was still opposition leader. He had been asked about his election prospects, and had replied: 'I don't know if I'll win. I mean, governments usually get re-elected, and I think a lot of people think that, too. But if we don't win, we don't win.' His office had neglected to put out the transcript, but I had seen it on the television news, so I pointed her towards one of the networks.

This was in August 2001, only a few months out from the election. Grats found the quote and, despite the circumstances behind the story, she reported it as the government 'gloating' over Beazley's remarks. There was no gloating. I was simply staggered that Beazley could have said something so sanguine about winning or losing an election.

The daily cut-and-thrust of politics was a constant backdrop, like white noise in an office full of computers. It provided the adrenaline to get you through the day, but the real rush came from being able to do things — big things. Not just criticise or spike from the sidelines, but help make decisions, every day, which might improve people's lives.

A few months after Christina died, Jonathan Cebon, the head of oncology at the Austin, called. I figured that maybe he needed to clear up something relating to her illness. Instead, he asked if I could arrange a meeting between Costello and The Australian Society for Medical Research to discuss an increase in funding in the May budget.

Two directors of the society, Dr Andrew Sinclair, of the Royal Children's Hospital, and Dr Matthew Gillespie, of St Vincent's, met with Costello, his then chief of staff, Mike Callaghan, and myself at the Treasury Place office in April, and argued eloquently for the increase, which had been recommended in a specially commissioned report.

They were worried that the report was going to be buried, and they pleaded for the government to nurture the culture that had produced such greats as Howard Florey and Macfarlane Burnet.

Peter was impressed, and Mike was especially engaged. The budget had lacked a centrepiece, and they knew instantly that they had found one. The 11 May budget duly included an additional $615 million for medical research — a doubling of existing funding. I pinched the directors' line, about nurturing the culture, for Peter's speech, adding Victor Chang's name to the list as well.

Mark Textor conducted a special focus group each budget, and would ring through to the prime minister with the results late at night. We would also get a tape of the audience reaction when people, with worm-o-meters attached, watched the speech to see which bits worked and which didn't. This particular night, the 'worm' went off the chart when the extra research-funding was announced.

There had been a small leak about the increased funding in one of the papers before the budget and, acting on this, Dr Cebon wrote to me, thanking me for interceding. I showed the letter to Peter, who, after delivering his speech, wrote on it: 'I saw Gus Nossal in the paper saying that Woolly [Michael Wooldridge] was the best health minister ever for getting this. In reality it was you who got it. Something good, from something bad.'

Dr Cebon sent another letter after the budget, thanking me for my 'pivotal role'.

They were both too generous, but their words were like balm on my wounded soul. Christina would have approved.

Dr Cebon, who is as clever a lobbyist as he is a clinician, made contact again a few years later. It was after I had left Costello's office, and while I was working in the Cabinet Policy Unit, attached to the prime minister's office. The Austin was planning to build a dedicated cancer-treatment centre, which it was naming after Olivia Newton-John, and she was spearheading the fundraising drive. They were desperate for money. Could I help? Of course.

I discussed it with both the head of the unit, Peter Conran, and Arthur Sinodinos, the PM's chief of staff, both of whom agreed that the government should support the project. It was sent off to the Department of Prime Minister and Cabinet, along with some other health-related items, where it languished.

We had to get the department to work out the formula and devise the programme through which this particular grant, and the other health-related payments, could be made. Although they were worthy projects, we couldn't just write out a cheque for them: we had to have a proper process to cover the payments so we could include them in the budget. We left it to the department to come up with the appropriate mechanism.

Weeks later, I asked the health adviser, a public servant, what was happening with the request. The budget was approaching, and we needed their response.

'They don't like the idea', he said. 'They don't want to do it.'

So much for Howard and the government bullying the public service, as critics often claimed.

It was time to bully, just a little bit. I was furious, and made it clear with a few f-words inserted that it was not for them to decide what they would or would not do, depending on what they did or did not like. Their job was to tell us how to get things done.

A $10 million donation from the Commonwealth for the centre was approved, and announced on budget night. The centre is currently being built and, in a touching recognition of Christina, who campaigned ceaselessly for improvements in patient care, the Austin is planning to recognise her in the courtyard of the new complex.

THE SUCCESS OF PETER'S BUDGET in 1999 was one of the few highlights for him in that second term of government. It was an unremitting grind, and the weight of the work was beginning to tell.

As well as the implementation of the GST, he was committed to a programme that included a continuing campaign of corporate-law reform, a strengthening of finance-sector governance that was to prove critical in Australia's ability to withstand the global financial crisis, and the overhaul of business taxation — and he was expected to carry the banner for the conservatives in favour of the republic.

There was a separate tax unit, under Phil Gaetjens, attached to the treasurer's office to handle a lot of the day-to-day work of GST implementation, and to act as a ready-response unit.

Just as each technicality was resolved, another more complex, more bizarre, and more preposterous one would rise up to replace it.

Clive Hamilton put out a press release on 1 March 1999 to advertise his forthcoming evidence as executive director of the Australia Institute to the Senate inquiry into the GST. The headline on the release was: '65 MORE DEATHS ANNUALLY DUE TO GST PACKAGE.' He said this would happen because of 'increased air pollution and traffic accidents if the government's proposed changes to fuel prices in the GST Package go ahead'.

A columnist in *The Land* warned of bushfire infernos if the tax changes meant that farmers could not afford the livestock to graze on the brush.

The Australian reported that Australians would have longer hair because they wouldn't be able to afford to get it cut as often.

Queensland's *Fraser Chronicle* ran a front-page banner headline: 'MUM: IT WILL KILL US.' And below it: 'FOOD WITH GST FRIGHTENS FAMILY OF NINE.'

When James Hardie announced it was moving operations offshore, it was portrayed as a reaction to the effect that the GST would have on building and construction, rather than the company moving to avoid a looming problem with asbestos claims.

The Australian Trucking Association warned that drivers could die from the extra pressure to cut costs because of the GST; winemakers threatened to go to jail rather than pay the tax; and, of course, it was going to destroy jobs and wreck the economy.

Even journalists who knew better wrote off none of these propositions as scare-mongering by people who should have known better. It was just run, and run prominently and endlessly.

In all the proposed changes to the tax system, there was an absolute insistence by the media that there should not be any losers. Not one. That would have been okay if the test was applied universally — that is, to Labor's tax proposals as well — but it never was.

Likewise, there was only muted pressure on Labor to support the government, or even to concede that what the government might be doing was warranted.

Peter's load was enormous, and the tolerance for him committing any errors was slim to zero. Michael L'Estrange confessed that he didn't know how Peter managed to store all the information in his brain. Pretty big head, pretty big brain, was the answer.

It was probably not the best time for Peter to do an extended interview with Peter Hartcher, then on *The Australian Financial Review*. I was dozing off as they talked, seemingly interminably, about business tax and the GST, and then roused when the subject got around to Peter's future — just in time to hear him say he had only one or two more budgets left in him.

It was obvious that the proverbial would hit the fan. Hartcher's article appeared around the time that Lachlan Murdoch heaped praise on Costello for his economic reforms and for having the courage to back a republic, so it kicked off another round of speculation on the leadership.

Peter's role in the republic campaign was, if anything, schizophrenic. Although he believed in the cause — strange as this might seem now — he got no pleasure in arguing for it in direct conflict with Howard and other conservatives.

He would rather poke himself in the eye than say, 'I am a republican.' Instead, he would say, 'I am for change …'

He did not like the model that had been chosen, nor did he have any affection for, or affinity with, the chardonnay set that had attached itself to it. Worse, Malcolm Turnbull, one of Peter's least-favourite people, was leading the 'Yes' brigade.

There were days in the closing stages of the campaign when he was clearly reluctant to take part, and we had to force him out to do interviews. When he did go out, he was a compelling advocate.

Howard and his lieutenants prosecuted the 'No' case in the same way they approached everything else: as if their lives depended on it. Howard believed that he had to win the referendum, otherwise defeat would be seen as a massive vote of no confidence in him. He feared a body blow from which he would find it difficult to recover.

After the inevitable defeat of the republican cause, Costello was subjected to a lot of vitriol from conservatives and monarchists. One day, he waved a thick wad of letters at me, all from alleged

Liberal Party supporters castigating him for his stand. 'This is all your fault,' he said.

I shrugged. It didn't worry me in the slightest. I was glad he had taken the stand he had.

Costello had no such reluctance on reconciliation. He wanted to walk across the Sydney Harbour Bridge, and complained bitterly to his colleagues and staff when Howard vetoed it. Together with other Liberals, he did the second walk later, in Melbourne. Michael Kroger was convinced that this would trigger a confrontation with Howard, but the moment had well and truly passed.

His less-conservative colleagues were now calling him LOM — Leader of the Moderates. Who would have thought that the poster boy for the New Right would make such a transition? He was acquiring a separate constituency.

When it came to the leadership, the conservatives in the Liberal Party would say that Howard came first, and then after him would be Peter. The trouble was, the love affair with Howard lasted a long time; and finally, when it ended, they still couldn't bring themselves to embrace Peter.

The agrarian socialists in the National Party were always deeply suspicious of Peter, and there was constant agitation for him to make bush tours, to prove he could relate to country folk. Peter agreed to such a tour in 2000, and in advance of it he did an interview on the ABC's 'AM' programme in which the interviewer, Mark Willacy, kept pressing him to say that farmers were whingeing or complaining too much. Peter wouldn't say it.

The next day, 17 November, *The Australian* carried a piece by Dennis Shanahan, headlined 'MINISTERS DECLARE WAR ON "WHINGEING" FARMERS', saying that the coalition had declared war on the National Farmers' Federation, accusing it of becoming a group of 'typical whingeing farmers'.

The story included a line from the National Party leader, John Anderson, saying that he believed the National Farmers' Federation was not prepared to acknowledge gains that the coalition had achieved for rural Australia. However, because of the 'AM' interview, Peter's colleagues assumed he was the sly briefer pinging farmers for being greedy.

A week later, during the tour, Anderson confessed to Peter that he was the one who'd rung *The Australian*. After he'd heard Peter's radio interview, and out of sheer frustration, Anderson had decided to round on the farmers for whingeing.

Poor Ando. He always was a bit of a tortured soul. The guilt got to him; it had clearly been playing on his conscience. Of course, Peter forgave him, but he was hurt by it. They were supposed to be mates. In the minds of other Nats, unaware of what Anderson had done, that story provided another reason to be wary of Costello.

The second bush tour was scheduled for August 2002 in Queensland, and was to be 'hosted' by Peter's good friends, Queensland senators George Brandis and Brett Mason.

Mitch and I sat down with Brandis and Mason to plan the tour. It's another golden rule of politics to pitch low and then, with a bit of luck and good planning, to exceed expectations. The last thing we wanted was to drum up extravagant pre-publicity. But the next thing we knew, there was a story in *The Australian Financial Review* by Tony Walker, headlined 'Costello's Longreach to the Lodge', likening the tour to the US caucuses that road-test leadership contenders heading for the White House.

Brandis, a clever lawyer and sometimes not-so-clever politician, was close to Walker, and it was exactly the kind of build-up that was not helpful. Our strategy was to carefully raise Peter's profile — not to make the prime minister paranoid about him.

After the 2001 election I had told Peter that, in my view, there was a greater chance that Howard would relinquish the job if he was given space. I did not believe that cornering or threatening him would work, and I thought that any attempt to do so would, in fact, have the opposite effect.

In those earlier days, Peter would agree; however, his instincts told him that Howard would never go voluntarily. Whenever it looked as if Howard was digging in, Peter would turn round and say, 'We're going to have to blast him out, you know that.' And before you knew it, the junior woodchucks were out there lobbing little hand grenades, which often rolled back onto our doorstep.

Peter promised to get Brandis to cool it, although it was hard to tell sometimes whether the junior woodchucks were freelancing or acting under surreptitious orders.

The previous year, a carefully planted story appeared in a Sydney paper to coincide with a visit by Peter to Bruce Baird's electorate. The story said that Bruce Baird was Costello's preferred choice for deputy.

It was stupid and presumptuous. I had a shocking migraine, and — in between episodes of throwing up in Peter's office bathroom — I had to spend more than a day with a pooper-scooper cleaning up the Baird mess. Christopher Pyne, who was the source for the story, protested that he was simply acting on instructions (from Peter).

So all that the *Fin* piece on the bush tour did was guarantee that a posse of hungry journos would be with us for the long drive from Longreach to Roma.

Glenn Milne warned me in advance that, while they might be happy with colour on the first day of the tour, by the second and third days they would be hungry for meat — and that there had better be some.

Thanks for that.

First, we had to sort out a few technical details. Brandis was insisting that we hire a convoy of vehicles to make the trip. He wanted six black four-wheel drives: he had visions of photos of the cars in a line, silhouetted at sunset on the open road. We had visions of wankery — and yet more work for those of us with the extra burden of the driving.

I had arranged for Vincent, my husband, recognised as the best advancer in the business, to do a dummy run of our route, and asked him to find us a small bus and driver, which he had.

Brandis had no interest whatsoever in a crummy little bus, and kept insisting on the black four-wheel drives. Finally, I said: 'Listen, George: no bus, no tour.'

We hired the bus. Brett and George, who are great company, kept us all amused on the bus by wearing their matching leather baseball caps. Bush boys they definitely were not.

The tour included a lunch stop in Barcaldine. George and Brett thought it would be a good idea if Peter had his photo taken in front of Labor's Tree of Knowledge. I hated that idea, too. Given all the suggestions that Peter had flirted with Labor as a youth, why would he want to be seen paying homage to a Labor icon? We managed to talk him out of that one, as well. Peter went into the pub and mixed with the locals.

He was a good mixer, and there were some great pictures for the photographers, to go with the ones already taken that morning. He had visited the School of the Air in Longreach, and the wife of the presenter at the local ABC radio station had baked him a cake for his birthday — much to the disgust of the young female reporter in the newsroom.

Then, talk about icing on the cake! As we were dozing off on the bus after lunch, heading for Blackall, it rumbled a bit, and then stopped. Oh god, not a breakdown! I'd never hear the end of it from George, and the analogy for the media — who, by the way, were following us in a convoy of four-wheel drives — would be irresistible.

It wasn't a breakdown, thank heavens. Instead, it was an example of magnificent divine intervention. Dozens of cattle were massed across the road. And there, herding them along, was the drover from central casting.

As I got off the bus, the delightful (and, now, sorely missed) Matt Price shook his head in disbelief and gave me a high-five. The drover was lean and handsome and laconic. And onside. Telstra mobile coverage? *Not a problem.* Drought? *We can cope okay.* He made no complaints, there was no hint of whingeing, and he didn't have his hand out for anything. And he was more photogenic than the Marlboro Man. The photos were sensational.

'Yep', I said to Matt, 'I arranged this, too. Nothin' to it, really.'

It didn't matter what happened after that — the success of the tour was guaranteed. On the last day, when Peter conducted the cattle auction in Roma that Bruce Scott had organised, he looked and sounded like a bushie, born and bred.

But for the Nationals, it was never enough. And for every step forward Peter made, two steps back usually followed.

WHEN HOWARD SAID in a radio interview that he would make an announcement on his future around his 64th birthday, it was not an idle, off-the-cuff remark. The formulation had been worked out long before to deflect questions on his retirement and the succession. Howard, his former chief of staff and eternal confidante, Grahame Morris, and his friend and former advertising executive, Geoff Cousins, worked out the line at Kirribilli some time after the 1998 election.

According to Morris, it was meant to be used during the 2001 election campaign, when the succession issue was bound to gain momentum. But it came out earlier than expected on Howard's 61st birthday on 26 July 2000, during an interview with Philip Clark on ABC radio. Howard said he would lead the government to the 2001 election, but after that would decide his future around his 64th birthday.

Morris insists that it was not designed to keep Costello in check, or to send a signal. But he admits that setting a deadline was a mistake. 'Who would have thought we would win four elections?' Morris now says.

There was little doubt in my mind then that Howard would stay. I had never seen anyone who loved his job so much. Plus, he was very good at it.

Peter was uncertain what Howard would do, and would act as if Howard owed him. He would murmur mysteriously every now and again about some arrangement between him and Howard, but he never really spelled it out. While he held out some hope that the prime minister would retire and hand over, he was not entirely confident it would happen.

In 2003, Howard had committed Australia to the Iraq War, had established clear ascendancy over Simon Crean, and was under no pressure to leave. On the other hand, Peter had only a small band of around 15 supporters. And he had suffered some serious body blows.

Despite promising to 'look through' the inflationary effects of the GST after its introduction, the Reserve Bank had instead overreacted and increased interest rates. Business and consumers were already trying to deal with a new tax and a new regime to account for it, and the bank decided, just in case people weren't unsettled enough, to give them another whack over the head. It was too much.

That's how we saw it, anyway, and our fears were justified when the national accounts, released in March 2001, recorded negative growth for the December quarter. Peter was shattered.

This had come on top of growing complaints about the Business Activity Statement (BAS), and two disastrous state elections — one in Western Australia, where Richard Court lost office, and the other in Queensland, where Labor increased its majority.

Petrol prices were going up, and the finger was being pointed at Peter for trying to skim more off refiners through the GST changes than they felt was justified — 1.5 cents a litre.

Costello was the bogey man, and it is true he was stubbornly holding out on changes to the BAS and the fuel excise, until it was obvious that the damage inflicted on the government, and on him, was becoming too great.

It was against this background that the infamous Shane Stone 'mean and tricky' memo was conceived. The 'memo' painted a devastating picture of the government, and characterised its principal players as 'mean, tricky, and out of touch'. It warned Howard that a swag of his backbenchers thought that he and Costello had gone out of their way to alienate traditional Liberal supporters, and complained that the government had to be dragged kicking and screaming to fix its mistakes.

For the record, Stone has maintained in an interview with me that the document was not a memo — it was actually the minutes of a meeting that he had attended in Queensland of most of the state's Liberal MPs. He and the party's state president, Con Galtos, and the federal director, Lynton Crosby, had compared their notes of the meeting and agreed on the content.

Stone rang the prime minister to tell him of the mounting fury and panic felt by the Queenslanders. They had instructed him to make sure he told both the prime minister and the treasurer. 'He [Howard] said, "Put it in writing — you have to document it properly"', Stone recalls.

So he did. Stone says he wrote it on his computer, printed off one copy — and one copy only — and then deleted the document from the computer 'so I could say to the PM, "This is the only copy."'

Howard visited Darwin soon after, and Stone went to his room at the Beaufort Hotel. With Howard were his wife, Janette, and principal private secretary, Tony Nutt.

Stone says he handed it over, saying, 'This is the only copy.'

'I understood it was dynamite,' Stone says. But he had a job to do, and he had done it.

'Howard would ring me and say, "We are working our way through those issues." He was clearly ticking them off. I thought, *This is terrific, this is great.*'

Reassured, he got on with his other business. Next thing he knew, he was walking around Sydney when his mobile phone rang:

> It was John, to say, 'Laurie Oakes has your memo.'
> I said, 'What memo?' He was a bit agitated.
> 'You know, that memo — the one you gave me in Darwin.'
> I was flabbergasted. I was close to his Sydney office, so I went straight there. I walked into the room, and he [the PM] was very agitated. Nutt and Sinodinos [the chief of staff] were there, and they all started pointing the finger at me.

The Bulletin published on the Wednesday, 1 May, but hit the streets on Tuesday evening. They held it back a little that night until Oakes could blast it all over the Nine News at 6.00 p.m. Howard's office had heard in advance that it was breaking.

It was bad news all round.

'I went for them,' Stone says, recollecting that Tuesday-afternoon encounter. 'I said, "Don't you dare accuse me of leaking it."

'I wasn't going to cop any of that. I had stood up to Keating and Hawke. They backed off.

'I wasn't going to be fitted up.'

Stone had been angry with Costello, and gives short shrift to Costello's later complaint that the events of that meeting should not have been put in writing and that, if there were complaints, they should have been made directly to him.

Stone reckons he tried that. He says that he and Lynton Crosby had sought a meeting with Costello before the Queensland election:

> We — the federal director and the federal president — waited over a month to be given a ten-minute audience with Peter to outline our concerns, then to be told, 'Don't you worry about that.'
> Lynton said, as we were leaving, 'Well, we know our place, and our view doesn't count.'

We were hugely irritated by the way issues like the BAS were being handled.

The research had us in freefall at the time. We were dead in the water. He wasn't interested. Other cabinet ministers who tried to raise things were rebuffed.

The day the story broke, Costello and his wife, Tanya, along with his personal assistant, Elizabeth McCabe, and I were in Washington attending the spring meetings of the International Monetary Fund. You know when your phone rings at 2.00 a.m. that it's never going to be good news.

Tony Smith was on the line to say that Oakes had got hold of some memo that Stone had written, and that he was faxing across the article.

After showering and dressing, I decided there was not much point telling Peter till around 6.00 a.m., figuring it was best if he got some sleep. I slipped the fax under his door, then rang his room to tell him about the disaster that had befallen us on this morning, and warned him to prepare for a torrid day.

He was puzzled, then furious, and then coldly angry. The 'Dear John' letter had become 'Blame Peter' — for everything. There were a lot of people, Liberals and Nationals alike, only too happy to do that.

Costello rang Howard from Washington. Howard was at Kirribilli, as was Stone, and Howard put him on the phone to Costello.

Stone basically told Costello that what was in the document was what his colleagues had been saying. 'He didn't ask me if I leaked it. I think he just assumed I did,' Stone says, although Costello later accepted Stone's later assurances that it was not him.

The source of the leak was never discovered, despite the prime minister commissioning Tony Nutt to carry out an investigation. The timing of its publication was also curious, given that the concerns raised in the memo about fuel excise and the BAS had been addressed.

The prime minister had kept the document in his briefcase after receiving it from Stone, and had given it to a female staffer to lock in the office safe only a few days before it became public.

Oakes says he was given the document on the Saturday before its publication; but, apart from saying that it was not Stone who gave it to him, and that it was clearly designed to damage the government, and not just Costello, he will not give any other details about how he came by it.

Stone says he has no copy of the 'memo' himself, and that he asked Oakes for a copy of the one he published. Oakes refused to give it to him. Oakes says he later destroyed it. The question is whether someone else made a copy based on the agreed version of the Queensland meeting, or somehow managed to copy the version Stone handed to the prime minister, or simply made their own notes of the meeting and then got them to Oakes personally or through an intermediary. I have tried, but failed, to pin down Oakes' source. Everybody has their theories. I reckon one reason Oakes would not hand over his copy of the 'memo' to Stone was because that copy, potentially, could have revealed the source.

Stone also wonders about the timing of the leak. Like Costello, Stone feels victimised by what happened.

'I was deeply hurt and wounded by the whole experience. I didn't deserve to be hung out there. I had done my job.'

The leak became the source of yet more tension with the prime minister's office. Every now and again, Peter would ask, heavy with meaning: 'I wonder how Nutt's investigation is going.'

If there was a conspiracy against Costello during those times, it was working a treat, and he would occasionally help it along.

Howard was utterly pragmatic when he had to be. Costello, like most good treasurers, found it hard to bend — even a little bit.

Howard brokered the deal with the Democrats to get the

GST introduced. Peter was extremely reluctant to give in to the Democrats' demands for the exclusion of food and the reduction of the tax cuts at the top end.

He emerged dispirited after one of the meetings with the Democrats, and wondered if it might be better to abandon the package entirely rather than see its perfect balance compromised.

I didn't think so. 'That's all very well, Peter,' I said, 'but what are we going to do for the next three years?'

His intransigence — over whether to deal or not deal with the Democrats, or to modify the BAS — did not help him with his colleagues, or with the public. By the time he was eventually forced into making compromises, as he was on the GST deal, then the BAS, and then the fuel excise, he had lost a few valuable layers of political skin.

Although Peter wounded Kim Beazley during the Aston by-election in July 2001, after the opposition leader said he thought that Australians were paying about the right amount of tax, Howard got the credit for the win.

The by-election victory was proof that the coalition was on the comeback trail, but its electoral dominance was cemented even further a couple of months later when the Tampa sailed into Australian waters, and when terrorists blew up the World Trade Center and the Pentagon. The election campaign was suddenly about immigration and national security. Howard slipped comfortably into the role of commander-in-chief. Concerns about tax, the BAS, fuel, and everything else fizzled.

Not all Liberals were happy with the tone and content of the campaign, though.

Costello went to see Lynton Crosby at campaign headquarters in Melbourne to suggest they should broaden the campaign and run a few ads on the economy. It wasn't just Peter's ego in play here. The economy was supposed to be one of the government's strong points.

Lynton had just received a new ad, and screened it for Peter on the small television in his office. It featured Howard from the campaign launch, standing in front of the flag and declaring: 'We will decide who comes to this country and the circumstances in which they come.'

Lynton seemed a bit embarrassed by it. He was debating whether or not to use it, describing it as 'a bit too Nuremberg'.

A few nights later, that ad was screening. Peter fully supported the government's border-protection policies. He had been part of the National Security Committee that had made the decisions, and he boasted that he was the one who suggested to Howard that he hold a joint press conference with Philip Ruddock to announce that the Tampa would be turned around.

But he didn't want the campaign just to be about asylum-seekers, fearing it would infect debate in the next term.

That night with Lynton, Peter was intent on getting his point across about the need for more emphasis to be given to the economy — as a reason for the government's success and for why it should be re-elected — even down to suggesting the types of ads that could be run. Lynton listened politely.

Peter was given ample opportunities over the years, both publicly and privately, to distance himself from Howard's immigration policies, but he never would. Whether it was during questioning at newspaper editorial-board meetings, or at meetings held under so-called Chatham House rules, where information can be used but participants not identified, he would maintain solid support for the government's approach to boat people and the detention of asylum-seekers, including women and children. I 'tricked' him into opening up a degree of separation later, but he quickly sealed the gap.

Any hint of separation from him during the 2001 campaign would have been the political equivalent of *harikari*, the Japanese ritual act of suicide by disembowelment — and he had no desire to do this, anyway. His objection to the 2001 election advertising was both pragmatic and personal.

What he wanted was some ads that would serve to highlight his success in managing the economy. This election was about him and his future, too. He had copped a lot of heat for his alleged failures and shortcomings; here was an opportunity to spotlight his achievements in a positive way, and they were being ignored. He was being ignored. He also assessed that the coalition would pay a price for its heavy focus on boat people if its opponents were able to claim that the victory had come off the backs of refugees. He was right.

We won the election, but everybody lost a little something, too.

CHAPTER NINE

Get out the bloody billycart

As 2002 drew to a close, we were getting on one another's nerves. We — the staff, that is — were desperate for a break. We knew that the prime minister would announce his decision about his future within a matter of months. In a rare and irrational outbreak of optimism, we — Mitch Fifield, Phil Gaetjens, and myself — had even held a planning session in a small conference room down at Treasury complete with whiteboard, to work out a possible transition and what Peter could or should be doing in the interim in the way of speeches and events.

We discussed personnel changes, both in his office and in departments, and what a Costello ministry might look like. One issue we could never resolve to our satisfaction was who should be deputy, and therefore treasurer. I was dead opposed to Abbott for the job, even though I liked him in spite of his many and obvious faults. I still like him, because he is red-blooded, but despair at his appalling judgement.

One of the reasons I didn't want to see him as Peter's deputy was that I could not bear to put up with the 'Who's on first?' jokes that would sweep around Australia and the globe. Journalists had already warned me they couldn't wait to start adapting the old American *Abbott and Costello* comedy routine about which player was in what position on the baseball field. Ridicule is an incredibly powerful weapon in politics, so long as it is not too vicious, and Peter himself had used it to devastating effect on his opponents. I knew how potent the Abbott and Costello gags would be, especially if one of them stumbled, as they inevitably would, or if there were any differences between them — as there inevitably would be.

Forget any other issues: a leadership team with the same names as an American comedy duo would be up against it from the start.

Costello and Abbott had been great mates, but the campaign on the republic, and Abbott's unflinching support for Howard, had created a rupture in the relationship.

Abbott was constantly being touted as a potential deputy for Costello, even though it was clear, since the republic campaign especially, that relations between them had gone into a deep freeze. So, by December 2003, when *The Weekend Australian* magazine ran a major profile on Abbott by Paul Kelly, Costello had pretty much had enough of all the talk about Abbott as frontrunner for the deputy's position. Costello was hugely unimpressed by the article's assertions and by Abbott's dismissive comments about economic management. Costello handed it to me to file away for future reference, with a key paragraph underlined. In the article, Abbott was quoted as saying he would probably run for the deputy leadership; however, he scoffed at the notion of becoming treasurer.

Kelly quoted a laughing Abbott as saying: 'I have never been as excited about economics as some of my colleagues; you know, I find economics is not for nothing known as the dismal science.' In Costello's books, that alone disqualified Abbott as a running mate.

Anyhow, towards the end of 2002, Costello was procrastinating, refusing to say if and when he was going to take his Christmas break — which meant that we couldn't organise ours, either.

A note was in order, so I slipped one into his in-tray:

Get fit. Walk or swim. It will help you sleep. Eat better. Drink less caffeine and alcohol. This also will help with sleep. Be nicer to everyone, staff, colleagues, waiters etc. This will help us sleep.

Take a long holiday over Christmas. It could be your last for a while, and it will give you the chance to reflect on your priorities, define the areas you want to (or can) change, and how.

He didn't respond, making me even crankier. Finally, I told him bluntly that he needed a break and that 'We need a break from you.'

That hurt him. 'You're lucky you don't work for Downer,' he said. This was mildly amusing, but not the right point.

We all got a holiday.

Terrorism, the war in Iraq, and the government's border-protection policies continued to dominate the political debate. The 2003 budget went on to spend heavily on defence and intelligence. However, even after all that spending, and after providing for a surplus of more than $2 billion, there were still a few billion dollars left over — so Costello decided to implement a surprise tax cut. The cuts were worth almost $11 billion, or between $4 and $11 a week: not huge, but better than nothing, especially given the circumstances at the time. The treasurer went to a lot of trouble to keep them secret, even from his own staff and the prime minister's office.

The cuts were derided by the opposition and by some newspapers for being piddling. But the person who really blew them out of the water, less than 24 hours later, was one of the government's own — the family and community services minister, Amanda Vanstone.

To minimise the potential for stuff-ups, we had a rule that only the treasurer and the prime minister could do interviews the morning after the budget. We divided up the radio and television talk shows between them, and they would tear up and down the press-gallery corridors like Energizer bunnies for hours, starting at 7.00 a.m.

The treasurer would address the National Press Club at lunchtime, attend Question Time, and then — for a few years, anyway — finish the night with a fundraiser in Sydney for one of the newspapers. Tony called it Groundhog Day. It was worse than budget day itself, but essential to continue the sales job and to make sure that all the messages stayed on track. Mark Textor's budget-night polling, which he would deliver by phone around 11.00 p.m., was a help there, too.

Amanda, much as I like her, wouldn't abide by rules even if she knew about them. So, on the morning after the budget, when she was asked in a radio interview (which she wasn't supposed to be doing) why welfare payments had not been increased, she answered in her usual direct manner. What was the point of giving, say, a $5-a-week increase, she asked rhetorically — you would be lucky to buy a sandwich and a milkshake with it. Of course, this was roughly the same amount as the tax cuts. It was too easy, then, for the opposition to turn Amanda's comments back onto the government. Immediately, any hope of selling the budget, or of Peter getting any kudos for his work — for producing a surplus budget that underpinned the nation's economic and national security while still providing for lower taxes — went down the toilet.

Months of hard work had been destroyed with a few careless words. The timing could not have been worse. The deadline that Howard had set to announce his decision on his future was rapidly approaching. If Peter's strategy had worked — that is, to deliver a solid, responsible economic document with a smart political edge that would give the government a bounce in the polls — he might have got a bit of a bounce, too, in the party room as well as in the electorate. He needed something to boost his stocks. He didn't get it.

Peter had no momentum, no numbers, and no prospect of engineering any. Two months away from his 64th birthday, there was no pressure on Howard to go; in fact, all the pressure was on him to stay.

On Monday morning, 2 June 2003, when he landed in Canberra, Peter called from the car and said that Howard wanted to see him. This could only mean one thing.

Peter dropped his gear in the office and then walked around to the prime ministerial suite. On his return, some time later, he walked straight into his office and closed his door. The red light of his extension went on, then off, and still he stayed in, writing down his notes of the conversation.

Then he called me in. Howard had told him he was staying. There was no ranting or raving from Peter. Sure, there was disappointment, but there was no ball of fury hurtling around the room and setting the furniture alight. We discussed his options. There were not too many. He could resign, he said, but he was worried about us, the staff. I reassured him. 'Don't worry about us; we'll be okay.'

It wasn't a serious consideration anyway. At that stage he had too much to lose, and hardly anything to gain. There was no discussion of a challenge.

It was clear that his numbers were well short of those he would need to mount any credible kind of assault. He probably had a couple of dozen votes, at best. A challenge would be a humiliation; an annihilation. If he resigned and went to the backbench, he would be without staff or resources.

Simon Crean was still leader, and nobody thought that he, or anyone else Labor had on offer then, could beat Howard. So, unless he wanted to drag down the government, and divide the party — which he did not — and run the risk of getting left behind, he only had one option, at that stage, and that was to cop it. Sweet.

Howard was going to tell the Liberal Party meeting the next morning of his decision. There was little we could do before then. We called Tony Smith and told him to come round. Peter related again what had happened — which was that, over a cup of tea, Howard had told him he was staying, and that Peter had told him he thought he should go.

We called together a few staff, and Peter consulted a couple of his colleagues and friends, but there seemed to be little point in creating aggro just for the heck of it. We went to Santa Lucia's in Kingston for dinner, where we commiserated.

Next morning I wrote a little spiel for Peter to deliver to the party meeting after Howard made his announcement. I thought it was critical for Peter to strike the right tone. He had to signal his continuing ambition to his colleagues, but also maintain dignity and grace:

> Colleagues,
>
> I believe there can be no greater honour than to lead the Liberal Party and to be prime minister of Australia — the greatest nation on earth. I hope one day, with your backing and the support of the people of Australia, that I will be able to fulfil those aspirations.
>
> I believe there is work to be done to ensure Australian society remains secure, prosperous and tolerant.
>
> I would be neither human nor honest if I did not say that I am disappointed today by the prime minister's announcement.
>
> I will continue to work tirelessly for the Liberal Party and my electors.

He added a bit extra, sending a signal that he would not model himself on certain others — in what was a clear swipe at Howard's own behaviour as deputy to Andrew Peacock, which apparently went over the heads of most of his colleagues — and he pledged to fulfil the role of loyal deputy. The backbenchers, only a couple of whom knew what had transpired before the meeting, applauded him warmly. They were impressed by the dignified way in which he handled himself in the party room during an incredibly difficult situation.

There was palpable relief that the team was going to stay intact. The combination of Howard and Costello, in that order, was what the overwhelming majority wanted.

However, at his subsequent press conference, Peter slipped and allowed his disappointment to show, both in what he said and the way he said it. In the process, he lost much of the goodwill he had inspired during the party meeting.

Again, during his press conference, he declared that he would like to see Australia remain 'secure, prosperous and tolerant'.

One word in there started a minor earthquake. 'Tolerant'. Was it code for something? Well, it was when it spat out of my computer, because I was feeling uncomfortable about women and children in detention, and about some of the attacks against Muslims. But it was not what Peter intended.

While sections of the media suggested that this was Costello tilting at Howard over refugee policies, this was not right. Peter, as previously stated, fully supported the government's border-protection policies.

The office received an avalanche of mail. Some congratulated him for what they thought he meant, others condemned him, and others mocked him.

It was a bit of naughtiness on my part. I knew exactly what I meant, and I guessed — rightly — what the reaction would be. I had bashed out the spiel in a few minutes, not long before he was scheduled to go to the party meeting where Howard was making his announcement, and decided to insert the word 'tolerant' deliberately. Peter hadn't focused on it, and I didn't draw it specifically to his attention. So it just kind of slipped through.

Now, with a couple of major speeches coming up where he had promised he would speak out, he faced the dilemma of explaining the phrase he'd used.

In the first of those speeches, in late June to launch a charity drive, he had toyed with the idea of naming and shaming senior churchmen who, while publicly condemning the government over the GST and tax reform, were lobbying behind the scenes for concessions on wine taxes. In the end, he decided against it.

Instead, he appealed to the clergy to do more to restore people's faith:

Less than half the population rates clergymen highly for ethics and honesty.

This is at a time when church leaders speak out more than ever on what they perceive to be moral issues.

The church leaders had a lot to say about Australia's involvement in Iraq. When the government was reforming the tax system, I was amazed how many church leaders were, in fact, tax experts who had sized up the moral dimensions of a value added tax.

Three years after the event, I am amazed how few of them care about whether their predictions were right or not.

But recent events have created the suspicion that, no matter how clearly the church imagines it can see the moral dimension of actions by others, it did not seem to get too worked up about the moral failure of some of its own priests.

First out of the blocks to attack Peter for his comments was … his brother, the Reverend Tim.

Never mind that the speech was made just a month after Dr Peter Hollingworth had been forced to resign as governor-general as a result of the controversy over his failure to sack a paedophile priest in 1993.

And never mind the almost-daily revelations of clergy either abusing children or tolerating those who abused children. We were certainly sick of the hypocrisy and all the lectures.

Tim saw it differently. He also seemed to relish going out in opposition to his brother.

He told *The Australian Financial Review* (28–29 June 2003) that Hitler had tried to stop the clergy criticising Nazi policy, and that if clergy did not speak out on moral issues 'there will simply be deafening silence in this country'.

Talk about over the top. And missing the point. By several hundred kilometres.

I had spoken to Tim a few times in the past in an effort to get him to be a bit more judicious in his comments to journalists, who liked nothing better than to play up any differences, real or imagined, between the two brothers.

Tim was always cast as the Good Brother and Peter as the Evil Brother, and Tim often played up to the stereotypes. I got the impression sometimes that he enjoyed it a bit too much. Now I tried to ring him again to suggest that he might like to read his brother's speech in full before rushing to compare him to Hitler, but he had left to go overseas.

The second, more important, speech was scheduled for 16 July at Gerard Henderson's Sydney Institute. Peter decided it should be about 'Building Social Capital'.

Mitch and I prepared a draft. In it, I included an idea that I had modified from an American system, to give students a discount on their Higher Education Contribution Scheme (HECS) fees if they carried out volunteer work in the community. It was called Auscorps, or Ozcorps.

It was a perfect fit for the speech. Peter explained tolerance in the context of social capital. And if you wanted to build social capital, what better way to do it than to encourage young people to engage with the community and with those less fortunate, while at the same time removing some of the burden of HECS. It also meant that Peter was fulfilling his promise to speak out on issues that he felt strongly about.

I had run the idea past Peter some time before. He really liked it, and said to hang on to it for when we really needed it. Well, we really needed it now.

We had already asked Treasury to look at Ozcorps, and to give us some idea of the cost involved, and had given its three-page response to Peter.

Under *Possible design of the proposal*, Treasury had said:

A person with a HECS debt would be able to gain a credit towards their HECS debt at a certain rate for up to a maximum of 200 hours a year.

The rate should not be too generous but should provide some incentive and reasonable rewards for voluntary work. One option is to use the Federal Minimum Wage of $11.80 per hour, giving a maximum credit of $2360 per year, or 61 per cent of the minimum standard HECS fee of $3854 a year.

Treasury said the administration of the programme could be linked to the ATO's (Australian Tax Office) existing arrangements for administering HECS, with the employing charity submitting a form on the student's behalf to the ATO, indicating the total hours worked.

With proper safeguards, it would not be possible for students to manipulate the programme to offset their entire HECS, and a parallel scheme could be implemented to reduce the upfront costs for TAFE. The bottom-line cost was not exorbitant.

Treasury estimated that if 2 per cent of total HECS debtors (then around 20,000 people) received the full credit of $2360 on their HECS debt in any given year, the total credit provided would be around $47.2 million. If 10 per cent, or around 100,000 people, received the full credit, the total credit provided would be around $236 million.

There was enough there to show it could work without draining away revenue, or compromising HECS. And it would encourage young people to engage with communities that needed help.

Peter was due to deliver his speech in Sydney at 6.00 p.m., and he was still going through it that morning, polishing and repolishing. He was quite a good writer, but painfully slow and always, always writing right up to deadline.

It was going so well, I said, that we would get good headlines in the morning, especially with the Ozcorps stuff. I should have just shut up, and maybe it would have slipped through, like 'tolerance' had.

Instead it triggered an alarm. He turned and went straight into his office and phoned the education minister, Brendan Nelson, to run the Ozcorps idea past him.

Costello walked back into my office and said that Brendan didn't like it, so he was dropping it from the speech. 'Give us another idea,' he said.

I felt flattened and angry. 'That's it. I haven't got any more.'

It was really the beginning of the end. There was a huge audience for his speech, and I felt vindicated but not happy when the bulk of the questions that night congratulated him on identifying the problem of discordant communities, but kept asking for a solution.

Ozcorp was not the only solution, but it would have helped. It was something.

I had to laugh when Kevin Rudd nominated it as one of the best ideas from his 2020 summit. If he only knew.

In fact, he should have known because Mitch Fifield used it subsequently in his pitch for preselection for the Victorian Senate vacancy created by Richard Alston's resignation, then later in his maiden speech. Fifield also wrote to Howard, suggesting it; but, while there was some initial interest, it was left to languish until Rudd discovered it.

John Howard had a remarkable ability to bounce back, no matter what wounds were inflicted on him. Peter Costello did not have the same facility. John's hide had been well flayed, and there were few barbs that could penetrate. Peter took everything to heart.

In my view, instead of retreating after Howard's declaration, Peter should have pushed forward even more aggressively — not by overt attacks on the prime minister's authority, but simply by getting out and showing he had the right stuff, and a few ideas. And I told him so.

'You should go hell for leather for the next six months.'

'Oh yeah, and then what?'

'Then we'll see what happens.'

In other words, get out the bloody billycart and just get on with it.

Instead he went into a funk. I had a week's leave, and in my absence he did an interview with John Lyons for the *Sunday* programme, and once again ran through his conversation with the PM where he had tried to convince him to go. No one wanted to hear it.

There was the occasional bright spot. He and Tanya went to dinner at the home of Qantas chair Margaret Jackson, where her extra-special guest for the evening was John Travolta. Peter was not often impressed by celebrities — well, not male ones, that is — but he found Travolta charming and amusing.

He asked Travolta about his dance all those years before with Princess Diana at the White House. Travolta told them that Diana had asked to dance with him, and seemed to know exactly how it was playing out when they twirled around the room.

Peter suggested that, after dinner, Travolta should dance with another of the female guests, then Peter could dance with her so he could say to people afterwards: 'I danced with the girl, who danced with the man, who danced with the Princess of Wales.'

Everyone fell about laughing, except Travolta, who didn't get it.

There was a lot that Peter didn't seem to get either. People were not going to feel sorry for him just because he felt sorry for himself for having only the second-best job in politics.

He was beginning to cop criticism for promising to speak out and then failing to do so. Andrew Bolt took him to task in *The Herald Sun* for pulling his punches, and advised him to consult a speechwriter if he didn't have the time or talent to write his own. That wasn't the problem. Some of his colleagues and commentators began pointing fingers at staff, blaming them — us — for the failures.

He wanted issues to get involved in; but, every time one was suggested, he either showed brief interest or none at all.

I wanted him to visit Cape York and strike up a relationship with Noel Pearson, who was taking a different approach on Aboriginals and welfare.

Although Peter did do so a couple of years later, he was initially reluctant. Climate change and water were not the issues then that they are today, so the environment didn't grab him, and Beazley had already tried to put his name on education.

He was in a bad way. He was going through the motions, but it was difficult to lift him out of his trough.

I came up with what I thought was another good idea, after talking to friends with teenage children. They were worried about alcohol consumption, and blamed the new rage for mixer drinks, or alcopops as they're now called.

I thought we should increase the tax on the drinks in the hope that the higher prices would act as a disincentive, and asked our tax adviser to get some figures from Treasury on how it would work and how much it would raise. Although — as Rudd has once again discovered — it was a lot of money, running to several hundred million dollars, I wasn't thinking of it as a revenue grab.

The budget was comfortably in surplus. It was meant to send a signal to teenagers and their parents that Costello, a father of a teenage son and two girls who would soon be in their teens, was aware of the problem and was trying to do something to tackle it. It was about the message, not the money.

But Peter didn't want to know. He had found the construction of alcohol taxes exceedingly difficult during the GST process, and had no interest whatsoever in revisiting it.

To be fair, the one issue that did move him was drug abuse.

Without telling the media, we had joined Melbourne youth worker Les Twentyman on a tour of 'hot spots' in the city of Melbourne and the western suburbs. Young kids with harrowing stories poured out their hearts to him.

Someone took a photo of Peter with the kids, and it turned up in the local western-suburbs paper. Nicola Roxon sent him the clip with a nice note, saying how good it was to see him take an interest. He followed up with a visit to the Odyssey House rehab centre.

I had a small wooden paperweight in the shape of a dice on my desk. Instead of numbers it had words, suggesting mood or activity — 'bed', 'eat', 'TV', 'jog', 'sulk'. Over the one saying 'pub', I taped 'fury', and kept it permanently on top.

When Mitch Fifield won preselection for Richard Alston's Senate vacancy, I told Peter I wanted Mitch's political adviser's slot. He didn't want to give it to me — he didn't want me to move from the press secretary's job which, according to him, was the most important job in the office after the chief of staff. No matter, I was sick of it. If he gave the adviser's job to my offsider, Dave Alexander, which was what he intended, I knew my job would become even harder.

On 8 November 2003, in an article in The Sydney Morning Herald, Margaret Simons quoted Maxine McKew as saying she had asked me to tee up lunch for her with Costello for her regular Bulletin feature, and I had said: 'Not in a million years, Maxine.'

Simons continued in the article: 'That, McKew says, is the problem. The Savvas of the world run the political scene, and they won't let people off the leash. Politics has become so polished, so posed, so institutionalised.'

She went on to quote McKew:

People have a nervous collapse when I've actually broken through and got someone to say something honest. It is either regarded as a gaffe or people say they must have been drunk, or publicly musing aloud, or they didn't realise the tape was running, or I must have had oral sex with them under the table. I find it absurd.

What had actually happened was that I had run into McKew in the ladies' toilets in the ministerial wing, not long after Kim Beazley had got into trouble following a lunch with her, and she asked to have lunch with Costello. 'You must be joking,' I said to her, and we both laughed.

We both knew exactly what she was after, and it wasn't going to be helpful to anyone — except McKew.

It was highly amusing after her election to see McKew come under sustained criticism for hovering below the radar. She was barely venturing out, much less even daring to broach the subject of 'oral sex'. Maybe someone had put her on a leash.

Still, the Simons article and McKew's comments niggled me and fed into my frustrations. The constant battles with journalists on the one side, and Peter on the other, were wearing me down. Maybe I was exercising too much control; maybe it was time for me to step away and let the real Peter rip. Whoever that might be. Maybe I had pushed him too far in the direction of my own beliefs and prejudices.

His dilemma was whether to carve out his own separate identity or to become Howard's alter ego, backing him to the hilt on everything, and acting as though the prime minister was his role model. My instincts favoured the first option. I admired Howard's resolve, even if I didn't agree with everything he stood for. His great strength was that everybody knew, or had a sense of, what he stood for. Even when he was deputy to Peacock, people knew what they would be getting with Howard: support for families and small business, and industrial-relations reform.

Peter was reluctant to be either too different or too similar. That indecision would be apparent, to Peter's detriment, in later polling when Howard was sliding.

If there had been any nervousness at all in the prime minister's office about Peter launching any kind of assault to blast Howard out, it would have disappeared after those two speeches. I sensed they felt, after this, that they would not have to worry about any direct strikes from the deputy.

It wasn't that I wanted Peter to take on the prime minister, but I wanted him to use the full force of his considerable intellect, personality, and office to make a compelling case for his own leadership credentials — much as Howard had done under Peacock.

Maybe by then I had outlived my usefulness. Maybe, if he had stopped listening to me and if he wasn't prepared to do what I thought he should, and the way I thought he should do it, it was time to let someone else have a go. Maybe it was time for me to start living my life again, as opposed to living his.

He would complain that I hardly ever praised him, and was often critical of him. It was true. I did keep praise to a minimum — there were plenty of others to ladle it on — and, in any case, in that period it was an understatement to say I was unhappy with his performance.

Part of the problem stemmed from the fact that I was as much a control freak as Peter was. It was way too personal. I came to see all mistakes and shortcomings as a reflection on me. If he misstepped, either in answering questions — usually the leadership ones — or if he looked messy, I could hear people saying: 'How could she let him do (say, wear,) that!'

I would insert myself into as many discussions or deliberations as I could — whether it was to suggest that the proposed Timor levy be struck only for those earning above $50,000, to protect people at the lower end, or that banks be required to show on their ATMs the fees that were being charged, or what issues we would tackle in Question Time and how.

Journalists are influential: they can force changes to decisions, have someone sacked, or somebody else promoted. Their contribution to the process is important, but it is too often negative, and nothing compared to direct involvement in actual decision-making every day.

Nothing can ever match that or beat it, but it is relentless. Staff are dispensable, and cannot afford to make a single mistake or to relax completely — even among close friends or family.

As Costello's press secretary, I insisted that all journalists' queries had to be directed to me. In seeking information from the prime minister's office, journalists had become expert at bypassing the press secretaries and going straight to the advisers or the chief of staff. I used to do it myself, but I would have none of this in Costello's office.

If I made mistakes as a press secretary, I was prepared to cop the blame. What I didn't want was hours added to my day cleaning up messes we created, as opposed to those that others created for us.

All contact with journalists had to come through me, and if necessary I would arrange for them to speak to the adviser, whom I would then brief on the parameters of the discussion — although I think Peter still freelanced a bit, which usually got us into trouble.

There would be no mixed messages going out from spontaneous conversations between different people in the office talking to the same journalist — or even to a different one.

Similarly with Treasury. I would 'advise' Treasury officials to direct media calls to the treasurer's office, unless journalists were simply seeking a clarification of a policy fact. Any questions about why or how the treasurer was embarking on a particular course was for him (or me) to answer, not for them.

It is not for public servants to answer for a government's decisions. Although Labor, especially at the state level, seems to favour this approach, especially when things are going wrong, it should be left to the politicians. The politicians make the decisions, based on what is meant to be the best available advice, and they will inevitably wear the consequences. Or accept the accolades.

Eventually, Costello reluctantly agreed to make me his principal political adviser, but the issue of whether I should still talk to journalists, given the rule I had instigated, could not be resolved. After six years of slogging and flacking and fighting, I resigned.

More selfishly, I could see what was coming. I felt I had done as much as I could, and I was anxious to keep whatever credibility I had left. A fat lot of good that did me. Even friends think I was still with Costello at the scene of his greatest disaster, the McLachlan affair.

Six years to the day after I joined him, I told him I was resigning: 'I don't think I've got another budget left in me.'

He laughed. He knew how that felt. 'When the magic is gone, it's gone,' he said.

Just before I left, I attended two meetings with him in Melbourne: one at the Royal Children's Hospital, where they were desperate for $2 million for a new MRI machine to scan newborn babies, and another at the Walter and Eliza Hall Institute, where they wanted $5 million for new infrastructure.

As we drove back to the office, I gave him one more piece of advice: 'Just write them a fucking cheque, Peter. We waste so much money on so many other things.'

'Stay and help me do it.'

'Too late.'

He did it without me, and more besides, but there were times over the next few years when I am sure — here goes that Greek thing again — I might have been able to get him to do and say what he had to, to get him where he wanted to go.

Instead, I went to work for the man who would make sure he never got there.

For most of the next three years, I worked in the Cabinet Policy Unit, attached to the prime minister's office. I went from writing columns ridiculing Howard, to writing columns for him. The irony of it didn't escape either of us.

CHAPTER TEN

Peter Peter Peter Peter

My six years with Peter Costello were stimulating, rewarding, productive, and hilarious but, ultimately, exhausting and frustrating. They were nowhere near as frustrating, though, as witnessing from the sanctuary of the cabinet suite the events of the three years that followed.

It was Peter Costello's great misfortune to be around at the same time as John Howard, the master politician of his generation, so he would always be seen as the second-best option. However, it is not overstating things to say that he stuffed up badly as he sought to supplant the prime minister. And more than once.

Jeanne Pratt asked Peter, at a dinner one night, why he wanted to be prime minister. It sounded as though she was asking why on earth anyone would want to do that job. A few days later, Peter asked for a screed to help him answer the question, but I put the request to one side. This was definitely one for him to handle.

There was never any doubt that Howard always wanted to be leader. He knew why he wanted to be leader, and he knew what he had to do to get there.

Howard's hunger and his resolve were there for everyone to see, every day. He made plenty of mistakes, particularly in his first incarnation, but he learned from them, and he learned not to publicly indulge his emotions. In his second incarnation as leader, his discipline and his focus were extraordinary, and until his final year his judgement was generally very sound.

He rose magnificently to the challenges of a series of disasters — Port Arthur, the Bali Bombings, the Asian tsunami — doing whatever had to be done to help, both financially and with words of comfort that did not descend into clichés or mawkishness. He was articulate, and could convey genuine compassion.

His work ethic was exemplary. He would commit fully to a policy or a position, and he would not stop until it was delivered. If something went wrong, he would not rest until it was fixed.

There were times when that commitment or, conversely, his failure to commit, translated into stubbornness, when he should have let go but he either couldn't or wouldn't. Pride and prejudice. In the end, that would cost him dearly.

He was unfailingly courteous. He would get irritable, but it was a rare thing for him — despite the pressures — to have a meltdown. I never heard him swear. I gave him a news rundown once, and in the process told him that one of the network news reporters had done his usual 'shitful job'. He didn't say anything, but I felt obliged to apologise for my bad language.

Peter also worked hard, but has been branded, unfairly, as lazy. Part of his problem was that he made things look too easy.

I always tell people that he has an enormous head because it has to encase an enormous brain. He is capable of absorbing highly complex and technical information, and plenty of it. He can remember where in his head it is stored, can summon it, and then communicate it in a simple, digestible form, without gulping for air or stopping every few sentences for a drink of water. Eat your heart out, Wayne Swan.

It is an incredible talent for a politician, especially a treasurer, and especially one who was responsible for reforming personal taxes, business taxes, corporate law, and the banking regulatory system without once being caught out on technical detail. He was probably one of the few treasurers able to comprehend his subject, rather than simply relying on a Treasury summary and a few glib lines. Eat your heart out, Wayne Swan.

Those abilities were a key ingredient in fostering and maintaining confidence in the coalition as economic managers. He sounded like he knew what he was talking about, because he did know what he was talking about. People marked him highly for that.

When he put his heart and head into it, he could deliver great speeches — spearing One Nation, supporting the republic, arguing the case for reform, defending values.

He is funny, well-read, and accomplished, and a decent human being.

One night, at dinner with Jim Middleton, he recited long slabs of Shakespeare — not the usual *Romeo and Juliet* or *Merchant of Venice* passages, but the less well-known. Jim was gobsmacked.

Another night, in a Sydney hotel, where he was upgraded to a suite replete with piano, he sat down and belted out 'The Piano Man' for Mitch and me. And he sang as well.

He can take the piss out of himself beautifully. He would often carry Lizzie McCabe's heavy computer bag for her, which had fragile stickers all over it, saying drolly, 'After all, it's got my ego in there.'

People were constantly surprised at his height. He is around 190cms tall. They would yell out to him, 'Peter, you are so big.' 'Yes, and I'm still growing,' he would say.

We were in danger of missing our plane one day, and when I started to run, he pulled me up: 'Never run to catch a plane, especially if it's taking you somewhere you don't want to go.' We were flying to Canberra. The people around us burst out laughing. I slowed down.

On another flight, as we prepared to land, he leaned over and declared: 'Do you know how much I love Melbourne?' It was loud enough for the passengers behind us to hear, and they started to giggle. One of them was Nicola Roxon.

He seldom swears; and if he has the occasional temper-tantrum, he doesn't make it personal or vicious. Not to staff, anyway. During his dispute with Malcolm Turnbull over tax, Peter threatened one day to crack him like a nut. Turnbull was not impressed.

In any case, I raised my voice to him more often than he did to me. Certainly, I slammed more doors in his presence to indicate my displeasure — like the day he patted the NSW treasurer, Michael Egan, on the head.

He would refer to me as 'the Greek', as in, 'What's the Greek up to today?' Or, if I was being especially vocal on an issue, he would turn to the boys later and say: 'It's the Greek in her, you know.' I would repeatedly correct him, telling him that I was actually a Cypriot, and that calling a Cypriot a Greek can be a bit like calling the Irish English. It made no difference. He was making a wider point. I got it.

He would often declare a 'Friday' and head out for Chinese. Only those who could be trusted not to nag him were welcome. After one of those lunches, he 'sacked' Smith and Fifield. They turned up at the office again on Monday. Peter used my credit card to ring them from the plane as we were flying off to a conference in the US.

He was still irked by their refusal to carry out whatever silly instruction he had issued, but was relieved that they were at the office.

He has little or no dress sense. Exhibit A: walking around Parliament House with T-shirt carefully tucked into tracksuit bottoms like a five-year-old. I would get rid of his worst ties by donating them to charities for auctions with a funny note extolling the virtues of high-quality polyester, and replace them with silk ones at birthdays or Christmas.

He would occasionally turn up at work in mismatched suit coat and pants, claiming he had dressed in the dark. Often he had to borrow clothes or accessories from staff, and John Olsen in Los Angeles once had to rustle up a suit for him because he had forgotten to pack one.

For his birthday, which coincided with a bush tour, we chipped in to buy him casual shirts to make sure he was properly fitted out. The boys bought him a Rod & Gunn shirt, which has a pointer dog as a logo stitched onto the front pocket. I made them take it back; one of my missions in the office had been to kill off the 'dog' tag that Kennett had lumped on him.

Although extremely bright — as a student he had considered doing medicine — he is also a dag and a bit of a klutz. He could use a computer. Just. All of his writing is done in longhand, in a scrawl that looks like a chicken doing wheelies across the page.

Others might be too vain, but Peter had no compunction about slipping into his freebie airline pyjamas on long flights. Then, with mask on, he would lie back and snore loudly for hours. The noise would ricochet round the cabin. David Leckie, a fellow passenger on one of our flights out of LA, helpfully informed the person in the seat beside him: 'That's our treasurer.'

When he changed back into his own travel gear, it was usually a check sports jacket that a Damon Runyon character could have worn comfortably to the racetrack. It was hard to decide which was worse — the Qantas pyjamas or his own wardrobe.

Rituals developed that had to be observed, no matter what. Before each budget we would go shopping for a new suit, shirt, and two ties — one for the night, and one for Groundhog Day. Mitch would have to iron the shirt for him on budget night. To get himself in the mood, Peter would put on his *Big Chill* soundtrack at maximum volume, and dance around his office to 'Heard It Through the Grapevine'.

Lizzie, who organised all his food, had to get him an iced doughnut (pink or chocolate) before each national-accounts press conference. For luck, I would give him a pat on the shoulder before each press conference, and make sure his hair and jacket were dusted down. If we were out, I would have to let him use my hairbrush. I stood behind him at doorstops, and tapped him on the elbow when it was time to call it quits.

Good staff can mean the difference between success and failure, no matter how brilliant the politician — and Peter had good policy, political, and personal staff. We made sure he was properly briefed before each and every outing, and he prepared for each interview and press conference as if it was a final exam. He would know the budget papers backwards, tabbing all relevant sections, doing everything humanly possible to make sure he was never caught out.

Still, we made a point of not taking ourselves too seriously, and we made sure he didn't either.

After the 1999 AFL preliminary final when Essendon, the hot favourites, was beaten by Carlton by one point, Peter was devastated. He was the number-one ticket holder for the Bombers and regarded that, above all else, as his crowning achievement. Tony Smith was a Blues man, and ecstatic. As it happened, Peter was still feeling the pain of a double whammy on Monday morning: Jeff Kennett had just lost the Victorian election and, despite their differences, Peter was cut up over that defeat, too.

Tony had his Carlton tracksuit top with him, and offered to buy me dinner if I would wear it in front of Peter. I put it on, grabbed the newspapers, tapped on his office door, and walked in. Peter looked up, saw me, let out a roar like a wounded lion, and threw his pencil at me. I dodged it, and we all burst out laughing. I am still waiting for my dinner.

Actually, Mitch and Tony owe me two dinners. On another occasion, we were flying on a VIP aircraft out of Melbourne. Peter always insisted on sitting in one particular seat, the one supposedly dedicated to the number-one VIP on board. The boys offered me another dinner if I would sit in that seat. Why not? Peter climbed on board, came to claim his seat, and there I was, feet up, determinedly oblivious to his discomfort.

He was agitated, but it would have been ungentlemanly for him to ask me to move. I finally put him out of his misery, and surrendered the seat.

Partly as a result of his upbringing, and partly because his job brought him into regular contact with the ultra-rich, he was deeply suspicious of wealth.

Laurie Oakes wrote a column in *The Bulletin* on 8 August 2006, saying that Malcolm Turnbull's money would work against him if he ever became treasurer.

Turnbull had enraged Costello by putting out an options paper on tax reform soon after his election to Parliament, but the enmity was born long before that. Costello had not warmed to Turnbull during the republic debate, thought he had failed as the party's federal treasurer, did not want him to win preselection in Wentworth, and always maintained that Turnbull had lousy political judgement. There was a visceral resentment there, and he knew that Turnbull's arrival in Canberra would trigger another bout of rivalry. Howard had backed Turnbull and kept promoting him, giving Costello even more reason to dislike them both.

When I raised the Oakes column with Turnbull at the time, Turnbull was not surprised. 'I heard the very same thing from your former boss. And in my own house,' he said. Costello had stayed the night at Point Piper, and after a few wines had proceeded to tell Turnbull exactly what he thought of him.

Costello's disdain for riches stemmed partly from his Baptist background. He would take himself off to meetings of the parliamentary faithful, telling us that we could join him if we wished. 'No, you can pray for all of us,' I would say. He is deeply religious, and after his disappointments in the leadership would wonder aloud if these things had been ordained. Because, if they had been, mere mortals like him could do little or nothing to undo or change them. Maybe there was some comfort for him in that.

He loved party pies, Maccas, and fish and chips. At the end of a long day on the road, we would suss out the hotel dining room for a club sandwich and chips. At his home, where we were often invited, it would be a barbecue.

The day after the 2001 election, even with rain spitting down, he hoisted up the big brolly in the backyard of his home and cooked everyone lunch. Okay, we had to bring meat and organise it all, but it was still endearing.

We enjoyed one another's company. It was more fun for us to be together than it was for him to be with some of his colleagues. He was paying a price for that, so we stopped our office lunches or dinners, and instead lined him up with backbenchers.

And yet. And yet.

Too many times, he would lose perspective, and his judgement would falter. When he should have fought he backed off, and when he did fight he used the wrong weapons.

He needed a bit more humility and a little less hubris. He could not see that praising others would make him a bigger and better person, not a smaller one. Conversely, if praise was heaped on him, he would get embarrassed. Maybe there was a connection.

He could never just take it on the chin. He would never forget a slight. He would mark news clips and hand them to me to store in the 'enemies' file'. I never had one. I did have a losers' file. Tony Abbott and other colleagues would have to go in there sometimes. As would journalists.

Howard had learned the hard way to deal with dissent. Criticism would send Peter into black places.

In June 2005, I ghosted a piece for Howard for the first edition of *The Party Room*, a publication edited by Mitch Fifield and Andrew Robb, which provided a forum for Liberals to air their views.

In a front-page story, *The Australian* reported the article as a new strategy to sell the Liberal Party as a party of ideas, in a move to control divisions within the coalition. *The Australian* observed that the prime minister's new political formula was designed to blunt the effect of divisions over immigration and tax because it accepted that differing ideas were 'the lifeblood of politics and provide essential stimulus for healthy debate'.

The piece for *The Party Room* was published after the resolution of conflict with backbenchers Petro Georgiou and Judith Troeth over immigration, but written while the dispute was still going on — to indicate that while the prime minister did not agree with every idea his colleagues put forward, they were all encouraged to contribute.

And I wrote it that way because I believed that the best way of managing dissent was to tolerate it — at least publicly — as a vital part of the political debate. Dissent (as opposed to gratuitous ill-discipline) can lead to better decisions, and is a safety valve. Howard added a couple of bits to the article, but he did not change a word.

Costello found it hard to resist the temptation to bite back, occasionally with brutal force. It didn't matter who it was — colleagues, bankers, economists, journalists, or editors.

Quite often, I would ignore his instructions to ring whomever to admonish them about whatever. He would get furious with me, insisting that the call be made, occasionally implying that my loyalties to my old mates were being put ahead of my new ones. In my view, unless the offence was particularly egregious, it was best to roll with the punches.

At the end of my first year, he thanked me for 'saving me from myself'. He was self-aware; it's just that too often he couldn't help making it obvious, no matter whether he was satisfied or sour. And people hated it. He failed to see the damage he did to himself — or, if he did, he couldn't help himself.

When the Reserve Bank lifted interest rates once too often and brought on the only negative quarter of growth in his tenure, in March 2001, the headlines ('Recession Looms' and 'Economy Hits the Wall') were horrific.

The following quarter, the economy bounced back. When he opened the envelope from the bureau of statistics in the morning and saw the positive growth figure, Peter was whoopin' and a hollerin' so loud thbat they would have been able to hear him down the corridors.

People outside could hear him when he sang. His voice ranged from booming baritone to piercing falsetto, and could penetrate the walls into John Anderson's neighbouring office. The girls in there always knew when he was in a good mood. On sensitive days we made sure that the heavy office doors were firmly shut.

His ecstasy over the good growth-figure subsided, and his thoughts quickly turned to revenge. He asked the girls to get him copies of the previous quarter's newspaper headlines. I told them not to. He persisted. He wanted to hold up the clips at his press conference and show them all how wrong they had been.

Just a little bit of nose rubbing never hurt anybody, did it? Not much. Finally, exasperated, I said to him: 'Why you would want a photo taken of yourself holding up a clip with recession in the headline is beyond me.' Message sent and received. Kind of. He did not hold up the offending clips at the press conference.

A year later, still burning, he fired off a pooey fax to his biographer, Shaun Carney, complaining about *The Age's* coverage:

> Twelve months ago the *Age* reported what didn't happen as 'Recession Looms' on 8 March 2001. Today it reports what did happen (Economy booms) as 'Pressure on Rates' on 8 March 2002. How come my photo is on the front page when there is a non-existent Recession but not there when there is an existent Boom.

Some time later, Leunig did a particularly vicious cartoon on refugees. A woman wrote to Peter, saying that Leunig's hands should be cut off. Peter was going to send her letter to the editor with a (supportive) note. I intercepted it and stopped it.

Peter was a social and economic conservative; his natural instincts were to the right of centre, and I kept pushing him to the left of centre, with issues like One Nation, the republic, and 'tolerance'. It wasn't that he didn't believe in them — I was reinforcing his instincts.

After I left, a different Peter would occasionally emerge, with other instincts reinforced. He became more strident in his attacks on Muslims, and derided 'mushy multiculturalism'.

It was confusing. Who was he, and what did he believe in? And if I was unsure, it was a pretty safe bet that others would be, too. Subsequent research confirmed it.

It is easy to blame Howard for blocking him, but Costello could have done more to help himself. Often he defeated himself before he began, complaining that, no matter what he did for them, his colleagues would still prefer Howard.

Politicians who want to succeed have to suffer fools, most of them from their own side.

They have to listen attentively to all the banal complaints or advice that their colleagues feel compelled to dispense, even when all they really want to do is talk about themselves.

They have to eat humble pie and look as if they love it, and then ask for a second helping. They have to admit mistakes and beg forgiveness, even when it is not their fault. They have to be across all policy detail at all times, and have the right policies all the time that will please or reward everyone, or else have an excellent reason why not.

They are never to forget who put them there, or take anything for granted, or ever — God forbid — be smug or complacent. They have to suppress almost every human emotion, yet be able to summon up just the right one for every occasion, and look and sound incredibly sincere when they do it.

When the media complains that politicians are all the same, politicians have to resist the temptation to be too different. They have to be different enough to attract attention, but not too different to be hunted down by the pack.

They have to know when is the right time to fight and how, when to retreat, when to seek revenge, and when to serve it up cold.

And all of this is truer for conservative politicians, given zero tolerance for their imperfections by the media. Alan Ramsey wrote it best when he contrasted the media's treatment of Bob Hawke over the crude Indira Gandhi joke with John Brogden's dismemberment for some minor sexual-harassment charges. One went on to become prime minister; the other was driven out of politics.

When universally applied, it is a winnowing process to ensure that only the strongest, the smartest, the most confident, and the most determined survive.

Peter would put his imperfections on display too often and too openly, and couldn't or wouldn't do what he had to do to win over his colleagues.

Howard never stopped wooing them.

Howard doubted Costello's maturity and application, and Costello thought Howard was past it. Resentment ran both ways. In the early years, at least, it was not life-threatening — just a discernible thread that coursed through day-to-day political life.

It started very early in the life of the government. In 1996, a few months after the election victory, cabinet had agreed to impose a wholesale sales tax on the states. It was decided that Howard and Costello would put it to the premiers at their meeting in June.

The premiers wouldn't have a bar of it. They blamed Costello, and viciously attacked him, using every dog metaphor they could think of in the process.

Howard cut a deal with the premiers — as he had to do — and left Costello hanging. Costello never forgave him. I reported those events for *The Age*, but didn't think too much about it at the time. I viewed it then as just one of those normal stoushes that prime ministers and treasurers get into, with no hard feelings later — all just part of the general cut-and-thrust of politics. It wasn't until after I joined Costello that I realised the depth of his resentment over the incident.

The dispute over the One Nation preference deal added another layer of tension. Costello's supporters started calling Howard 'the white man' — a snide reference to the PM's positioning on One Nation.

For their part, Howard's office and his supporters were building up Peter Reith as an alternative possible successor to Howard and a competitor for Costello. Later, it was Tony Abbott and, after that, Malcolm Turnbull.

Costello liked Reith, and valued his support in policy and parliamentary battles, but was dismissive of any talk about Reith as a leadership rival. 'One bald guy with glasses becomes prime minister, and they all think they can do it,' he told a group of friends one night.

These were minor eruptions destined to end in a much larger explosion. Yet, for ten years, the Howard–Costello working partnership delivered enormous benefits to the government and to the people. A lot of marriages don't last that long. And if they do, it's for the sake of the kids. For 'the kids' here, feel free to read 'the party'.

The success of the previous Labor government had been built on the strength of its two main characters, Hawke and Keating. It was the same with the coalition. Howard's reformist zeal, political smarts, utter determination, and ability to rise to an occasion were indispensable assets — as were Costello's command of his portfolio, his ability to cut through with a message, and his parliamentary performance.

We would often wonder in the office who would be Costello's Costello if he became leader. It was difficult to think of anyone who could do what he had done. Costello might have been able to match Howard, but there wasn't really anyone to fill the gap he would leave — perhaps apart from Downer, although the relationship between them was glacial.

Howard and Costello were a deadly combination and, despite their differences, they never forgot the real enemy. The coalition would not have won four elections in a row without Howard, and

Howard would have struggled to do it without Costello.

But just as Hawke and Keating were doomed, so were Howard and Costello. Kevin Rudd and Julia Gillard will go the same way, unless Rudd is smarter about the timing of his departure and succession.

There was an expectation — more a hope, really — among the Costelloites that Howard would announce his departure soon after the tenth-anniversary celebrations of his prime ministership. They were counting on Nick Minchin to deliver the tap on the shoulder. But Minchin never did approach Howard directly. He believed that there were only two people who might have influenced him to go: one was his good friend and Canberra housemate, Alexander Downer; the other, Howard's chief of staff, Arthur Sinodinos.

Minchin laid out the case to Downer a number of times, at home and on VIP flights around the time of the tenth anniversary. He pointed out that the Liberal Party only had one hero, and that was Menzies. Minchin believed that Howard was a great prime minister and that if he left while he was on top, the Liberal Party would have two heroes to look up to. It would be like bullion in the bank vault that they could use to rebuild and regenerate the party.

Downer thought it was an interesting argument, but saw no need for any push against Howard. At that stage, Howard looked immortal.

Perhaps he might have been persuaded to do so if Costello had invested time and energy in trying to convert him to his cause — or even by offering him the treasurer's job — but he didn't and, in Downer's book, that also counted against Costello.

In any case, Downer, who relished the blood sport of politics, had little to gain from a switch. He seemed in awe of Howard, and he would have got the treasurer's job from Howard if Costello had left.

In early 2006, the Nationals leader and the deputy prime minister, Mark Vaile, had what he describes as an 'informal discussion' with

Howard about his plans, born out of a 'How are your people going?' kind of chat. Vaile says that the conversation left him with the clear impression that Howard would leave at the end of the year, in order to give Costello a clear run at the job before the election.

In Vaile's view, this was the right thing to do, and he told the prime minister so. He respected both men and had worked closely with both of them over the years, and firmly believed that the end of the year would be a good time to hand over.

Vaile thought that would give Costello enough time to break free from the shackles of Treasury before the next election.

'The bottom line is, I felt if there was to be a change, that it should take place in 2006 to ensure Peter had a chance away from the tough job of treasurer,' Vaile told me.

'I was comfortable with whatever decision the Liberals made but, if it was going to happen, it needed to happen in 2006.'

In view of what transpired, the tenth anniversary would have been the best time for a transition, or the best time for Howard to tell Costello what he had told Vaile. He did not. They did not have that kind of relationship.

In the early years, they could discuss anything to do with policy in the most intricate detail, but they could never really discuss freely with each other their personal ambitions. Intricate, yes; intimate, definitely not. They were not that close, and the trust was not that deep.

They both paid a huge price for their inability to connect and communicate. And so, in the end, did the Liberal Party.

CHAPTER ELEVEN

Invasion of the body-snatcher

The tenth anniversary of Howard's prime ministership was celebrated widely, if not universally, in March 2006. Howard was in full command. Costello was finding it harder to suppress his frustration and impatience.

Howard had surpassed Hawke's record to become the second-longest-serving prime minister. He had hinted to staff after the 2004 election that he would not be staying for the whole term. He would never say it directly to them, and they would not presume to ask him directly.

He liked to make his decisions at a time of his choosing, and he resented it if he thought anyone was trying to probe or push. So they let him be, trusting he would get around to it before it was too late.

Bill Heffernan, a prime ministerial confidante, would make regular forays to the Costello office, urging patience and making soothing noises. Costello had heard it all before.

Towards the end of 2005, Costello was talking tough to his supporters. He promised his great friend Michael Kroger that, this time, he wasn't going to blink. He told others that he was not going to get 'sucker punched again'.

He made his timing clear to his backers. He would deliver the budget, and then confront Howard and insist on an orderly takeover.

Howard had planned a long trip overseas with an official visit to Washington. It certainly looked and smelled like a lap of honour. He and the rest of the party were seduced by the attention he received. Pipe bands, bells and whistles, and flourishes can do that to you.

Those of us watching at home were appalled. It looked like an almighty indulgence.

Costello embarked on a tour to sell himself, as distinct from selling the budget, and Rupert Murdoch kicked off the leadership speculation again by telling reporters on his way to the White House dinner for Howard: 'He's probably planning to go out at the top.'

On 14 May, Piers Akerman, who was close to both Costello and Howard, wrote that people with close ties to the Howard camp 'are now admitting that the times may suit an elegant departure'.

The Costello camp was jubilant; surely this was a signal. Their jubilation was short-lived; they soon saw other signals.

Rod Kemp, who was not renominating for the Senate, and was minister for sport and the arts, rang Costello in early July to tell him that he had had a call from the prime minister. The prime minister had told Kemp: 'You don't want to go just yet.' Kemp told Costello that the PM was not planning a reshuffle, or anything else, any time soon.

More significantly, Grahame Morris, Howard's former chief of staff, and the person closest to him outside the immediate family, said in an interview on the ABC's *Lateline* on 7 July that Howard would make up his mind in November or December and that, 'if he chooses to go', it would give the new leader nine months to get organised. Plenty of time.

This was seen by the Costello camp as a deliberate intervention. *Here we go again*, they thought. *He's just going to keep stringing it out, and pretty soon they'll be saying the election is too close and there won't be enough time for a changeover.*

Those comments by Morris reverberated over a critical weekend.

Morris says that the Costello camp was wrong to see the

Akerman column and his comments as signals of anything, and that he had not been deliberately dispatched to send a message. But he was speaking with inside knowledge. Morris had indeed discussed possible retirement plans with the prime minister. He had a softer take on his conversation with Howard than the one Howard had left with Mark Vaile.

Morris says that his conversation with Howard had taken place earlier in the year, and it was agreed that they would meet at the prime minister's Kirribilli residence towards the end of 2006 to review his options.

The thinking was that if the prime minister decided the time was right for him to depart, he would announce it over Christmas. This would give Costello time to settle in over the silly season and before the resumption of Parliament, and allow him a full year to put his stamp on the government.

According to Morris, there was no reason for the prime minister to consider it any sooner than that. Morris' view was that no one in the party, and no one in the country, wanted him to go.

'Was there 100 per cent certainty he would make up his mind to go? No,' says Morris.

'Was he happy to consider it in a sensible, orthodox way? Yes.

'Did he have in his mind the possibility of an orthodox handover? Yes.'

But the possibility of any orthodox handover then or later was killed on Sunday, 9 July when *The Sunday Telegraph* ran a story by Glenn Milne, in which former minister Ian McLachlan said that he had a note from a 1994 conversation between Howard and Costello, which purportedly had Howard saying that he would quit within two terms of becoming prime minister.

The publication of the McLachlan story by a reporter seen to be twinned with Costello — in much the same way as Danny DeVito and Arnold Schwarzenegger were twins in the hit movie-comedy of the same name — was dynamite.

Costello insists he did not leak it, and this is now accepted by everybody, but that was not the case at the time. Was its publication then and in that way a coincidence?

No bloody way.

Milne had heard whispers of a deal six months previously, but all he had were a couple of mismatched bits of jigsaw until the Friday afternoon, the same day that Morris went on *Lateline.* Milne was told by a Liberal Party 'machine man' with links into the Howard camp, who was desperate to engineer Howard's removal, to ring McLachlan because he knew all about it.

Shane Stone says McLachlan had told lots of people about the note.

'I knew about the note in the wallet for years,' Stone says.

'Ian wasn't backward about telling people about it. My view was, so what? I didn't believe the leadership of the nation was predicated on little bits of paper. If Peter felt there was an obligation or commitment, Peter needed to take him on over it in the party room.'

McLachlan told Nick Minchin in 2005 that he had the note. Minchin gave him one piece of advice: 'Screw it up and throw it away.' He feared the damage it would cause if it ever got out.

No matter, the great crime of the McLachlan note was not the leaking of it, but the handling of it.

As is so often the case in politics, it is not the unprompted disasters or the mistakes that bring down governments and politicians, but the way they respond to them. The way that Costello responded sealed his fate.

Costello had plenty of warning that the story was going to break. Milne rang Costello's press secretary, Dave Alexander, on Saturday morning to tell him he was running with the story. Dave rang Costello and told him. Costello and McLachlan also spoke, and Costello effectively gave McLachlan the go-ahead to speak on the record to Milne.

If he had wanted to, Costello could have told McLachlan to shut up, or he could have downplayed it with Milne. He did neither. A decision was made to detonate the bomb.

Costello had hours to run through his responses and his strategy.

Milne deliberately left it until much later, around 7.00 p.m. on Saturday, to ring Howard's press secretary, David Luff, who was having a rare night off and getting ready to watch the football on television. By then, Milne's story was done and dusted. Milne didn't want to give the prime minister or his office time to run interference.

Milne, never known to downplay any of his stories, told Luff to remember where he was and what he was doing at that moment because he had a yarn that would change the way the government operated.

'Righto', said the affable Luff, and he listened as Milne ran through it. It was the first that Luff had heard of it. Luff then rang Howard, who was at Kirribilli, to tell him. Howard made little in the way of comment, except for a few 'mmm's here and there, but he was keen to know every single detail of the story.

Luff then had to go to the Phillip Street office to try to hunt down previously reported comments by Costello when he had been asked about the leadership and whether or not there was a deal between himself and the prime minister on any handover. Luff could find nothing conclusive in the files that would contradict what was now being said by Costello and his supporters.

Luff texted Sinodinos to tell him about Milne's story. It was also the first that Sinodinos had heard of it.

Sinodinos had a very bad feeling about this. He saw it as proof that the government was fraying at the seams. He had a vision of the road ahead: a breakdown of discipline; bad blood between the two main principals; and, ultimately, the downfall of the government.

Sinodinos was born in Newcastle of Cephalonian parents, but when it came to this he could easily have descended from the Delphic Oracle.

Given that Costello knew about the story well in advance, he or his office could have called anyone in the prime minister's office and warned them that it was going to break. Or, once the prime minister and his office found out, they could have called Costello to find out what the hell was going and to discuss how they might handle it.

Instead, both sides decided to sit pat that night and all through Sunday while they assessed the fallout. That was another mistake. If both men had spoken on either Saturday night or Sunday, and agreed on a form of words, the story might have had a very different ending.

Andrew Robb, who had worked with McLachlan at the National Farmers' Federation, and who was federal director of the Liberal Party when Howard took over from Downer, had also known about McLachlan's note. He was dismissive of it. He did not believe there was any such thing as a deal struck between the two on the leadership, because the negotiations had continued well after the meeting that McLachlan had attended.

Nevertheless, on the Monday morning — the day after the story broke — Robb had to ring Costello on another matter, and decided to counsel him. He told Costello to be careful in what he said and how he said it. He told him that it was an opportunity for him to put the relationship and his previous behaviour in context.

He told Costello it was a chance, if he used the right tone and words, to get the upper hand, and that he should seize it.

Instead, what followed was a wholly unedifying spectacle of a leader and his deputy playing 'Liar liar, pants on fire' in public.

Costello would have been infinitely better off, even if he had believed there was a deal, to have done as Robb had advised. He should have taken the high moral ground, declared it was a long time ago, that many rivers had flown under dozens of bridges since that conversation had occurred, and that Howard, as a highly successful prime minister, had earned the right to determine the time of his departure.

This would have ensured that the heat was kept on Howard, but Costello just could not bring himself to do it.

On his morning walk on the following Monday, the prime minister said there was no deal, but there had been lots of discussions — and proof that there was no deal lay in the fact that there had been discussions on the leadership for weeks after the alleged deal took place.

Costello followed up with a doorstop outside his Treasury Place office, where he said that Howard had volunteered the undertaking, 'and I took him at his word. Obviously, that did not happen'.

In other words, the prime minister was not a man of his word.

The stoush triggered an avalanche of support for the prime minister. It was not just Howard's colleagues who rang him. Howard told staff that even Don Argus, the chairman of BHP Billiton, told him that he should not leave under such circumstances. Argus now says he has no recollection of such a conversation.

While heartened by the support, Howard was incensed by the leak and by Costello's public statements.

Privately, Howard was highly agitated, accusing Costello of impugning his integrity, and vowing that he was not going to allow his deputy's remarks to go unchallenged. His staff tried to get him to respond in a more dignified fashion at a press conference, but he let loose again on his Tuesday-morning walk. Although more circumspect, he was keen to put Costello in his place:

> The leadership of the Liberal Party is not my plaything; it's not Mr Costello's plaything.
>
> It is the unique gift of the 100 men and women of the federal parliamentary Liberal Party, and any member of the parliamentary Liberal Party who forgets that is indulging hubris and arrogance.

The way Costello responded brought universal derision. Friends and foes alike shook their heads in disbelief.

As he prepared to go into Tuesday's cabinet meeting in Sydney, Costello told journalists: 'My parents always told me, if you have done nothing wrong you have got nothing to fear by telling the truth, and I told the truth.'

He succeeded in sounding both sanctimonious and sooky at the same time.

Inside, Howard was busily taking counsel from staff and colleagues. Costello's actions provoked accusations of disloyalty. Sinodinos broached the highly sensitive subject of sacking Costello. Sinodinos suggested that, given the circumstances, the prime minister should consider removing Costello from the treasurer's portfolio.

Howard was reluctant to move against his deputy. He wanted to see how events would play out. He did not want to rip apart the government, or do anything that would make matters worse. Or make Costello a martyr. He was still hoping that the situation was salvageable.

However, he was ropeable that Costello was effectively calling him a liar. He had a sheaf of folders, and he waved them around in front of his staff. He kept his own record of meetings and conversations, including those ones, and he could prove, if he had to, that his account was right.

Sinodinos believed that the situation was untenable. There were already problems between the two, and this would only make it that much worse. Costello was always tight with information, and trying to get him to tell the prime minister's office what was in the budget was always an ordeal.

In 2003, Costello kept his budget tax-cuts a secret until the last possible moment. In 2006, the prime minister's office was not told about the superannuation changes until a few days before the budget was put to bed.

Howard would ring his advisers seeking information on what was in the budget, only to be told that they couldn't get it and that he would have to ring Costello himself to ask for it. It was a constant source of irritation, at the very least.

Now, here they were, calling each other liars. Sinodinos' view was that no one would believe they could work together again, even if they managed to reconcile.

Sinodinos was right.

Before the cabinet meeting, Howard had also sounded out Vaile on the views of the National Party. Vaile reported to him that the party wanted him to stay. Vaile told him that the party's marginal-seat holders believed 'it was a safer bet' with him there. They were sticking by Howard, as they would until the very end.

Vaile says that, during the discussion, Howard repeated that it had been his intention to leave at the end of 2006. But, given what had just transpired, he 'would not be seen to be pushed out'.

Vaile had not known about the McLachlan note, and does not believe that Costello was responsible for its leaking, but felt that Costello's handling of it was disastrous. He knew what Howard's response would be, 'purely because of his personality'.

'He was never going to be pushed or shouldered out. He would go at his time of choosing,' Vaile told me.

'It still remains my view that if this particular event had not unfolded as it had, there was a very strong possibility that he would step down.'

Despite suggestions that he had warned the prime minister his departure would trigger a split in the coalition, Vaile says this is not true. He does concede, however, that he had expressed concern to Howard about the need to maintain the stability of the government.

Vaile recalls the cabinet meeting that day as the 'iciest' he had ever attended. Howard and Costello sat next to one another, as usual. The prime minister opened up by referring to the unpleasantness, and intimated that he and Costello would be meeting separately afterwards. He threw it open for discussion. Vaile had already told his fellow Nationals ministers not to buy in if the subject was raised.

After a short silence, Minchin gave each of the principal characters a short lecture.

'There are hundreds of thousands of Liberals out there devastated by what has happened,' he said. 'Both of you have a responsibility to fix it.'

The meeting then began tackling the usual polyglot issues: visa processing for unauthorised boat arrivals; funding to locate HMAS Sydney; drought relief; the agenda for an upcoming Council of Australian Governments' meeting; and a paper on options to draw Muslims more into the wider Australian community.

The prime minister and treasurer made appropriate interventions on submissions. It was surreal.

Costello and Howard met that evening, and then Costello flew back to Melbourne. At a press conference the next day, he said he had asked the prime minister to carry out a smooth transition. It was obvious that a challenge, if it was ever on, was dropping off Costello's agenda.

Costello had met with Minchin for almost two hours before his press conference. Minchin warned him not to challenge. He told him that the mood of the party was against it: they wanted Howard to stay as leader, and if Costello launched a challenge he would do very badly.

Minchin was sympathetic to Costello, and believed that Howard should have gone voluntarily before this stage. He pays tribute to Costello for holding back and for not tearing down the party; but, like everyone else, he despaired at Costello's handling of events.

The following Monday evening, more than a week after the story broke, Costello met with a tight group of supporters. Over takeaway pizzas, they gathered at Michael Ronaldson's city apartment which, although sparsely furnished, was superbly located in the Philadelphia building in Spring Street, with views over Treasury Gardens and the Melbourne Cricket Ground.

There was precious-little brotherly love to spread around

that night. As well as Ronaldson, there was the South Australian moderate and then chief Costello backer, Christopher Pyne, plus Costello's two former staffers and now MPs, Tony Smith and Mitch Fifield.

Costello seemed calm and collected, and was anxious to hear the advice of his colleagues. There were three options: challenge, resign, or sit pat. He got mixed advice.

Pyne and Fifield thought he should challenge. Ronaldson thought he shouldn't. After assessing the numbers, Smith thought he should stay where he was and not challenge — advice he would later regret.

They all knew that the numbers were not there. At the absolute maximum, Costello might have been able to muster 30 or 35 votes, roughly one-third of the Liberal Party room.

Pyne and Fifield argued that even though the numbers might not be there the first time, they never would be unless and until people were forced to make a decision. With the first challenge obviously doomed, they argued, Costello should resign and go to the backbench. Then he should bide his time before launching a second challenge. It is a classic technique, and one that Paul Keating had used effectively against Bob Hawke.

Ronaldson thought this was madness, and argued that the fact that the numbers fell a long way short of a credible showing was reason enough not to challenge.

In Smith's view, the wobblers would fall away when it came time to vote, so that there was little or no chance that Costello would get even a third of the vote. His resignation would precipitate chaos within the government, and any subsequent election-defeat would be laid at Costello's door.

But he told him: 'It's your life; it's your call.' Pyne also told him, with two for a challenge and two against: 'It's your call.' They all promised to back him to the hilt, whatever decision he made. The meeting lasted around an hour.

At the end of July, when Howard announced he would stay on, Costello acquiesced. I did not think at the time that Costello would resign or challenge, and I told Howard so.

Nor did I believe that Howard could or should go under such circumstances, although for months beforehand — in Greek, English, and Gringlish — I had discussed it with Sinodinos any number of times, knowing the depth of Costello's feelings, warning that Pompei was going to erupt, and arguing that it would be best if the prime minister acted before the explosion rather than after.

Arthur and I were in furious agreement. Still, there were only two people who could resolve it, and they had not been communicating properly for some time.

It was possible to discuss all manner of things, in either language, with Arthur. His value to the office and to Howard was immense, but even he was powerless here.

Howard's forced departure after the publication of the McLachlan note would have triggered a bloodbath in the Liberal Party and a rupture with the Nationals. It is highly unlikely, in those circumstances, that Costello would have been able to lead a united party to an election.

The Liberal Party is a fractious beast at the best of times, with members of Parliament believing it is their right — no, duty — to speak out every time they disagree with their own government's decision. Howard had not tamed the beast, but had learned to manage it. Costello did not have as deft a touch in dealing with colleagues.

I was no longer on Costello's staff. If I had been, I hope I would have been strong enough, with the help of a few others, to convince him to quit as treasurer and deputy leader. His position was untenable.

I thought then, and still do, that Costello should have resigned and gone to the backbench. It would have been the honourable thing to do. It would also have showed some ticker and, with clever positioning, would have paid off for him and perhaps the government.

Regardless of any numbers, it was an intolerable situation for him politically and ethically. How could Costello continue to work with, and pretend to be loyal to, a man whom he had accused of lying?

The government would have been much weaker without Costello as treasurer; there is no doubt about that. Costello's very absence would have strengthened his own position — assuming he behaved himself appropriately, that is.

In 2003, there was every risk that the caravan would have moved on without him if he had resigned. In 2006, and later in 2007, the caravan was stranded in the desert and had nowhere else to go. It would have made no difference who led the Labor Party, whether it was Beazley or Rudd.

The government was showing signs of age, and its decay would be reflected in the polls. If Beazley was spared, it would only be because he was streaking ahead in the polls; and if he was not, Rudd would still have been elected leader, with the same disastrous consequences for the coalition.

The Liberals would have turned to Costello as their only saviour.

Instead, Costello stayed where he was, sullen and frustrated. He went into another funk. Some of his supporters gave up trying to talk to him, because sooner or later discussions ended in a fight. Even Rod Kemp, who had been as close to Costello as anyone, despaired about his friend.

Costello believes that Howard never intended to go. We don't know for sure but, after the 2004 election, Howard had led Vaile, his staff, and others to believe that he probably would leave at the end of 2006, giving Costello enough time to establish himself in the job.

After the McLachlan affair, Howard told his staff that if he had not been pushed, he probably would have gone. He said he had been waiting for the High Court to rule on the government's industrial-relations legislation, and once this was settled — successfully — he intended to leave.

The court ruled in the government's favour in November 2006.

Much as he might have liked to, Howard knew that he could not stay forever. He knew that his seat, which had a rapidly diminishing margin, would be under threat; he knew that he should go out while he was on top; and with the workplace reforms that he had held dear for so long finally enacted, he knew that there would be no better time.

Perhaps, if Costello had brushed aside the McLachlan revelation and waited, things might have turned out very differently. But he couldn't wait, and Howard wouldn't be pushed.

Perhaps, if Howard had told Costello what he was thinking, Costello might have been prepared to give him more space. But they did not have that kind of relationship. Trust and goodwill had been eroded to such an extent that this was impossible.

If they had spoken when the story broke, they might have been able to get through with a couple of bruises — and not, as happened, with huge chunks of flesh missing.

The repercussions of the McLachlan saga within the government were enormously destructive and continuing. Both the leader and the leader-in-waiting were now damaged goods — not because of anything the opposition had done to them, but because of what they had done to themselves and each other. Brilliant!

Brian Loughnane organised a strategic-planning session for the next election at Liberal Party headquarters about six weeks after the leadership debacle. Peter Conran and I went, but no one from the prime minister's main office was invited to attend. It was seen as a slight by the office, and proof that down at Menzies House they were preparing for a transition — especially as David Gazard from the treasurer's office was present.

The meeting was sombre. Morale was running below sea level. Everybody well knew the problems, and pollster Mark Textor summed them up succinctly. The main one, of course, was the relationship between the prime minister and the treasurer.

'As a result of the leadership [stoush], they think John Howard is a liar, and Peter Costello is incompetent,' Textor said.

'They think, *Well, what else would Howard lie about if he lied about this?* And as for Costello, they thought he was smart, but he has completely fucked this up. And they think, *If the prime minister is not prepared to endorse him as the next prime minister, is he any good?*'

Could it get any worse than this? Yes. No matter how bad things are, they can always get worse.

Textor predicted that, if the next campaign was about industrial relations, 'We will lose the election.'

'If it is about defending the details of industrial relations, we will lose the election without doubt. They don't understand what we have done.'

Major difficulties were showing up in seats in New South Wales, in areas where the government had travelled well in the past.

People couldn't understand why Australia was in Iraq — or Afghanistan, for that matter — and previously strong showings in immigration and national security were softening.

There was only one glimmer of hope for the Liberals. Kim Beazley was still leader of the Labor Party, and the Liberal research on him must have been the same as Labor's. He was seen as weak. He didn't look as if he could stand up to the challenges of the economy or much else and, more, he didn't really understand what the new Australia, with its ever-increasing prosperity, was all about.

People worried that he would take the country backwards, and allow himself to be bullied by the premiers, unions, Greens, and any other lobby group.

The day he mixed up Karl Rove with Rove McManus, we knew he was finished. Bloody idiot! Why did he have to go and do that? There would have been louder screams in our offices over that tongue-trip than in Labor Party offices. We knew it would only be a matter of time before Rudd replaced him, and it was not something that we looked forward to or took lightly.

Rudd was elected after I left the gallery, so I had not dealt with him as a journalist, but I knew enough to know what he was like.

One day, standing in the queue at Aussie's, the coffee shop that provides the only piece of real humanity in the new building, I felt a tap on my shoulder.

'Hello, you're Niki Savva, aren't you? You know my brother Greg — I'm Kevin,' he said. We had an amiable chat then, and whenever we ran into one another. I crossed paths with him in Members' Hall when Crean's leadership was falling apart and Rudd's soundings of a possible run were being firmly repulsed by his colleagues.

'Hang in there, Kevin. I've got a theory about you — you'll get there,' I said to him. Not that he needed any encouragement from me, of course.

'Yes, and when I do, I'll give you a job,' he said. Yeah, right. Add that to the list of broken promises.

Rudd is like Howard, but not in the way he later postured as Howard Lite on the economy. He is as socially conservative as Howard, and more so than many liberals.

He was absolutely relentless, and he was disciplined. He was obvious — perhaps too much so — in his hunger for the job, and he was Miss Piggy when it came to acting, but he knew how to frame a message and stick to it. Or, to be more precise, he stuck to the ones that Hawker Britton framed for him.

He looked like Howard — except that he was younger. He looked as safe as Howard. He looked like he could be Howard's son, sounded like Howard, and did everything he could to encourage the comparisons with Howard.

It was creepy. It was the invasion of the body-snatcher. Howard went to sleep one night, Rudd slipped in, smoothed out a few wrinkles, and stole his skin. It was incredibly effective.

Invasion of the body-snatcher

The bottom line was, we knew that if we couldn't steady, we were stuffed.

CHAPTER TWELVE

Economy great; government stinks

The political year began well in 2007 with the prime minister's Australia Day address to the National Press Club, announcing a $10 billion package over ten years to save the Murray–Darling Basin. It was a visionary programme, designed to tackle a serious threat to our economic and environmental well-being. Nevertheless, a few of us were nervous about it. There was one major defect — not in the package itself, but in the process that had led to its construction.

Treasury had been left out of its formulation until the very end When we returned from holidays, I learned that Treasury had not been included on the committee that had been pulled together by senior officers in the Department of Prime Minister and Cabinet — partly because they wanted to put the package together quickly, as the first major hit of the year, and partly because they wanted to keep it tight. This was a recipe for disaster, and I warned Peter Conran to expect Treasury to retaliate for what it would interpret as a deliberate slight.

Treasury had not shown any particular expertise on water, as Treasury secretary Ken Henry would later claim when he launched his critique of the government's policy approach. My fear was based on the fact that the simmering jealousies between the two great departments would be certain to spill over into the public arena, and that the splatter would not land on the public servants, but their masters. Which is exactly what happened when Ken's supposedly private speech in April found its way into the media.

When I was still working for Costello, I well remember a dinner which Peter, our chief of staff, Phil Gaetjens, and I attended at Treasury, hosted by Ken and attended by the most senior members of the department.

After the main course, Costello decided to go round the table and ask each of the top brains in Treasury to nominate the most pressing challenge facing Australia. Costello wasn't looking to put people on the spot, but wanted some idea of where they thought the country should be heading, and what the government's priorities should be. Plus he was casting around for issues he could use to set himself apart.

Ken nominated the three Ps — productivity, population, and participation. In other words, how to deal with an ageing population and the difficulties this would pose for the economy, the workforce, and society generally. It was a serious issue in vogue at the time, and one that Peter had already taken up with gusto.

At least two others nominated early-childhood education. Another couple mentioned the environment, in the sense of its need for protection. All of these were important issues in their own right.

Not one referred to climate change; no one even mentioned water.

The closest contact I had with Ken and water was on a visit to New York in 2000. Peter had decided we should all go for a walk in Central Park to shake off our cobwebs after the long flight. It was autumn, a beautiful sunny day, and we happened to come upon the lake and the boat shed that rented out tin rowboats.

Peter thought that what we really needed to do to get rid of the jet lag was to row on the lake. He had seen it in movies, and loved the idea of it. So they hired a boat. There was Peter, Ken, Lizzie McCabe, and me perched in a small tinnie.

Peter and Ken struggled with the oars to get the tinnie out to the middle of the lake. We did a few tight circles close to shore before they got the hang of it, with Peter shouting instructions at Ken, telling him to row harder or row this way or that, all of which Ken took in good humour, while Lizzie and I laughed our heads off at these two inelegant blokes, carrying on like, well … fish out of water.

While we were in the middle of the lake, my mobile rang: it was journalist John Vause, then with Channel Seven, asking where were we. 'Um. New York.' This was not a lie, just not the whole truth.

In 2007, the tinnie that the government was in was looking more and more like the Titanic. The water package was in dire straits — thanks to the eternal bickering among the states and Henry's later verbal assault — as was the government itself and its main players.

There was a distinct pattern to the year. The government would steady, briefly, and then crash. The only way we could cope was by indulging in black humour. We joked among ourselves whenever we had two good days in a row. That's about as far apart as the disasters were spaced, and as long as the discipline would last.

The media was sick of us and wanted us gone. Almost 12 years is roughly two lifetimes in today's media cycles. Even if they were not philosophically opposed — and most of them were, antagonised even more by issues such as 'children overboard' and the detention of asylum-seekers — they were desperate for something new.

That much was obvious. The journalist in me could see it from their perspective. It had been the same after 13 years of Labor.

It was not that they all fell in love with Rudd — thanks to his infamous temper and foul language, and the bullying tactics of his staff — although some of them did. He was about as well-liked in the Press Gallery as he was in the caucus. And while the government was looking a bit tatty, it was a long way from rotten.

Unemployment was the lowest it had been for 30 years, inflation was still reasonably in check, and interest rates were manageable, even though they were creeping up. In fact, the country was going through an almost unparalleled period of prosperity.

Some commentators found it hard to reconcile the two conditions: economy great; government stinks.

Most reporting focused relentlessly on the grey clouds around every silver lining. Good economic news was rarely reported prominently, if at all, or was slanted to portend something more dire. If unemployment went down, it meant interest rates would have to go up, with 'HOMEBUYERS TO BE BE HIT AGAIN' — not that a record number of people were in jobs. If inflation went up, it was not that the economy was growing strongly; instead, it was a case of 'INTEREST RATES SET TO RISE'.

The media and Labor launched strikes against the government, but in the end they were nowhere near as effective or as deadly as the ones we executed on ourselves.

Rudd's ascension to the Labor leadership wrought an instant reversal in party-political fortunes. Labor went up dramatically, and the coalition began to unhinge. Polling done for the Liberal Party by Crosby/Textor just three days after Rudd's elevation showed immediately that the government was in deep trouble.

In a memorandum on 7 December based on focus-group interviews, in what was a brutal internal assessment for the party and the prime minister, and which was subsequently presented to the internal review of the election defeat conducted by the Liberal Party, they warned of the change in sentiment:

> Top of mind, these Queensland soft voters thought the leadership change was a good thing because they felt that in Kevin Rudd they now have a credible choice at the next election.
>
> The change of Labor leadership has also caused soft voters to reflect on the age and stagnation of the Howard government and what they see as the by-products of that stagnation — broken promises due to complacency and general disillusionment.

Further, soft voters tended to re-evaluate the 'experience' of the Howard government from a positively positioned experience that provides strong, disciplined, stable government to a negatively expressed perception whereby the Howard government uses its experience for abuse of power and the self serving political manipulation of issues, the media and voters.

John Howard himself is now more readily seen (by many of these Queensland soft voters at least) to have been PM for too long, with some losing appreciation of the benefits to them and to the nation of over a decade of stable government and the strong, decisive leadership of John Howard.

However soft voters generally assessed that Australia is now at a peak (and on consideration credit the Howard government with getting us to this point) but feel that we have started a 'decline' with the new IR laws (particularly) and the war in Iraq strongly underpinning this negative perception.

And for those soft voters that think John Howard is doing a good job, an acknowledgement that they need to look beyond him because 'all good things come to an end' and the government cannot sustain their position at the 'top of the crest' because there is no apparent succession plan.

In contrast to the early 'Latham' groups, perceptions of Kevin Rudd were almost wholly positive or at least non judgemental, with virtually no negative opinion, just a few questions about his background and experience qualified by a 'wait and see' attitude.

A few days later, quantitative research showed that the coalition's primary vote in key marginal seats had dropped three points to 35 per cent, and that Labor's had increased a whopping 11 points to 45 per cent.

The government's weaknesses were its longevity, its industrial-relations policies, the war in Iraq, and the Australian Wheat Board scandal. All of them had helped to erode its credibility.

And as if that wasn't enough, the government helped Rudd and Labor along with a combination of inaction and incompetence or bravado. Areas of neglect, such as climate change and broadband, looked as if they were getting band-aids slapped on them, while the sore of industrial relations was allowed to fester.

Howard would later tell confidantes that one of his biggest mistakes in government was getting rid of the no-disadvantage test in his second major wave of workplace reforms.

In some ways, having a majority in the Senate was the worst thing that could have happened to the government. There was no parliamentary check on it, while it felt the pressure to do *something big* and not waste a hard-won majority.

The reformers argued, and Howard himself believed, that if ever there was a time to push through major industrial changes, this was it. The key players in the cabinet, including Costello, thought the same. One cabinet minister I have since spoken to recalled that the most compelling case for major change came in an initial submission from the minister for employment and workplace relations, Kevin Andrews, pointing out the brake that the no-disadvantage test was putting on the signing of individual contracts.

It was the view of the hardliners that, if they genuinely believed in the principle of individual contracts — and they did — the no-disadvantage test had to go. It's a bit hard now to explain the mood and the rationale at the time.

Senior people in the government, cabinet ministers, and many advisers either underestimated the disastrous consequences that would flow from the removal of the no-disadvantage test or believed that it would be possible to overcome them. They thought they would be able to sell the policy because they believed employers would play fair, and that a booming economy, which was delivering record low unemployment and rising wages under the coalition — along with Howard's well-documented backing for and support from the battlers — would convince workers that they would be safe.

When you look back at the way it all unfolded, you think: *How could they be so naive? Or so misguided?* I guess you had to be there.

Before the GST was introduced, the government had spent months laying the groundwork, convincing the electorate that the tax system was broken and needed fixing, before going to an election for a mandate.

There was not the same kind of preparation before WorkChoices was introduced as there was with the GST. There was no foreplay, no flirting or courting, no wasting time on seduction — just the old 'Wham! Bam! Thank you Ma'am!'

The industrial-relations reforms seemed to come out of nowhere. The internal polling showed that people could not understand why the reforms were necessary, given that everything was going so well, unless it was to fulfil an ideological ambition.

Within the government, although there was an appreciation of the degree of difficulty involved, even the hardest of hardliners, the former finance minister Nick Minchin, now concedes he underestimated the extent to which the ACTU would mobilise in opposition.

At one meeting with Arthur Sinodinos, Peter Conran, and his deputy, David Quilty, Howard was reminded of his promise on proposed new industrial laws in 1996, just before his first election victory, when he pledged that 'under a Howard government you cannot be worse off, but you can be better off'.

That line had been devised by a group including Sinodinos and Peter Reith almost a decade before, to reassure the Howard battlers that they had nothing to fear from a coalition government. After 2004, even though everyone was aware of the challenges that lay ahead, the weight of arguments by all the principal players was in favour of bigger reform.

Tony Nutt was one of the few who argued against going too far. He warned that the battlers would be alienated, and that the government had little to gain in pursuing such an agenda.

Ironically, Nutt, who had argued that the changes would be too difficult to sell, was also the man in charge of all the government's sales and advertising programmes, including the one that would prove so costly and, ultimately and inevitably, ineffectual.

On 4 March 2005, a briefing note to the prime minister from the Cabinet Policy Unit (sent ahead of the first substantial cabinet discussion on workplace reform) summed up the mood, foreshadowed the opposition, and warned of the need for a strategic plan to withstand the attacks:

> We really have only one shot in the locker in terms of further major IR reform and it is critical that the reforms are not only bold, but that they actually do increase flexibility, enhance productivity and reduce the cost/red tape entailed in workplace relations.

The note expressed disappointment in the cabinet submission for failing to address these areas, and also ran through a number of other issues that it either failed to address or did not address satisfactorily, including minimum conditions, the role of the AIRC, and the possible use of the corporations powers.

It concluded:

> Because we only have 'one shot in the locker' it is critical that we get these reforms right.
>
> Before it gives the go-ahead, cabinet must have all the information needed to fully assess the extent to which the proposed changes will and will not meet our core objectives.
>
> It also must have a strategic plan to withstand the attacks from the reforms' opponents in a way that maintains our political support from hard working Australians.

Ahead of the next scheduled cabinet meeting in the third week of May to discuss the many complexities of the package, which still had to be sorted out, the prime minister was advised that, although the legislation would be complex, 'pressure must be kept on for the earliest passage — certainly by the end of the year':

> There is no doubt that once the decisions in this submission are announced, the political fight with Labor, the unions and the States will commence.
>
> There is no point letting them get up a head of steam by waiting seven months to introduce the legislation — a timetable that will also look like we are 'reform shy' or at least 'not reform ready'.

The prime minister was also counselled against any staged approach to the reforms, as some were suggesting:

> Also there seems little logic in pursuing reforms now (for implementation in mid-2006) only to revisit them in 2007 for an agenda 'to 2010 and beyond …
>
> What does this say about the shelf life of these reforms? Surely we need to cast these reforms in a long-term, productivity-boosting context — say, in a 15 year time frame out to 2020. By suggesting otherwise, we could wear all the pain of a full-blown scare campaign, but still be exposed to the charge that these are merely interim measures.

Given his approach a few years before on the introduction of the GST, John Howard would have been mindful of the pitfalls of a two-step implementation process. Even so, softer options, including a scaled-down version that would increase protections for small business while still clamping down on union power, were considered and discarded in the general argy-bargy.

Howard succumbed to his own instincts and the arguments of almost everyone around him, as well as business, wanting to go *big*. As a consequence, when the package was released, he was unable to give any guarantee to the Howard battlers that they would not be worse off. Every measure before had provided a safety net; now it was being ripped away.

And the unions, recognising that their very survival was at stake, made it a fight to the death.

Peter Conran, John Kunkel, David Quilty, and I were having our breakfast coffees as per usual at Aussies one day when Ian Hanke, a bull-terrier-type political operator working in Kevin Andrews' office, wandered up. It was in the early days of the process, and things appeared to be going well. The Greek in me always regarded that as a bad sign; something was bound to go wrong. And on this, you didn't need to be Greek to know we were heading for the old 'wham bam', and definitely no 'thank you, ma'am'. A few of us had been shut out of the formulation process, so all we could really do was watch it play out.

I asked Hanke what the strategy was for dealing with the media once unions started to wheel out individual cases of workers being screwed by employers. Having lived through the GST campaign, I felt it was easy to predict the road ahead. Hanke doubted that that was what would happen, so I bet him $50 that that was exactly what they would do. I am still waiting for my $50.

By the time Howard reversed the policy and inserted a new safety net, in early May 2007, it was too late. The unions had already won the public debate, and any concession given by the prime minister was seen as a trick or simply a ploy to win the election.

HOWARD ALWAYS REGARDED CLIMATE CHANGE as a second-order issue, failing to acknowledge that when all else is going well, second-order issues filter their way to the top.

He would later claim that the government had been caught in a 'perfect storm' of a long drought, the Stern Review on the Economics of Climate Change commissioned by the British government, and

Al Gore's documentary *An Inconvenient Truth*.

Of them all, Gore had the biggest impact on Australian middle-class voters. On the political stump, Al Gore is about as charismatic as a piece of fibro; but his movie managed to frighten the pants off millions of people.

Howard stolidly refused to be one of them.

When the pressure became too great to ignore, he pulled together a task force at the end of 2006 to examine options, but he was not about to switch and ratify the Kyoto Protocol. Even though Australia had effectively met its targets without ratifying the protocol, it didn't matter.

Howard was caught in his own perfect storm. No one would have believed him if he had switched and yet, instead of looking resolute, he looked stubborn and old-fashioned. Or just plain old.

Cabinet ministers took advantage of the prime minister's absence from a meeting in mid-2007 to discuss ratifying the Kyoto Protocol. Alexander Downer, Peter Costello, and Malcolm Turnbull all agreed that it should be signed, or should have been signed. Even the greatest sceptic in the cabinet, Nick Minchin, conceded the political arguments in favour of signing.

Minchin argued, however, that if Howard did sign so close to the election, it would be viewed so cynically that it would only create more damage. In any case, he doubted that Howard would have been able to carry it off convincingly.

Downer and Costello believed that any benefits would be outweighed by the costs — principally that the electorate would see it as hypocritical, given the emphatic arguments that the government had mounted previously against ratifying.

Turnbull, then environment minister, kept insisting it was not too late. Within the cabinet, he was a lone voice. He reckoned later that he tried again in September, by circulating a letter, rather than a formal submission, arguing for a discussion in cabinet urging ratification. It failed for all the same reasons.

Aboriginal intervention was no band-aid or patch-up. It was unfinished business. Howard was genuinely appalled by the findings of the *Little Children are Sacred* report, and furious at the cursory responses of the Northern Territory government, which Kevin Rudd had also echoed initially.

Urged on by the head of his department, Dr Peter Shergold, and by his minister, Mal Brough, both of whom he respected, and buttressed by his private talks with Noel Pearson and Sue Gordon, he launched an all-out war — complete with troops — on abuse in Aboriginal communities in the Northern Territory.

Even Noel Pearson's support on this, and then later on the preamble to the Constitution, could not convince people that Howard was genuine in his attempts to right a great wrong. Or, even if they were convinced, they gave him no credit for it.

Howard never believed that the exercise was a vote-winner. In fact, he knew that in the Northern Territory it would probably cost him votes.

There was a curious paradox in the reaction to the intervention. It won almost universal approval from commentators, but the electorate reacted more cynically, and the government slid again in the polls. It wasn't a case of too little, too late, but too much, too late.

The root cause of all the government's problems was undoubtedly the fractured relationship between the prime minister and his treasurer. They had never really been close, but had managed a productive professional relationship for more than a decade. That was no longer the case. They were barely speaking to each other, and the atmosphere between them was poisonous.

Staff in the two offices continued to talk, otherwise the breach would have been complete, but it was no substitute for the irreconcilable breakdown of trust that had occurred at the very top.

To make matters worse, Howard's once-sure touch was faltering, gradually at first, then dramatically and irretrievably. The government's greatest strength — Howard himself — was slowly but surely turning into its greatest weakness.

He never lost his resolve, or his propensity for work, or his determination to overcome obstacles, or his ability to stay focused and civil under pressure. It was his judgement that began to falter. And his luck ran out.

On 11 February, Howard was slotted in to do the Laurie Oakes interview on *Sunday*, ostensibly to foreshadow a massive aged-care package. During the course of it, he made some highly critical remarks about Barack Obama, then the glamour candidate in the Democrat primaries.

Howard's comments, that al-Qaeda would be praying for an Obama/Democrat victory, were unnecessary and gratuitous. They also signalled something else: an inability to get either the tone or the content of his messages right.

He realised immediately after the interview that he might have mucked up when he rang his foreign-policy adviser, Andrew Shearer, to see what he thought about his remarks. He had not discussed them beforehand with Shearer, and Shearer could only confirm what Howard suspected too late: they would attract a barrage of criticism across two continents.

The $1.5 billion aged-care package sank without trace.

Then there was the prospect of mortally wounding Rudd in early March; but, incredibly, the government managed to find a way of killing one of its own instead.

Brian Burke was back in the news in Western Australia, and journalists explored inconsistencies in Kevin Rudd's earlier accounts of his meetings with Burke when it seemed he had been courting the support of the corrupt politician in his attempts to undermine Beazley and seize the Labor leadership.

Rudd knew he was in trouble, and his responses showed it. The government went for the jugular. Costello's performance in the house was electrifying as he declared that anyone who had dealt with Burke was 'morally and politically compromised'.

Senator Ian Campbell, the human services minister, was particularly impressed with the treasurer, and rang one of Costello's supporters to say so. Unfortunately, Campbell failed to mention to Costello, or anybody else, either then or in the lead-up to the attacks on Rudd, that he had met with Burke the previous year to discuss an indigenous cultural centre. When that meeting became public, Campbell — partly because of Costello's remark — was removed from the ministry, and Rudd slid out of the net like a slippery eel.

On 26 March, the member for Kalgoorlie, Barry Haase, asked the prime minister a stock-standard Dorothy Dixer about workplace reforms and how they had helped to strengthen the Australian economy. No question to the prime minister from his own side is spontaneous, but sometimes the answers stray from the prepared script; this time, the reply was a beauty.

Winding up his tirade against unions, the PM said: 'Working families in Australia have never been better off.'

Even if it were true, it was an extremely unwise comment to make, and it echoed all the way through the year as Labor used it ruthlessly to paint him as uncaring and out of touch.

The polling went from bad to awful. In March, negative opinions of John Howard were hardening ('he's been in the job too long'; 'he has to be pushed before he responds'; 'he's suffering burn-out'; and so on), while positive opinions of Rudd were growing (he was said to be 'strong', 'compassionate', 'likeable', and 'articulate').

For younger voters, Rudd offered an exciting prospect of 'generational change'. And, just as worryingly, even though they are roughly the same age, on this issue he was ahead of Costello.

Incredibly, even though he had only been on the political stage for five minutes, soft voters (those who could still be persuaded either way) thought they knew what they would be getting with Kevin Rudd as prime minister — an education revolution and action on climate change — but didn't have a clue what they might get from Costello.

According to the Crosby/Textor research given to the internal Liberal Party post-mortem on the defeat, voters in the period between July and September 2007 had 'little appreciation of what Peter Costello would offer, apart from a "good economic brain"'.

Soft voters acknowledged that Howard had been a great prime minister (they were starting to talk about him in the past tense), but they were looking to the next prime minister to carry on his work. They were looking for a younger version of Howard, and they weren't looking to Costello. They thought they had found him in Rudd.

The invasion of the body-snatcher was working a treat.

Throughout, the union movement was running its highly effective campaign against the new industrial-relations laws. Despite labour shortages, they were succeeding in making workers feel anxious about their job security.

Another break for the government came in May with the revelation in Melbourne's *The Herald Sun* that Rudd's wife, Therese Rein, had underpaid almost 60 employees in her multi-million-dollar employment business. The question was how this could be squared with Labor's unrelenting campaign against the government for allegedly short-changing workers.

Rudd threw out some diversionary bait about politicians and their wives leading separate lives, declaring that women were not simply 'appendages of middle-aged men'.

Peter Dutton, the assistant treasurer, swallowed it whole. Dutton was upset that Rudd had not shown enough respect for women who stayed at home, and demanded an apology.

Rudd was out at dinner that evening, and when journalists relayed Dutton's remarks to him, he was ecstatic. Rudd had succeeded in switching the debate from allegations of Rein's unfair work practices to one about whether wives were entitled to separate lives.

The prime minister, unsettled by Rudd's ascendancy and the disastrous polls, was beginning to question himself. In March, he told confidantes that if only Costello had waited, he probably would have had the job by the end of 2006. When we heard what he had said, we did not regard it as an attempt to rewrite history.

In the lead-up to the 2004 election, two of his most senior advisers had presented the prime minister with a policy option for major federal–state reform. They had been waved aside by Howard, who said it would not be his problem; someone else would have to confront it. In other words, he would not be around to do it.

Arthur Sinodinos and others went through that campaign convinced it would be his last.

Then, in April 2007, Howard was given some private qualitative research that gave him some hope. This research, different in tone from the earlier Crosby/Textor findings, showed that while people were interested in Rudd, and seemed to like him, they had not yet made up their minds. They were not convinced that Rudd and Labor were ready to govern. They thought he was a bit slick and too programmed.

This research showed that, on the one hand, Australians felt that the nation's prosperity was locked in and would continue regardless; on the other, they were insecure about their own circumstances, largely because of WorkChoices. They were also worried about how their children and grandchildren stood to prosper in the great Australian middle class.

The research showed that people had not given up entirely on the government, but they wanted the government to get its act together and present a united team.

Crucially, they wanted to be convinced that Howard and Costello could still work with one another. And they wanted tangible proof of it. They wanted to see them in action, together.

They were also waiting for the government to lay out a clear roadmap of the priorities it wanted to tackle in the future.

At that stage, there was still a sliver of a chance for recovery.

It never happened.

We had been worried that the return from Guantanamo Bay of David Hicks — a man who had betrayed his family and his country, but who had managed to win considerable public support, thanks to his father's tireless campaign — would overshadow the budget.

The separation of the two events won some breathing space, and a window opened for the government to showcase its economic credentials.

It made no difference. The budget, which included substantial tax cuts and funding for education, came and went and left no bounce. It lay like a dead cat in the middle of a busy freeway.

CHAPTER THIRTEEN

Dear John …

There never was — and there never will be — any kind of credible reconciliation between Howard and Costello. In that final year, whenever voters looked up to check what was happening, more often than not all they could see were middle-aged men busily inspecting their navels to see if any new fluff had arrived.

It was not a pretty sight.

There was a general air of despondency in the executive wing and the Liberal Party, and it was in this atmosphere that Shane Stone decided that somebody had to do something.

In 2006, Stone, the former Northern Territory chief minister and former party president and 'memo' author, had been encouraging a tight circle of friends within the Liberal Party, including Alexander Downer, to consider a leadership change.

He got short shrift.

'Everyone was caught up in the tenth anniversary, riding high. I was confronted by people saying, "Why? Why do you want to say these things now?"' he told me.

He now bitterly regrets that the one person he did not raise it with at the time of the tenth anniversary was the prime minister himself.

Stone, although not particularly fond of Costello, had been conscious for some time of the need for a smooth transition, and he did not want to see Howard go out a loser.

He was one of the few people game enough to have raised it directly with Howard a few years before, while he was still party president, and most likely after the 2001 election:

> I remember saying to him: 'You have got to be careful in this business. There's only one week between Palm Sunday and the crucifixion. If they can do it to Jesus, imagine what they could do to you. The mob are like that.'
>
> He [Howard] said: 'That's a good one — I haven't heard that before.'
>
> 'I said: 'I am being serious.'
>
> He heard me, but he wasn't listening.

In May 2007, he was convinced it was all over for Howard, and he decided to tell Howard in person that it was not too late for him to retreat with dignity. He arranged a one-on-one meeting with the prime minister to have another go.

'I believed that the time had come. It was over. I just sensed it,' he says, recounting his feelings at the time. 'When it turns, if you have been in the business, you realise it has turned. It was fast becoming irrecoverable.'

This time, he did not put it in writing, except for a small note to himself to remind him of the points he needed to make:

> I was particularly concerned there was no 'go to' person in his office. Arthur had gone; I was worried Conran had been marginalised; Nutt was trying to be both principal private secretary and chief of staff, and it wasn't working.
>
> I said to Howard: 'There is no go-to person. There is no one.'
>
> He said: 'Tony.'
>
> I said: No, it's not working; it's just not working.'
>
> My concern was for him [Howard]. I didn't want to see him in a situation where, after everything that had happened, he was

flung out by the electorate. I was desperately concerned about how it would end.

The Northern Territory might have been the smallest jurisdiction, but I didn't get chucked out, I didn't get rolled in the party room, I didn't get defeated by the electorate.

There is a big difference between picking yourself up and walking out of a room and building, and waking up Sunday morning defeated. Better to leave a year too early than a week too late.

So he put it all to Howard. And what happened?

I was listened to politely.

You know, 'Thank you for expressing your views', but I got a sense that, while he heard, he hadn't listened.

I was a bit annoyed. I thought to myself, *Mate, there are people who care about you — you ought to bloody listen.*

John Howard had this idea, even if they went down, it wouldn't be as bad under him as it would under Costello. That was the theme.

Howard had heard, even if he hadn't taken heed. He wasn't stupid. He could see what was happening.

By June, Howard was canvassing a tight circle of friends and family, wondering out loud if he had made a mistake in not going. There was deep concern about his performance. Sotto voce, and only ever among themselves, his most senior aides confessed that he realised he should have gone in 2006.

In June, Arthur Sinodinos, who had left Howard's office six months before, was one of those who believed that unless the PM could get his act together, he should get out. He and Stone had kept in touch, and Stone had told him beforehand he was going to speak to the prime minister.

The air of desperation was suffocating, and Howard knew that he could not ignore it. It was like a thick, black fog hanging over everybody.

He kicked off the cabinet meeting in mid-July by asking his ministers to give frank assessments of the government's problems and what could be done to restore their fortunes. He told them not to hold back, and not to worry that he might get upset at what they had to say.

Reports later had the prime minister asking, 'Is it me?' He did not say this exactly, but that was the subtext. What he was seeking was advice on how he could resuscitate his leadership — short of exiting, that is.

Nothing much came of it. They all knew they were in diabolical trouble. Brough, Downer, and Costello all said later that their only option was to fight on. None of them, at this stage, thought seriously that the prime minister should, or could, leave. Or, if they did, they weren't prepared to say so.

Brough remembers that Howard also had a dinner at the Lodge with his cabinet ministers around the same time, and in the more relaxed surroundings had said to them: 'If you think it's me, I want you to tell me.' Minchin, who thought that Howard should have gone in 2006, but now believed that he had no choice but to stay and lead, made some reassuring remarks. Costello said nothing.

Around the same time, Mark Textor had dinner with Costello in a private dining-room at the Ottoman, Canberra's most popular Turkish restaurant, and a hangout for politicians and apparatchiks.

Textor told Costello in graphic detail the magnitude of the defeat confronting the government. Textor says he had no ulterior motive, other than to make sure that Costello was fully aware of how bad the situation was. Neither did he suggest to him at that dinner, he says, that he should make any move on the leadership.

But he did not hold back on any of the gory details, telling Costello that the government stood to lose between 20 and 40 seats.

Textor, who believed that there should have been a switch, even if he did not press Costello on it that night, might have skewered himself at that dinner as cleanly as the Ottoman's shish kebab.

Later, when he thought about their conversation, he worried that his frankness might have only succeeded in frightening off Costello.

If there was any chance of recovery, it ended on 6 August with the publication in News Ltd's tabloid newspapers of supposedly confidential polling conducted for the Liberal Party by Crosby/Textor. This polling was so secret that only a very select few people — or so it was thought — had been allowed to see it.

The *Herald Sun* headline, 'Old, Tricky and Losing', was devastating. The Liberal Party had confirmed for people in its own document what they were already thinking. There were mutterings in the prime minister's office that either Textor or Loughnane should be sacked, even if they were not directly responsible for the leak. But, given the proximity of the election, the party could not function without a director and pollster.

The talk subsided, but the bitterness remained, especially when staff from the prime minister's office recalled that they had been excluded from the strategy meeting a year before at Liberal Party headquarters.

The story was written by the Sydney *Daily Telegraph*'s Malcolm Farr. The paper's editor, David Penberthy, later told people that he had been given the Crosby/Textor research by Mark Arbib, then NSW Labor state secretary.

Penberthy had rung David Luff on Sunday evening to tell him they had the story. Luff happened to be with Howard at the Lodge, and relayed the destructive news to the PM. In a display of remarkable discipline, there was no weeping or wailing from Howard. Uppermost in his mind was how to deal with it, and to speak to Crosby and Textor to determine what exactly had found its way to the media.

When they were confronted by the prime minister, they denied any knowledge of, or responsibility for, the leak. They told Howard that, if he really thought they were responsible, he should sack them.

Textor says that the firm hired a computer expert to conduct an extensive and expensive investigation into the leak. The expert found that a computer glitch at the Liberal Party's federal secretariat on the day that Textor sent his research to Loughnane had been responsible for the polling finding its way into the wrong hands.

Maybe. Conventional wisdom has it that if it's a choice between a conspiracy and a stuff-up, go for the stuff-up. Even so, whether glitch, hackery, or treachery (and, within the Liberal Party, there is a prime suspect), whoever got it to Arbib was trying to engineer an outcome: destroy the leader.

Although outwardly steady, John Howard was already psychologically vulnerable, and the apparent act of high treason threw him further off balance. If the leakers were seeking to create a crisis that would precipitate a move to install Costello, their efforts were futile.

With all this going on, you would have thought that Liberals would have been lining up outside Costello's office, begging him to take over. They were not.

As was his wont, Peter had sliced off a few more pieces of his own flesh. He had many good qualities, but disguising or suppressing his wounded feelings and bruised ego were not among them.

Costello had done two interviews with Howard's biographer, Peter van Onselen, and when the book was published in mid-July it revealed the treasurer as a resentful and critical man. Even if his criticisms were justified — and not everyone thought they were — once again it did nothing to endear Costello to colleagues who already doubted his suitability for the top job.

Then, within days of the leaking of the Textor polling, *The 7.30 Report*'s Michael Brissenden went to air to disclose details of an alleged conversation that he and two other journalists, Paul Daley and Tony Wright, both then on *The Bulletin*, had had with Costello at a dinner on 5 March 2005.

The gist of the story was that Costello had vowed at that dinner to destroy Howard if he did not hand over the leadership, and that he'd claimed that Howard could not win the next election.

Brissenden broke the story on 14 August. It was the night of Costello's 50th birthday, and a party was in full swing at the Queen's Terrace café in Parliament House, which everyone from John Howard to Glenn Stevens to James Packer attended.

The story went to air just as Peter and Tanya finished making fine speeches about their life and family. It was a glimpse into what might have been.

Costello denied the substance of the story. It didn't matter.

I had been to countless dinners with Costello and journalists. If the conversation got tricky, I would remind the journalists that everything was off the record — that is, never to be used — even though I always believed nothing was truly off the record.

Eventually, everything found its way into the public domain. Unless, of course, it was boring or inconsequential. I would constantly remind Peter that if he didn't want to see it in print, he shouldn't say it. As I keep saying, a friendly journalist is not necessarily a friend.

I made a point of going to those dinners, even though as a journalist I hated press secretaries who, on rare occasions, invited themselves along with their boss. They always tried to get in the way of a good story, and they usually did.

It was exhausting as well as fattening, yet I would sit opposite Costello at the table, night after long night, refusing to drink, glaring and tapping my fingers gently on the table if he became too — shall we say — frank. He would get the hint and shut up. He never objected to these discreet interventions, and in fact he found them a useful check. If it was a particularly sensitive time, I would be careful to arrange meals only with those who could be trusted to show some discretion.

As a journalist, I would stay up drinking all night with colleagues;

as a press secretary, I was almost a teetotaller.

During my interview to gain top-secret security clearance, when I was asked if I drank, I said, 'Hardly anything now.' And before? 'Yes, every now and again.'

'Do you miss it?'

'Hell, yeah.'

A combination of long hours, sensitive subject matters, alcohol, and journalists on the prowl was a recipe for disaster. The easiest to eliminate was alcohol.

The revelations by Brissenden and his mates reminded the public once again of the poisonous relationship between the two men at the very top of the government. More than that, it presented a picture of a government run by people obsessed with themselves and their own ambitions.

Another story surfaced soon after that should have splattered Rudd's reputation, yet only served to enhance it. We had passed through the looking glass, and had entered a parallel universe.

On 19 August, *The Sunday Telegraph* revealed that, on a trip to New York as shadow foreign minister, ostensibly to observe the UN, Kevin Rudd had gone to a strip joint called Scores to make a very different kind of observation.

He claimed he had been so drunk that he couldn't remember whether he had had a lap dance or not, or if he had been asked to leave because of inappropriate behaviour. Of course he couldn't.

If it had been a coalition government minister, there would have been media outrage that someone on a trip at taxpayer expense had been drunk and possibly disorderly in a seedy bar. At the very least, the pack would have insisted that the rorter pay back the money. Instead, Rudd was painted as a regular kind of guy, doing a regular-kind-of-guy thing.

Uriah Heep was never one of Dickens' most endearing characters, but Rudd managed to make him look likeable as he humbly begged forgiveness from his wife and the public.

If it had been revealed that Rudd had volunteered to act as a sponsor for one of the Scores girls for a work visa because of the Australian skills shortage, he would have been hailed as a hero for helping solve the crisis. Have another spoonful of earwax to make the good medicine go down.

He couldn't do anything wrong, and we couldn't get anything right. At least, that was the way everything was being cast.

Despite this, one last opportunity presented itself to Liberals to do something so dramatic that it would force people to reappraise the government and look more critically at Rudd: change the leader.

Circumstances conspired to wreak miserable failure: competing ambitions, lingering resentment, cowardice, pride, and a goodly amount of contempt. As if trying to change the leadership wasn't difficult enough, it was further complicated by a play for the deputy's slot.

When Alexander Downer finally realised it was all over for his close political ally John Howard, he became the principal architect and coordinator of the push to replace him with Costello.

Downer was slated for the deputy leadership; but, when Mal Brough found out about this, he made sure that Downer knew he wouldn't get it without a fight.

In the end, it was all too hard.

Everybody has a brain snap at some point. The pressure, the demands, the expectations, the hours, the constant pounding of critics — it all takes its toll.

When we watched Howard and George W. Bush at their joint press conference in Sydney that week, we witnessed something truly remarkable. Bush, who could seldom string words into sentences, looked and sounded articulate in comparison to Howard. That's how badly Howard felt and performed, and how far down he had come.

Howard conducted his private meetings with the most powerful men in the world — Bush, Russia's Vladimir Putin, and China's Hu Jintao — in an utterly professional and intelligent manner. He didn't skip a beat, and his performance won him the undying admiration and respect of his staff.

Yet everywhere else was turmoil. His eyes and ears in the party were reporting back on the unrest, and in the days leading up to APEC he had already told his closest confidantes that 'all options were under consideration'.

When Newspoll was published on Tuesday 4 September, it showed Labor at 59 per cent and the coalition at 41 per cent. The previous polls had been bad, but this was horrendous.

For almost a year, Downer had been hoping it would turn around for Howard, that eventually people would wake up to Rudd, and that Howard would revive. But nothing seemed to dent Rudd's appeal.

Downer says he arrived in Sydney on the Sunday for APEC, and met with Howard at his request that day and every day thereafter. Both of them were painfully aware of just how dire was the situation confronting the government. The question was what to do about it.

The poll was evidence that Howard could not be resuscitated. Despite having dismissed Minchin's concerns the previous year, Downer now reluctantly concluded that Howard's leadership appeared terminal. People had simply stopped listening to him.

Minchin believed it was too late to switch. Howard had decided the year before that he would be staying, and it was incumbent on him to now lead the party to the election. In Minchin's view, there was only one way a transition would succeed: if Howard left voluntarily. Anything else would be suicidal.

Downer did not believe it was too late: he thought that the prime minister could use APEC as his crowning glory, and at its conclusion announce his departure. Nevertheless, he maintains that he did not go to see Howard to tell him to vacate his position.

Downer's conversations with Howard revolved around one critical point: would Howard's departure leave the government better off, or would it deliver a fatal blow from which it would never recover?

Howard did not think for one moment that Costello would do better than him.

Downer was conflicted, and remains so. He was despondent about Howard's decline, and angry that Costello had made himself so resistible.

He says now they recognised that the public had 'grown weary' of Howard, but there was no objective evidence that Costello could do better. On the contrary, Downer reckons all the polling showed he would do worse, that the Liberal heartland did not want Howard to go, that Costello had been negligent because he had failed to woo his colleagues — or even court Downer himself, for that matter, given he could hold the key — and that Costello was brought undone by his own vanity.

It all added up to a lack of faith in Costello's judgement and character.

After days of thrashing around, Howard told Downer that if his colleagues asked him to go, he would. But they would have to do so publicly.

Downer was already receiving feedback from his colleagues and staff. His chief of staff, Chris Kenny, and senior adviser, Tony Parkinson, thought that a switch was the only option, and Downer saw this as further proof that even Howard loyalists had abandoned the prime minister. When Howard gave Downer the green light in his hotel suite on Thursday, 6 September to take formal soundings of cabinet ministers, Downer was already on the case.

Downer had spoken with Costello. He had called Costello and told him that Howard was considering resigning the prime ministership. First, he wanted to ensure that Costello was prepared to take it on. He was.

He also wanted to make sure that Costello did not say or do anything that would wreck the chances of a handover. Nothing would kill it off faster than the slightest hint that the push was being engineered by Costello or his backers.

A few ministers rang Stone to ascertain his views. Stone told them that it was not too late, and that Howard should go. He did not want to see Howard defeated.

Once again, Mark Vaile reported to Howard that the National Party marginal-seat holders did not want him to go. They still believed that Howard was a safer bet than Costello.

Mal Brough, who describes himself then as a 'Howard supporter, not a Howard loyalist', was not at APEC, but he had heard about the meeting in Downer's suite.

Bearing in mind the prime minister's instruction to 'tell me if it's me' from the Lodge dinner in July, Brough decided that he had to tell him it was indeed him.

He called Kirribilli on Friday and left a message for the prime minister. Howard rang him back that evening.

Brough says he was having dinner with friends and family at a Brisbane restaurant, and that when the prime minister called he walked outside, pacing up and down along a wet Brisbane street to talk to him:

> I said to him straight out: 'This is the hardest phone call I have ever had to make. You said to me once, "If you don't think I can win, tell me."'
>
> He said: 'Do you think I should go?'
>
> I said: 'With great reluctance, yes. People are not listening to you; it doesn't matter what you say or do. There's no logic to it.'

What Howard said next remains imprinted in Brough's memory: 'I have had a good innings. All good things come to an end.'

Then Howard told Brough that cabinet had to take responsibility for his departure. Brough did not think that was right:

> I said: 'You also have to take some responsibility.'
>
> He asked me: 'Do you really think you can win with Costello?'

I said: 'No, I am not saying that at all. I know we can't win with you. With Costello it might only be a 1 per cent chance, but I am at the point where I think that is what we have to try.'

When he hung up, Brough was convinced that Howard had decided to go.

Reconstructing events, Brough says: 'Then Downer turned up about five minutes later [at Kirribilli], and I think that was when Janette said, "Over my dead body", and that strengthened his resolve to stay.'

Back in Canberra the following week, Brough tried to convince his colleagues that the matter had to be resolved by the Wednesday, and not through intermediaries. He did not want Downer carrying messages back and forth. He was pressing for a special cabinet meeting to discuss it, and, he hoped, help bring about the declaration that Howard said was essential for his departure.

Brough was in the middle of talking to Brendan Nelson about this when Nelson got a call to go down and see the prime minister.

Brough was also called down on his own. It was clear to him that Howard did not want a cabinet meeting, and that he was picking off his ministers either singly or in pairs of like-minded souls.

Brough remembers that Janette was sitting, like a warrior sentinel, in an office adjacent to the prime minister's, with a clear view of who came and went. She could see them, and they could definitely see her.

Brough delivered the same message again to Howard, this time in person.

Brough had already told Costello what he had done, and he spoke to Downer. Brough says Downer was arguing that, if Howard went, it should be a Costello–Downer leadership team.

There was no way that Brough was prepared to cop this. 'I thought that was barmy. It was unworkable,' Brough recalls.

So he told Downer that if Howard left and Costello moved up, he would contest the deputy leadership.

Downer says some of his colleagues at the Quay Grand had suggested he should be deputy, and he had told them that he did not care either way. His main interest was in clearing the way for Howard to stand down at the end of APEC. But Downer says that if there had been a ballot, he would have won it.

People close to Downer are convinced he was preparing to front the prime minister with Costello the following week to insist on his departure. Any prospect of this was killed off, however, by a misguided leak to Sky News on Tuesday, 11 September that some of his ministers had asked Howard to step down.

The leak was intended to keep the pressure on Howard to force him out.

As soon as the story broke, I headed round to the press office. We had heard the whispers. We had been hearing them for weeks, if not months, and now they were being broadcast to the world as fact. Tony O'Leary was tied up, so I told David Luff and Ben Mitchell that it was all over, and that the PM should call a press conference to announce his resignation. It wasn't what I wanted to happen; it was what I thought should happen. In my mind, there was no way he could recover. It was over.

Luffy and Benny said little in response and just looked incredibly glum. They put their heads down and got on with it. When he got off the phone, O'Leary was his usual ferociously loyal self, ready to take on all comers.

It turned out that Howard had already decided he was going to stay, and now the leak made him dig in.

Ironically, Downer and Minchin were forced onto the airwaves to declare their full support for the prime minister. We all fell in behind Howard. There was no other choice: he wanted to fight, and we had to fight with him.

However, the objective part of me doubted that Australians would vote for a man who had publicly lost the support of even part of his party. If some of his own ministers believed he was no longer up to the job, and were prepared to tell him so, how could the punters be convinced that he was?

If anyone, especially junior staff, asked me what I thought would happen, I would recite my best-case scenario: with a bit of luck, we might just flop over the line.

I wasn't trying to kid anyone. I didn't want them to lose heart. Plus, we were prepared to slog away, day and night, to see if we could make it happen.

In their heart of hearts, his senior ministers all knew it was over, but they could not, as a group, bring themselves either to deliver the killer blow to Howard or fully embrace Costello.

It is clear from his remarks to Brough that Howard knew in his heart of hearts that it was all over, too, but he could not bring himself to admit to it publicly.

Stone summed it up: 'John always said he was there at the will of the party. Then, when confronted, he said: "You will have to throw me out."'

Stone is a big fan of Janette Howard, and pays generous tribute to her for her political wisdom and for keeping Howard on track in countless campaigns. But, he says, even her political antennae failed her at this critical point.

Downer maintains that Janette was 'not instrumental' in Howard's decision to stay, and that it was Howard himself, spurred on by grave doubts about Costello's electability and judgement.

Even so, it was madness for Howard to say, as he did, that he had consulted his family and that they had told him he should stay. It was madness for the cabinet ministers to baulk at making a public declaration. And it was madness for Costello not to front him back in Canberra after the story broke.

Howard and Costello knew one another very well — every flaw, every strength, every driving impulse. Costello knew that Howard would not go unless he was forced.

Even though Costello was the one who kept saying, 'We're going to have to blast him out,' no one was willing to light the fuse when the time came. Costello knew that Howard would not go voluntarily, and Howard knew that Costello would not have the strength to force him.

Howard's detractors in the party saw his refusal to go at this point as evidence that he had never intended to go, and that the only way he would go out would be in a box.

They believed that he, like every prime minister before him, had convinced himself that he was the only one who could lead his party to victory — and that, even if he couldn't, he would still do a better job than the other bloke.

It is also true that the McLachlan episode had hardened Howard against Costello. He wasn't of a mind to give Costello any break at all — not even the opportunity of fighting an election he was likely to lose.

And, just as importantly, he did not want to be branded as a quitter. His own pride and stubbornness demanded the cover of a public execution that his colleagues could not and would not deliver. In my view, when Howard initially insisted on the public declaration from his ministers that they wanted him to go, it was to provide himself with a cloak for an exit he did not want to make, but which he thought he would be compelled to undertake. After he resolved to stay — when it was clear that the numbers were not there decisively for Costello — it became the weapon that enabled him to stymie and stifle his opponents. It showed just how clever a politician Howard was. And how determined.

Costello was fully expecting a handover, and was ready for it — and then, as quickly as it came, it slid away. Minchin believed it was all over from the minute that Howard said his ministers would have to declare that they wanted him gone.

Once again, the Costelloites were split on what he should do. Smith thought that a change could only work if Howard went voluntarily; otherwise, they would run the risk of a wrecking campaign being launched by the former leader.

Smith believed that the only ones who could convince Howard to go were those closest to him — Downer, Minchin, and Abbott — and there had to be confidence that Howard would accept the decision with grace. Costello, or Costello's supporters, would be the last people to be able to convince him.

Smith believed that, in the best of all possible worlds, Howard would make the decision to go, acknowledge to the electorate that he knew they wanted change, and then argue persuasively that he was giving them not only change for the better but, with Costello at the helm, safe change as well.

By this time, Pyne, who had been one of Costello's stoutest supporters, was losing faith. He saw the whole episode as just another nail in the government's coffin. One thing he did not believe was the anti-Costello polling that Labor was putting around. All it did was prove to him that Labor did not want change.

In any case, he thought it was probably too late for change, and his major preoccupation then was to hang on to his own seat.

Fifield, along with senior members of Costello's staff, did not think it was too late, and urged Costello to confront Howard. They told Costello that Howard was finished. They said it was up to him to go and tell Howard that it was over and that he had to go. They told him he should threaten Howard with a challenge in the party room if he refused to go.

They believed that Howard would not dare call his bluff, because he would know that, even if he won the vote, the government would not recover from the bloodbath.

Costello's confidantes also told him that he should hold out the promise of a significant job for Howard after the election, assuming that the coalition won, and guarantee that he would render him legendary status through word and deed within the Liberal Party.

Defeat seemed inevitable, they told him, but this was no reason not to go for it. 'Yes, it looks hopeless, but you are the only chance for averting defeat,' they told him.

There was just a remote possibility that he could win the election. Labor's 'fresh' approach on issues like climate change and broadband would be countered, as would their mantra of generational change. Howard might not have been able to switch course on issues like Kyoto, but Costello could.

And while the punters might not like him, they respected his economic management.

Costello was not convinced, though. He didn't want to get blood on his hands. He wanted the party to come to him and anoint him, and for Howard to cede. Neither of those things was about to happen.

His only chance was to grab it by the throat — to take Howard by the throat — but, physically and psychologically, he could not bring himself to do it. In some conversations, he seemed defeated and sorry for himself. Why should he take on such a poisoned chalice? If they lost the election, as it seemed certain they would, he would cop the blame. Who needed that on their record and on their conscience? He had offered himself and been rejected before, and wasn't prepared at this late stage to go through it again.

As much as anything else, it was this fear of failure that ensured he pulled up short. The fear that drove Costello to prepare remorselessly for every media appearance, every budget — to ensure he never stumbled or erred — also held him back and stopped him from taking that one extra step needed to eliminate Howard and to prepare to fight what looked like an unwinnable election. Textor sensed it after dinner that night at the Ottoman.

That same fear would probably have made Costello a first-class prime minister, because he would have worked very hard to do well. But first he had to get to the leadership, and he just couldn't summon the strength to get there.

He had already, twice previously, asked Howard to go, in 2003 and again in 2006, and Howard had refused; so now, Costello told his friends and advisers, it was someone else's turn to do it. It was up to them: if they wanted Howard to go, they should go and tell him.

Those who wanted Costello to be bold were angry and frustrated with him. They could not budge him.

In his account of the meeting on the morning of Wednesday, 12 September with Howard, in *The Costello Memoirs*, Costello says he demanded that Howard make a public declaration that none of his ministers had been disloyal to him. Further, he writes, 'I also told him that, if he was going to stay on, he should make clear precisely when he intended to go.'

It was a long way short of what the situation demanded, but it was as far as Costello was prepared to take it.

One person who did have the ticker to take it further was Andrew Robb. When speculation was running during APEC about the leadership, Robb got feedback from his blue-ribbon electorate of Goldstein that they wanted to stick with Howard. It was the kind of feedback that the others were getting, and that had made them freeze.

Robb also was not at APEC, was unaware that Downer was on a mission, and had reached a different conclusion from his electors. He rang Downer independently on the Friday, and told him that he thought it was all over for Howard and that he had to go.

When the quasi-coup petered out days later, and Howard appeared on *The 7.30 Report* to say that he would leave in the next term and hand over to Costello, the mood in Goldstein changed dramatically. Robb went to two electorate functions on the night of Friday, 14 September and lunchtime the following day.

There had been a revolutionary mood-swing. It was as if Howard's remarks had given people a signal that it was okay to switch to someone else. They would rather it was Costello, not Rudd; so, most definitely, did Robb. And Robb was sure there would have been the same mood-swings in other electorates, too.

Robb rang Tony Nutt, and told him he would be in Canberra on Sunday night and would like to see the prime minister. Nutt arranged for him to meet Howard at the Lodge at 8.00 p.m.

It was just the two of them: no personal staff, no household staff. The prime minister offered Robb a cup of tea, and then went off to the kitchen to make one for Robb — a drop of milk, no sugar, thanks, PM — and one for himself.

They spent an hour together. Robb took half an hour to go through the reasons why he thought Howard should vacate. Robb might talk slowly, but that's because he usually thinks before he speaks. Even so, his language was pretty dramatic.

'I think we are heading for a train wreck,' he told the prime minister.

Howard responded with a part question, part statement of fact: 'You are asking me to resign?'

Robb said: 'No, I wouldn't do that. I think it is legitimate you not resign under your own volition, as if you are running away. You are not that kind of person. Your colleagues should ask you to resign.'

Robb agreed wholeheartedly with Howard's precondition that he would only leave if his cabinet told him to. He informed the prime minister that he was going to spend the next 24 hours speaking to cabinet ministers in an effort to engineer just that. He was going to organise a mutiny.

Then, in the second half-hour, Howard gave Robb his reasons for not leaving. Robb had been hoping for some special insight, but he never got it. It boiled down to Howard believing that the government had a better chance of winning with him at the helm rather than Costello.

Note the distinction: a better chance of winning — not that he would win.

By then, Howard was well aware that he was not only headed for defeat in the general election but in his own seat as well.

They shook hands, and Robb left. Robb says he felt good about what he had done because it was the right thing to do and he had done it in a civil fashion. Robb, who has been around the traps a long time and with a lot of players, says this about the man he had told to get out: 'I have never worked with anyone who is so decent in his professional dealings with people.'

Robb told Costello about his mission. 'Good on you,' Costello said, glad that someone had taken up the cudgels on his behalf.

Robb did spend the next 24 hours talking to his colleagues, but was stopped dead in his tracks by Tuesday's Newspoll, which showed that the coalition had gone up to 46 per cent and Labor down to 54 per cent. It was just enough to kill off any chance of mustering the numbers.

One percentage point less in the coalition's vote, and Robb would have continued with his mission — and Australia's political history might have turned out differently.

As federal president, years before, Tony Staley had engineered the leadership handover from Downer to Howard. But now there was no one as tough or with as much authority in the Liberal Party to fix this.

Howard would not go unless he was forced; cabinet ministers could neither bring themselves to force him out nor bring themselves to beg Costello to take it; and Costello would not initiate a direct strike.

There was no guarantee that a change would have secured another election victory, but at least there would have been the prospect of it.

With Howard, the chances were zilch; with a new leader, it was possible. Years before, *The Advocate* had taken a photo of Peter at the Parklands High School in Burnie, Tasmania, in front of a wall hanging of the class slogan, 'Anything is possible'.

If only he believed it.

In the public's mind, Howard was finished. People didn't hate him; they had just had enough of him.

They had doubts about Costello — they weren't sure what he stood for, and weren't convinced that he was tough enough for the job.

If Costello had challenged, it would have shown he was tough enough. And if he had treated Howard and all his colleagues with generosity and grace in the aftermath, people would have respected him for it.

Howard was smart enough to know that if he behaved as a wrecker during the subsequent election campaign, he, not Costello, would have paid the price.

Howard loved the Liberal Party more than he disliked Costello, and would not have wanted that as his legacy. That would have been worse than being branded a coward — or a loser.

Instead, the government limped its way to the polls with a leader forced to declare that he would be handing over to someone else. It was as good as telling people that they could go ahead and vote for someone else.

And his deputy, resentful and thwarted yet again, withdrew even further.

Howard and Costello were both crippled. The only person with all his limbs intact was the body-snatcher, Kevin Rudd.

CHAPTER FOURTEEN

Murphy's Law XL

Mark Latham was both the best thing and the worst thing that ever happened to the Liberal Party. He was Arthur and Martha to himself, and Victor Victoria to the Liberals. Or the other way round. Take your pick. Equal and opposite.

He was the best, because he helped deliver a huge victory; and the worst, because he helped deliver a huge victory.

Instead of ostracising him, Labor should induct him into its vast pantheon of heroes, next to Gough. Without Mark Latham as opposition leader, there would have been no Kevin Rudd, Prime Minister.

In 1996 the Liberal Party had secured one its greatest victories ever, and in 2004 almost equalled it, largely thanks to Latham, with the unexpected bonus — or curse — of the Senate majority.

The win made everyone think that John Howard was invincible, and it made Howard think that he would be vilified — just as Malcolm Fraser was — if he squandered his majority. So it spurred him and others on to WorkChoices.

The Liberals were living under the delusion that it would take Labor another two elections to get back, so they could afford to misbehave. Discipline broke down as MPs thought that, no matter how bad the situation was for the government, Labor would never get its act together, and that John Howard would ride to the rescue if necessary. Maybe John Howard started to believe it a little bit himself — although, in that final year, try as he might (and he never gave up trying), you could tell that he knew the situation was beyond recovery.

After the 2004 campaign was over, when I saw the prime minister and congratulated him on his victory, he threw his hands up in the air and did a half-turn. 'We killed 'em,' he said, and gave me a hug and a peck on the cheek.

It wasn't a victory dance, more a spontaneous expression of delight. The increased vote and the increased majority weren't what he'd expected. But when he'd asked people 'Who do you trust?', there was no other answer they could sensibly give.

Howard was always a bit hyper on the campaign trail, but in 2004 he exuded confidence and control, even if he didn't feel it, driving the themes and the policies. Back then, it was a much more decisive and focused John Howard in charge. It was not unusual for policies to be left to the last minute, but it didn't matter so much because it was in a very different context, with very different opponents.

It was Howard's idea to offer a 30 per cent childcare rebate, which he told his advisers to formulate as the starter's gun was fired for the 2004 campaign. They worked on it for 48 hours straight, and when it came out it undercut Labor.

The pensioners' utilities allowance was also born during that campaign.

Howard held firm — encouraged by his wife, Janette — to outmanoeuvre Latham with the Tasmanian timber workers. He watched Latham avoid the workers by going through a back door, and decided that he would front them all in Launceston's Albert Hall. It was gutsy, and it paid off when the Liberals picked up two Tasmanian seats, Bass and Braddon.

Howard was the one who came up with the scheme for the federal government to set up technical colleges because he was fed up with the states' failures. The announcement of the scheme won the biggest applause at the policy launch that year.

In 2004, if the campaign even looked like veering off from the economy, it would be swung back. Pronto.

For example, one morning in Melbourne, journalists travelling with Howard were herded onto the press bus ready for departure. The prime minister's team had decided that day to keep the focus firmly on interest rates.

There was just one minor problem. Even as the journos sat on the bus, waiting to be told where they were going, the location was still being organised. David Luff was on the phone to a young couple in Chris Pearce's electorate of Aston, giving them a heads-up that the circus was coming to town, and warning them to expect journalists to ask them about everything, including their mortgage, and their views on Iraq and David Hicks.

But the dynamics in 2007 were very different. The prime minister was not the same person, he had lost his aura of invincibility, and there were not the same people around to help him and the campaign.

As in the ministry, where some of the previously reliable heavy-hitters had departed, the staff ranks had thinned out, putting even more strain on those who were left. Arthur Sinodinos was gone, as was David Quilty, who had been deputy to Peter Conran in the Cabinet Policy Unit and was, like Sinodinos, a complete package — whip smart about both policy and politics.

There were still good people there, but the burdens were heavier, and the tasks much more difficult.

At the request of the prime minister, Shane Stone spent several weeks at campaign headquarters to help with fundraising. He couldn't believe how bad it was.

'It was hopeless, hopeless,' he said later. 'Loughnane had lost his authority. Tony [Nutt] was running things. They just couldn't make a decision in campaign headquarters.'

There were about 130 people at campaign headquarters, the

biggest number ever, and in a building that cost an absolute fortune in rent. It was a massive bureaucracy, and the person at the top of the pile was not in control. Many of the staff felt that they were working in a vacuum, or to no real purpose. Others, particularly in the policy areas, were being ground down.

There was a complete role-reversal between government and opposition. Labor looked confident; the government, rattled. Labor was setting the agenda, and the government was being forced to react.

As the prime minister prepared to call the 2007 election, the Liberal Party was the most ill equipped it had ever been to fight one.

The daily distractions and the constant tension between the key offices meant that the government lacked both a narrative and a coherent policy-framework, and the discipline or resolve at the top to forge either.

Policies were put together and then would lie dormant. Housing affordability, for instance, was running as a big issue. The prime minister wanted to provide a tax deduction for mortgage costs, which would have been very expensive and would have represented a major change in longstanding policy. The treasurer was not interested: he didn't believe it was worth the money, and he felt it wouldn't solve the problem anyway.

After much back and forth between the treasurer's office and the prime minister's, a broader savings measure, billed as a home savings account, was set to be announced in August. Then there was a leak, so the prime minister decided to sit on the policy. Labor got there first, and announced its own housing package to much fanfare.

There was another proposal before the government to sell off the site at Badgery's Creek, which had long been set aside for a second airport for Sydney. Nobody really believed the second airport would ever be built, so the proposal was to turn the site into a kind of satellite city, which would have opened up more land for housing.

Howard raised it in cabinet. Joe Hockey, Malcolm Turnbull, and Tony Abbott were extremely nervous about it, fearing it would provoke a backlash against them because it would obviously mean more flights at Sydney's existing airport — which meant that more planes would fly over city (that is, their) electorates. Howard was keen on the idea, even though his own seat of Bennelong would have been similarly exposed, and he consulted local members such as Danna Vale and Pat Farmer. They, too, were opposed.

That proposal died. With so many battles raging on so many fronts at the time, there weren't many — or, more accurately, any — ministers or backbenchers willing to take on another fight. There were a few good ideas left in the bottom drawer that Labor picked up — like Ozcorps, and increasing the tax on alcopops — and this might have been another one.

The government also allowed itself to be skewered on childcare.

Measures had been introduced in the 2007 budget to pay the childcare rebate at the end of the tax year through Centrelink, rather than through the Tax Office, which had previously meant that recipients had to wait an extra year for payment. While this cleaned up some untidiness left after the implementation of the 2004 policy that had first pledged the rebate, a number of senior ministers and policy advisers felt that the government had done enough on childcare, and that there was no real need for it to do more in this campaign.

Mal Brough had, however, managed to slip a line into the 2007 budget papers foreshadowing a move to quarterly payments. When a newspaper article alerted Costello to what Brough had done, he was furious. He believed that Brough had cut across the relevant decision by the expenditure review committee.

Brough had to hold the phone away from his ear when Costello rang him to chew him out.

The result was that the quarterly payments were not announced before the start of the campaign by the government. Instead, Labor picked up the idea and announced it first as its own.

There were suspicions that bureaucrats working on the government's policy, who had gone to help Labor in its campaign, had slipped the technical details of the implementation to Labor. This might or might not have been paranoia. Even so, the coalition was trumped on its own policy, and it enabled Labor to regurgitate, after the coalition tried to catch up later in the campaign, its well-tested lines that Howard had lost touch with working families, and that he would say and do anything to win the election.

By the third week of September 2007, the government was in appalling shape. The APEC madness had succeeded pretty well in knocking the stuffing out of everyone.

Even though a fifth term looked increasingly unlikely, we still — just weeks out from the election — had no agreement on any policy of substance to put to the voters. In the weeks leading up to the election, Conran, Kunkel, Bailey, and I had been pushing for a monster tax package with 'dirty great tax cuts' as the centrepiece.

Handouts here and there were not economically productive, and lower taxes were supposed to be core business for the Liberal Party. If we were going to go down, our view was that it might as well be with all guns blazing, with a tax package so big that it could be sold as major structural reform. And maybe it would jam Labor.

We kept pushing. The PM was ambivalent about tax cuts, and needed convincing that they were a better bet than spending. He thought there was more bang for the buck with other options and had, even in the middle of the APEC debacle, called for a paper on his old favourite, income splitting.

He had championed income splitting for decades, because he believed that the tax system severely disadvantaged single-income households in which one spouse was not working. He much preferred a system whereby a single-income household could split its one income between the two spouses, so they could each get the benefit of two tax-free thresholds — as would happen if each was working in a two-income household.

Fortunately, this fell by the wayside; but, inside the prime minister's office, there was little enthusiasm for our 'dirty great tax cut', as we kept calling it, and my old boss, the treasurer, was anything but engaged. Even his own staff, normally so tightlipped, were expressing frustration at their inability to get Costello to focus on the campaign and any policies that might have been needed to fight it.

Peter and I had not spoken much since my departure from his office. He hadn't been happy when I'd left, and madder still when I'd gone elsewhere. During one of our little spats while I was still in his employ, he said to me: 'You won't go off and work for someone else!'

'No, probably not,' I said. 'But you won't get anyone as good as me, either.' This was my not-so-subtle way of telling him that he couldn't take me for granted, and that he should heed my advice.

Who was the bigger Greek?

So I had not only left him, but I had gone to work for someone else. In between my time with him and my employment in the Cabinet Policy Unit, I was 'parked' for about six months — first in David Kemp's office, and then in Robert Hill's — much to Peter's chagrin. He made no secret of his displeasure.

The only vaguely sensible discussion between us after I left occurred at the end of 2005, almost two years after my departure from his office, when our home was destroyed in a bushfire. He rang to commiserate (as did the prime minister).

Costello had had a particularly bad few months, which had ended with him declaring, yet again, that he would not challenge for the leadership.

I said I thought that somebody up there didn't like me, and he said he felt as if he had killed a Chinaman.

Our brief chat ended with my reassuring him that both my problems and his were 'all fixable'. Houses burn down all the time and are rebuilt. Careers can be resuscitated. It is a painful process, but you do what you have to, and get through it.

By September 2007, we were not getting through anything — not even wet paper bags.

Desperate to break the logjam and to get him involved, I sent a note to Costello urging him to fight for tax cuts as a centrepiece of the re-election platform. I felt that we needed an issue big enough to carry us through the long weeks of the campaign. We had to have something to talk about that fitted with the only thing we could still boast about — the economy.

There had been some talk of tax breaks for education expenses. But this would neither fix education nor tax. And income splitting was definitely not going to capture anyone's imagination.

'A major reform of the tax scales is the way to go. It not only fits with our message to boost productivity, grow the jobs market and wean people off welfare, it goes to supposed Liberal values as well,' I wrote to Peter.

'Do tax first, not last. It should not be the leftovers, but entrée, mains, and dessert.'

I finished with: 'Unless *you* fight for it, it won't happen. And there is as much at stake for you as there is for anyone else — if not more. It is your legacy, too.'

After he received my note, Costello rang and said he supported the idea, but needed everybody's help to convince the prime minister and his office. I assured him we would help.

'We have got nothing to talk about,' I said.

'I know,' he replied. I didn't mean him and me — I meant policies. He did, too.

The package was formulated. But even on the very day it was to be released, the day after Howard had called the election for 24 November, there was a wobble.

In his usual way, Peter had held all the information so tightly that the prime minister only saw the tables a few hours before he and the treasurer were scheduled to hold their joint press conference to unveil them.

One table showed that the tax cuts for middle-income earners — those on between $60,000 and $75,000 a year — were a measly $11.54 a week, while those on $35,000 to $45,000 would get about $20 a week.

Howard was incensed that what he regarded as his target group looked like it was being diddled. He marched around to Costello's office with Nigel Bailey, who had joined Howard's staff as his economics adviser, to seek an explanation.

Tax cuts had already been announced in the budget, to come into effect on 1 July 2008; taken together, they showed that middle-income earners would get $20 or more a week.

Two more columns were quickly added to the press release. Taking into account the cumulative savings of tax cuts already announced, combined with the new ones, they showed that those on $70,000 a year — the prime minister's key group — would be a bit over $34 a week better off.

Howard was mollified, and the press conference went ahead.

Everybody held their breath, waiting for the negative reaction to the cuts for middle-income earners, but it never came. The package gave the government good lift-off. The coverage was positive, crediting the government with seizing the initiative with a $34 billion package, and putting Labor on the spot. Private polling showed a spike in support for the coalition.

It got the campaign back onto issues — principally, the economy — and away from the 'leadership' theme that the prime minister had used when he called the election, and which had infuriated campaign headquarters.

Labor was caught out, but Rudd caught up in a few days and released his matching package with twist — funding for computers.

Hardly anyone talked about ours again. There was little or no advertising support from the Liberal Party for its own tax package.

There were, however, plenty of coalition ads aired about the unions getting back in control under Labor. Textor reckons that they helped, even though he had warned the year before that if the campaign was about industrial relations, the coalition would lose. Workplace reform was a negative for the government, but unions in power under Labor was a positive, according to Textor — and the issue was run all the way through the campaign.

Joe Hockey, in his inimitable fashion, would claim during the election that 'our fear campaign was based on fact'; in fact, Labor's fear campaign was streets ahead of ours.

A week later, the leaders' debate on Sunday, 21 October ensured that the focus would switch back to personalities and away from the issues, as the public got an extended look at the two men side by side: the original Howard, and the cloned Howard.

For the prime minister, it was an unmitigated disaster. He closeted himself with almost all his most senior policy advisers on Saturday night and all day Sunday at the Lodge. Not one of his three press secretaries — O'Leary, Luff, or Mitchell, all of them expert in preparing the PM for the media — was included in the debate preparation. The result was information overload, and not one single cut-through line.

The man who had come up with 'Who do you trust?' in 2004 to encapsulate everything that was right about himself and wrong about Latham was a very different man from the one who would front up to Rudd on 21 October.

In 2007, he wanted to say in his opening remarks in the debate: 'I know people are suffering.' His advisers almost gagged, given the unparalleled prosperity that the country was experiencing; they saw it as yet more evidence that Howard had been psyched out by Rudd.

During the preparation, Howard got hung up on broadband. He spent almost an hour trying to get across all the technical jargon and properties of broadband, until finally Kunkel told him that he now knew much more about the issue than Rudd ever would.

'Relax,' Kunkel urged.

Howard had lost or drawn all the debates in all the previous campaigns. In 2007, he was worse than he ever had been, and against someone who had been born without charisma.

Ministers and staff gathered in the prime ministerial suite after the debate. Howard quickly downed a few glasses of white wine. They tried to keep his spirits up, but everyone knew he had done badly and was in bad shape.

On 7 November, when the Reserve Bank announced, for the first time ever, an increase in interest rates in the middle of an election campaign, it was — despite the protests to the contrary — an overtly political act and, as events have since shown, completely unnecessary. The sub-prime crisis had been bubbling away in the United States. It didn't take a genius to realise that a volcano was about to erupt.

Yet no one was ever allowed to criticise the bank's actions — even if it had made a mistake. The last time I checked, the governor had not been made pope. Independence does not bestow infallibility.

In a perverse way, however, the interest-rate rise itself was not unwelcome. Once again, it gave the government the opportunity to talk about the economy, and to ramp up its rhetoric about the risks of trusting Labor.

On the day that the rate-rise announcement was made, Howard had flown to Brisbane. God knows why. There seemed to be no real reason for it, other than to wait around for the Reserve Bank's announcement. Then, in the middle of his press conference on interest rates, where he was expounding on the government's superior economic-management skills, the hotel's fire alarm went off. As bad luck would have it, a member of his advance team, Susan Bruce, had decided right at that moment to use the toaster in her room. The burning breadcrumbs from her toaster had set off the alarm.

The PM ploughed on with his press conference while the alarm was roaring, because he thought he was going to air live on Sky. When he found out later that it had not been broadcast live, he did a pretty rare thing for him: he had a meltdown. Given the circumstances, his staff thought it best not to tell him how the alarm had been triggered.

Naturally, the 'alarm' surrounding the economy and interest rates featured heavily in radio and television news all day and all night. It was too good a metaphor to ignore. When I think about that improbable sequence of events now, I can't help laughing. Back then, those of us who had hair were tearing it out.

Completely fulfilling and exceeding Murphy's Law, it got worse. The prime minister once again got himself into a sorry mess over 'Sorry.' He had said sorry to Australians because interest rates had gone up; but when he was quizzed about it the next day, he tried to argue that it was possible to say sorry without apologising.

He just couldn't let it go.

It reopened the whole sorry mess over the stolen generations, and buried what was a first-rate speech by the prime minister, largely prepared by John Kunkel, which was delivered in Melbourne that day and which had been designed to keep the focus on the economy and the government's priorities.

We were toast.

In his Treasury Place office, Howard was puzzled by the reaction to his 'sorry' remarks, even as his staff tried to explain to him — in the nicest possible way — that he had just killed off any chance of getting the debate back onto the economy.

He couldn't work out what people were going on about. In his mind, there was a distinction between saying sorry and making an apology. What was the big deal?

Janette Howard was there, too. She could understand what the fuss was about. She wondered aloud why he had said it.

Good question.

Upstairs and across the corridor in his office, Costello had been hoping that the interest-rate rise would turn the debate back onto the economy. He was also wondering why Howard had got himself into such a sorry state again. It was very different from 2004, when it was just the economy, stupid.

Easily the worst example of the corrosion of confidence in the dying days of the government was the fate of its health policy. It was symptomatic of so many things, but especially the leeching away of spirit and purpose.

Conran and his deputy, Gavin Jackman, a highly respected social-policy expert, together with the relevant advisers from the prime minister's office, had worked tirelessly for months before the campaign began to draw up a list of options. But they couldn't get anyone to focus or decide on which ones they wanted.

Rudd's announcement in August that he would take control of all public hospitals if necessary — accompanied by his cleverly scripted decisiveness that 'the buck will stop with me'— rattled the prime minister. He wanted a major health package.

Howard's advisers thought that Rudd's idea was madness. While it might have populist appeal, there was no way it could work in practice or ever be implemented (and so far, well after the event, they are being proved right). But health was an area in which the government was vulnerable, and where the prime minister was anxious to outdo Rudd.

In the lead-up to the APEC meeting, Howard called all his senior policy advisers to a meeting in the cabinet room at the Phillip St. offices in Sydney. The head of the Cabinet Policy Unit, Peter Conran; his deputy, Gavin Jackman; the economics adviser, Nigel Bailey; the social-policy adviser, Perry Sperling; his chief of staff, Tony Nutt; and his political adviser, Stephen Galilee, all went through the proposed 30-day election-campaign grid, mapping out which policies were likely to be released on what day.

It went for several hours. The prime minister was engaged and across the detail. Advisers were relieved. At last they were making progress, and their morale and confidence lifted.

It was soon pricked. At the very end of the meeting, the prime minister summed up their hard work by saying: 'Well, that's all very good, but it's not going to make one bit of difference.'

It threw some of his advisers. Was he raising the white flag even before the real fight had begun? This was so out of character for Howard that they couldn't believe that was what he meant.

The older hands took it in their stride, figuring that what he was saying was that the campaign would not be about policies, so it didn't matter what they came up with. It was going to be all about him and Rudd. Which, in the end, it was.

It was still pretty dispiriting for the newer advisers. If it wasn't going to be about policy, all their hard work would be for nought. They pressed on regardless; they had no choice.

During long days and into the night during the campaign at headquarters in Melbourne, a small team led by Conran, and including Jackman and Bailey, put together a four-year $18.1 billion integrated package for hospitals, covering every aspect of their functions, including primary care, emergency departments, and acute care.

It proposed a massive additional $16.9 billion extra in direct funding for public hospitals, $688 million for other measures to take pressure off hospitals, and $541 million to increase the number of doctors and nurses. Among other things, it provided for a doubling of the number of transition-care beds, from 2000 places to 4000 places, so that older people could be moved out of hospitals and into more appropriate care; the establishment of 50 emergency Medicare GP clinics, with 25 clinics open for 24 hours a day; and a doubling of existing capital funding for nursing homes, with a special focus on rural areas.

They met the prime minister at his Treasury Place office on 30 October to brief him on the package. Also present was the health minister, Tony Abbott. Abbott had flown to Melbourne to attend a launch way out in the eastern suburbs with the prime minister the following morning.

Howard was concerned. Wasn't Abbott scheduled to debate the opposition health spokeswoman, Nicola Roxon, at the National Press Club in Canberra at lunchtime the next day?

Yes, he was.

Howard asked Abbott if he was sure he could get back in time for it. Abbott assured him that all the arrangements were in place. He told the prime minister he had chartered a plane and that he would get there on time.

Famous last words. Abbott was late for the debate, he swore at Roxon, and she beat him anyway. Another day; a different disaster.

At the Treasury Place meeting, the prime minister approved the $18 billion hospitals package. That package never saw the light of day. It was killed off a fortnight later.

The prime minister had decided not to unveil the health package at the official launch, but to save it for the last weeks of the campaign, to make a final big hit and build up a bit of momentum. Rudd had got the jump on Howard on health before the start of the campaign proper, and Howard planned to repay the favour when it would be too late for Rudd to do anything about it. As things turned out, he ended up being snookered and psyched by Rudd.

When he officially launched the Liberals' campaign on 12 November, the prime minister announced, among other things, the upfront payment of the childcare rebate, tax-free home savings accounts for all Australians yet to purchase their first home, and a new tax-rebate for education expenses.

He and Costello had already announced the $34 billion in tax cuts at the start of the campaign, and that had gone extremely well. But now the additional spending was not going very well at all.

There was no pleasing anybody. The punters were sceptical; the media, hostile; and economists, scathing.

The spread and magnitude of the combined packages looked and sounded as if the prime minister was stuffing wads of money in the cracks of neglected areas, trying to buy people off with multi-billion-dollar handouts rather than with ideas or inspiration. And he hadn't even got to health yet. In 2004, the spend-athon that Costello subsequently complained about had worked — or at least it hadn't ricocheted like a stray bullet; but, in 2007, there was a much lower tolerance for big spending. People wanted to be wooed, not bribed. They wanted to know that if the government was re-elected, it planned to do more than just spend money. Whatever problems they had or thought they had, they were doubtful that extra money from John Howard would solve them. In fact, they were beginning to think — were, in fact, being urged to think — that extra spending would only make things worse.

Up until the Liberal launch, Rudd had matched Howard dollar for dollar, or had even promised to spend more. Then, all of a sudden, Rudd called it quits. Labor cleverly exploited concerns that the government was overspending and was dangerously overheating the economy — concerns which now look hollow and manufactured. But, back then, there were resonant warnings from economic commentators and other race-callers about the effect that the spending would have on interest rates. They succeeded in raising community anxiety, and cast doubt on the government's economic management — the one area where it had been unassailable.

When he launched Labor's campaign on 14 November, wearing the economic conservative's suit he has since donated to the Salvos, Rudd declared that 'reckless spending must stop'. Labor held back on its spending and made the government look profligate, desperate, and out of control. Howard judged that he had no choice but to stop, too.

The morning after Rudd's launch, Howard rang Nigel Bailey and told him that the health package had to be scaled back. They trimmed off a few billion. Bailey relayed the instructions to Conran and Jackman.

About an hour later, Howard called again, and said it was still too big and needed to be stripped down even further. Another few billion was trimmed. Then, before Bailey could get to Conran and Jackman to tell them the latest, the prime minister called again, just before lunch, and told Bailey that he wanted it stripped down to the bones.

It wasn't death by a thousand cuts. Three was all it took.

Howard was the one who was being sliced up, every day, in every way. It would have been as painful for him to go through it as it was for those who had revered him for his political acumen to watch it happening.

Howard had assessed the fallout from Rudd's remarks, and had concluded that they would not be dismissed as a 24-hour wonder or a catchphrase in the media. They had bitten, and bitten hard. From then on, anything that Howard announced would be made to look like either a cynical vote-buying exercise or an assault on sound economic management.

The health policy was released, but it was a shell: only 2000 transition-care beds were pledged, and there were no precise figures on hospital funding. It was a document full of good intentions, with little or no detail about what it would cost to implement them. It was meaningless. But the prime minister had stopped the 'reckless spending'. After that, the coalition did not release any more policies.

Calmer heads thought that the health package should have been released anyway. Bugger Rudd — the government would have had something else to talk about. Plus it was a good package in its own right that would have made a difference to health care.

But Textor and others thought it would not have made any difference. In their view, there was only one focus in the campaign: the personality contest between Rudd and Howard, and Rudd was winning it. Rudd was communicating ideas, and we were throwing money at everything.

Not surprisingly, morale at campaign headquarters was sinking as surely as the Titanic. 'Dysfunctional' was the word most campaign workers used to describe relations between them and the PM's travelling team, which largely comprised his personal staff, his wife, Janette and, increasingly, his son Richard.

There was constant tension between the two camps. The travelling team suspected that the campaign heavies were trying to promote Costello at Howard's expense, and the campaign heavies worried that the Howard family was having too much say.

There were good reasons on both sides for the suspicions, but the increasing paranoia made for an unproductive and unhappy environment. The campaign was difficult enough without the mutual distrust.

The campaign heavies thought that Howard and Costello should be doing more of substance together. They argued that, given Howard had said he was going to hand over, the public should be allowed to see the team working together, or to see Costello on his own handling more of the responsibilities of leadership.

In September, a campaign note by Crosby/Textor for the Liberal Party, also given to the committee conducting the post mortem, had recommended that Costello should be given a higher profile and the lead on certain issues and messages. 'The Liberal campaign has a communication gap,' the note from Crosby/Textor said:

> *Who* sells the Liberal forward agenda is an important consideration because many of these soft voters have largely switched off to John Howard as the messenger, especially knowing that he will be retiring in the next term as they don't necessarily see him as having an investment in seeing things through.
>
> The Liberal campaign can help overcome this communication gap by having Peter Costello announce (or co-announce) more future agenda plans to demonstrate to the electorate that he firstly, supports the sort of policies that are John Howard's hallmark and secondly to show that he has an investment in seeing things through.

Using Peter Costello as a vehicle to announce future plans is also needed (consistent with previous advice) to help raise Costello's credibility as the future leader and prime minister, more than just as a good treasurer.

While this might sound sensible and logical now, all it did at the time was raise the hackles of the Howardites, and they worked harder to exercise control.

The involvement of the Howard family also caused resentment.

One evening, Brian Loughnane, Tony Nutt, Mark Textor, and advertising executives, including Ted Horton, were called to the Howards' hotel suite. It was around 9.30 p.m., and dinner was served. The latest TV ad was called up on a laptop, and Mrs Howard, along with others, offered her opinion about it. This was not unusual. She was present for many discussions, saw most of the campaign ads, and almost always expressed an opinion.

But some of those present resented being called to the suite late at night, and felt that ads should be seen in a more formal campaign environment, where they could be discussed properly — not dished up like an afterthought with the remnants of the night's dinner.

Although the staff had pretty much got used to Janette's involvement, it still rankled with a few people — even though her opinions and observations were usually sound.

In 2007, the tension was exacerbated by the fact that Richard had also been brought into the campaign, and was travelling around with his father, the prime minister. Everybody competed to get their point across to the PM, but it was difficult if not impossible to cut across family members, and Richard's involvement and perceived influence was causing some angst at campaign headquarters.

Throughout the campaign, according to one senior campaign worker, TV ads that had been produced which attacked Rudd were vetoed by Howard because they were too personal. The advertisers and marketers felt hamstrung.

The advertising gurus later claimed that they did not know about the tax package before its release — not many people did — so they did not have enough time to work out how to sell it. They claimed that they had no clear idea about what exactly they were supposed to sell for the next term.

Apart from endless prosperity.

That seemed like a big-enough issue to a few of us humble staff. These days, ads can be turned around in 24 hours, so we couldn't work out why we never saw any ads on the tax package. What was missing was leadership and clear direction.

In 1996, as campaign director, Andrew Robb would choose the ads. He would usually — but not always — consult the leader, and Howard was happy to trust Robb to do his job.

In 2007, there was little that Loughnane was trusted to do, and he lacked the clout and the confidence to go against the wishes of a man who had won four elections in a row. There was no independently minded federal president or other party office-holder to take charge and drag everybody into line.

No one seemed to have a grip on anything.

It was a train wreck in the making, as Robb had warned. In politics, as in life generally, catastrophes usually strike not because one thing suddenly goes wrong, but because a series of things go wrong. In 2007, almost everything that could go wrong did go wrong, and then some. It was Murphy's Law XL.

Howard was spending a lot of time, every weekend, in his own electorate fighting off Maxine McKew. She didn't even need the extra attention, but all that did was make sure her profile was raised and that she got a run on the news bulletins. Behind the scenes, the polling in his electorate was atrocious, and it would send him into a spin.

My job was to stay in Canberra and run the prime minister's press office.

We had a phone hook-up every morning at 7.10 with campaign

headquarters, the prime minister's team, the deputy prime minister's team, and the treasurer's office. It was the same drill every morning: Loughnane would recite what was in the morning papers, then briefly run through the itineraries of the main players. Nothing of any substance was ever discussed on those calls. Nor was it encouraged.

If anyone had anything important to say, it was done later and privately. The daily hook-up with the leaders was the same, although ministers on the call complained later about the prime minister's occasional tetchiness.

Most of the television correspondents stayed in Canberra most of the time, finding it easier to draw packages together from the central location, so it made sense to have someone who knew their way around to mind the shop.

Part of my job was to field ministers for talk shows, but it was a constant battle to find people available to go out, or who could be trusted to go out. A few would go out when they were not wanted, and would say things that were unhelpful.

The people who had given the government a distinctive character, such as Amanda Vanstone and Tim Fischer, were gone. Those who could be counted on to land blows on the opposition, such as Peter Reith, were gone. And those who could be counted on to run consistent and coherent lines were few.

Then there were the likes of former NSW Liberal leader Peter Debnam, who was such a political genius that he ran around in his undies — sorry, I mean bathers — in the state election campaign, and who publicly and gratuitously chided Howard for his stance on climate change and nuclear power. That chewed up another day.

The media was only too willing to take up anti-Howard stories, and there were too many people willing to supply them. Paul Bongiorno, for example, was one of the senior people in the gallery who made clear his distaste for the government, and who couldn't wait to see it booted out.

In his news package reporting on the clearly menacing Latham–Howard handshake in the dying days of the 2004 campaign, one of Bongiorno's offsiders had described it as a 'final gesture of goodwill', so it was a bit hard to take Ten's political coverage seriously, despite its self-promoting logo.

Ten's news menu always seemed to be laden with anti-coalition government stories, and its 2007 campaign coverage was, if anything, worse than in the past. It ran a story early on in the 2007 campaign claiming that the Liberal member for Robertson, Jim Lloyd, had suggested to the prime minister during a street walk in his electorate that the government should consider introducing a GST on food. Lloyd insisted he had been reminding Howard that John Della Bosca, husband of his Labor opponent for the seat, Belinda Neal, had suggested a few years before that the GST *should* have been imposed on food. I took it up with Bongiorno, asking for the network to correct the record. They were initially reluctant; and, by the time they got around to it, Lloyd had been badly wounded.

It was hard enough getting good people out to spruik reliably on the government's behalf, and in my view there was little point in serving up ministers for *Meet the Press*. Hardly anyone watched it, and people could make more headway with a doorstop on Sunday.

Bongiorno was furious that he was having trouble getting anyone senior on his show, and worried about what his superiors in Sydney would think. He warned me that there would be 'grief' if we did not field senior people for his programme during the campaign.

'Is that a threat?'

'No, it's a promise.'

To my mind, it made no difference whether they went on or not; there would still be grief.

But trying to keep some politicians away from cameras and microphones was like trying to stop cobras swaying to flutes, or moths flying into flames — even former journalists like Tony Abbott who should have known better.

Abbott was not Robinson Crusoe, but he had a particularly bad campaign. He found commenting on polls irresistible; he beat up on Bernie Banton, the asbestos campaigner; and then he was late for his National Press Club debate with Nicola Roxon. Finally, and most regrettably, he advised Jackie Kelly to make light of the filthy Lindsay leaflet scandal by likening it to a *Chaser* prank.

When the NSW state director, Graham Jaeschke, called me the night before to warn me that the story on the dodgy leaflets was going to break, I felt sick to my stomach.

The fake leaflet that had been distributed in Jackie Kelly's electorate, purporting to be from the non-existent Islamic Federation of Australia, and claiming that Labor supported terrorism, was reprehensible. It was bigoted, stupid, dishonest, and incompetent. It was anything but funny. Once the story broke, I wondered how anyone would be able to bring themselves to vote for us.

The prime minister and his team were in town that day for the traditional address to the National Press Club. It was Thursday, and the election was on Saturday.

I vented loudly and passionately about it to Tony O'Leary who, to his credit, impressed firmly on Howard just how badly the affair would play out in the dying days of the campaign. Howard condemned it, but the damage had been done.

I had always tried to act honourably, as did my close workmates through all those years. Despite this, I had faced hurtful and untrue accusations from some journalists, who had been briefed by Labor that I had been part of a dirt unit.

My 'dirty' tactics had largely consisted of reading transcripts and pointing out to journalists any inconsistencies in policy positions or comments among Labor's various spokesmen. I played tough; I didn't play dirty. Perhaps I had been a little too successful in landing hits on the opposition — and they found a nasty payback, using journalists I had once considered friends.

Mortified about what my friends and family would think, I had to spend some time shaking off those charges about my alleged foul play, and was helped along the way by a couple of journos who had a bit more trust in my integrity. Still, the episode had smashed long-standing friendships, so I felt especially betrayed by what those few rogue Liberals had done in Lindsay. Suddenly, all my protests about how we didn't do things like that sounded hollow.

I felt ashamed, and as if my own name had once again been blackened. I had already decided long before this — win, lose, or draw — that I would leave after the election. But this was an unworthy way for my last campaign to close.

On the last night of the campaign, Howard and his team flew from Townsville back to Sydney. The polls had shown a narrowing of the gap, and Howard was trying to lift the spirits of his weary workers — as well as give himself some hope to get through what would be his longest day.

'It's closing up; it looks like it's closing up,' he said.

Nutt brought everyone back down. Yes, it was closing up, but it was not going to be enough. He ran through the problems as he saw them, chief among them being the selection of candidates in key seats where long-serving members had retired. The Liberals had become too indulgent in their choice of candidates, Nutt believed.

On that last night, Howard was described as hopeful, but not confident. The atmosphere on the plane was subdued.

His concession speech on the Saturday night was extraordinary. Unlike Malcolm Fraser, he did not allow his bottom lip to quiver, and he remained stoic and eloquent.

When I saw Howard a couple of days after the election, I gave him a hug, and tried to soften the blow by reminding him that, given today's political and news cycles, 12 years surpassed Menzian rule.

'Yes,' he said. 'I think that's right.' He was, if anything, quite matter-of-fact about it. Arthur Sinodinos described him, at the end, as 'gritty'. That was a pretty good description, I thought. Howard's self-control was amazing. There was certainly little or no Greek in him.

At final drinks in the cabinet suite later that day, Howard paid generous tributes to his staff. There was no wallowing and few tears. Everyone was exhausted, and it was not as if the result was a huge surprise to any of us.

Unfortunately, Howard had been right about the campaign itself. Policy had not mattered one little bit. It was all much more personal.

In a clear-eyed assessment after the campaign, written for the federal director, Brian Loughnane, Conran echoed his former boss's sentiment, and alluded to the other problems as well.

As head of the Cabinet Policy Unit, then later as chief of policy formulation at campaign headquarters, the talented Conran had had a difficult time of it, but always remained incredibly cheerful. After an especially tense meeting, if you asked him how it went, he would laugh and say, 'Best ever.'

'We had some very good policies, but they were largely irrelevant to the overall campaign,' Conran wrote to Loughnane when it was all over:

> A massive tax reform and pension support plan, a savings reform which was a real revolution, an education rebate that was more comprehensive than the ALP's and a better health policy.
>
> Perhaps we didn't sell them as well as we could have or put a better narrative around them but I'm not sure that would have resulted in commentators adopting a different approach.
>
> That said the policy development process was to my mind unsatisfactory. Little if any attention was given to election policies by the leadership group during most of the year.
>
> Policy positions on most major issues were finalised only some days prior to the campaign and changed, not unnecessarily

during the course of the campaign. While this meant maximum flexibility it also meant alternative options were not considered. And it impacted on the story.

There seemed to be a perception that the policy gurus could produce outcomes and did not need much guidance. In part that is the way but in future, leadership must be engaged much earlier.

Conran paid generous tribute to his team, and he magnanimously accepted responsibility for the process not being up to the standard he would have liked. It was not their fault that it failed. They worked their guts out. Conran, Bailey, and Jackman had done a brilliant job — the best ever, as Conran would say — under the most trying circumstances, aided and abetted by Stephanie Wawn and Jenny Howse.

The research and summations by Crosby/Textor handed to the internal review shows that the election was lost on the day that Rudd became leader, although there might have been a chance with a Liberal leadership-change.

Certainly, all the private and public polling showed that, from the day Rudd ascended, the Howard government's days were numbered.

People were too relaxed, too comfortable, and in the mood to swing. As well, the government seemed to have gone out of its way to alienate key constituencies. Small 'l' liberals, and the so-called doctors' wives, were put off by some of the harsher social or immigration policies — even by the perceived abandonment of Hicks and the war in Iraq — and Howard's once-loyal battlers felt betrayed by WorkChoices. When Labor finally chose a credible leader, they had a licence to switch.

From the moment that Rudd became leader, almost everything that Howard said or did was seen as a tactical response designed to win an election, and not as a sign of leadership.

People still regarded him as a great prime minister, but he

seemed to have achieved everything he had set out to do, climaxing in the hugely unpopular WorkChoices. When he went too far on that and had to back off, it was not because he cared about them as people — just as voters.

The consumers were determined to trade in the old model for the new one. Young Howard for Old Howard.

No one can say with confidence that the result would have been different if Costello had been leader. It might have been better. It might have been worse. A lot would have depended on whether both Costello and Howard behaved themselves.

Costello would have had to act as if he was not God's gift to the electorate and the Liberal Party, and Howard as if he really wanted Costello to win. Their working relationship in the past had secured four election victories. A fifth was not out of the question, and they both stood to gain much from it.

What solace would there have been for Howard to lose the leadership, and then be blamed for causing Costello to lose the election? If Costello had lost, Howard would have had plenty of time for public retribution. And there would have been no mileage for Costello as leader denigrating Howard or the Howard government's legacy. It was his legacy, too.

What comfort, really, does Costello have to draw on now? 'I told you so' doesn't really cut it, I'm afraid.

Howard might console himself by saying that the defeat would have been greater under Costello, but it would have been much better for the Liberal Party, and for his own state of mind, if he had left at the time of the tenth anniversary. Or at least spoken openly to Costello about his plans.

The McLachlan affair and all the bitterness that overflowed as a result might have been averted, and Howard would have fulfilled the desire he had expressed years before to spare the Liberals the trauma that Labor suffered as a result of the Hawke–Keating struggles.

His legacy would not have been tainted by the twin defeats of losing both the federal election and his own seat, and the Liberals would have had another hero to look up to.

They both bear ultimate responsibility for what happened. At critical points, neither of them could summon the courage or the common sense to do what was necessary, and there was no one who could convince them or compel them to do it. Their failure over the leadership exposed their fatal flaws.

It would certainly have been a different campaign with Costello as leader in 2007: the ages of the combatants would not have been the factor that it was, and voters looking for change would have got it, without having to vote against a government that had delivered on many fronts.

The very act of wresting the leadership from Howard would have forced people to assess Costello differently — not as someone who had merely wanted the delivery boy to knock on his door with a neatly wrapped package of party leadership, but as a fighter who had wanted something so badly, and had believed in it so much, that he had been prepared to risk everything to get it.

The leader would not have been distracted by the prospect of losing his own seat. The campaign against WorkChoices by the unions would have been as potent — maybe even more so — but Rudd's attacks in other areas, such as climate change, would have been blunted.

Costello would have said sorry, or apologised — whatever was necessary — to Australia's indigenous people. He might have even had time to announce the appointment of a female governor-general. These two important symbolic gestures would have cost nothing and meant a lot.

Changes at the top by state Labor governments have shown that a new leader forces voters to see even rotten old governments in a new light ... and the Howard government was a very long way from rotten.

With so much at stake, it would have been worth a shot.

CHAPTER FIFTEEN

Finally

The coalition didn't get everything right, but in the areas of economic management and providing help for families, it succeeded handsomely. The rich might have got richer, but the poor certainly did not get poorer.

Despite that, it was punished severely by a sated electorate. People had quite simply had enough.

For about a year after the election, we had an informal coffee club called the Ugly Sisters — Conran, Kunkel, O'Leary, Mitchell, Bailey, and me — and, as we slurped our cappuccinos and lattes, we fumed and railed over all the mistakes and injustices. We fought all the old battles over and over and over: Howard versus Costello; us versus journos; us versus the Labor Party; us versus the Liberal Party; and us versus the world. We talked about our previous lives, had a few laughs, and consoled ourselves.

Anyone who says they have no regrets is lying or stupid, and none of us is blind to what went wrong — even if some of us have trouble admitting to it. In that final year in office, it was pretty much everything. We did our best but, much as we tried, we couldn't control everything or everyone.

We remembered and acknowledged (or most of us did) that when it was good it was very, very good, and when it went bad it was lousy. It was valuable group-therapy.

Now the Liberals face a prolonged period in opposition, divided within and taunted from without by Labor and its acolyte analysts tearing into the Howard–Costello legacy, spinning every which way to blame the conservatives for any of the misfortunes of today, and barely able to give credit for the prosperity they delivered.

It is pathetic and infuriating to watch ten years of your life being ground into dust. And there is some sadness, too, as the circles complete themselves.

The Higgins preselection first sprang up on my radar more than 20 years ago when I was chief political correspondent on the Melbourne *Sun*. The amiable but going-nowhere Roger Shipton was under threat from John Elliott, although there were vehement denials at the time that the businessman was angling for the seat.

Derek Parker was writing a book about the Press Gallery, and chose the wrong day to ring to ask me why, in the face of those denials and the apparent lack of evidence, I persisted in writing that Elliott was manoeuvring to get into Parliament so he could make a run for the Liberal leadership.

Having come under attack from several different directions over the story, I was exasperated. 'It was a quiet day,' I offered up to Parker as my excuse for once again writing a story that people were trying to knock down.

He quoted my response in his 1991 publication *The Courtesans: the press gallery in the Hawke era* to help substantiate his claim of consistent and wanton bias against the then opposition leader John Howard among journalists in the gallery.

Before that, at a function in Melbourne, I had introduced myself to Elliott. 'Well,' he said, 'I like your husband.' Vincent was then working at the Liberal Party federal secretariat. Elliott was halfway through smoking a cigarette, dropped it into his unfinished cup of coffee to extinguish it, turned on his heel, and walked away.

By the time the Elliott stories were proved right, Shipton was under threat from another quarter. The talented and charismatic

Finally

young lawyer from the so-called New Right, Peter Costello, had been recruited for the campaign by his great friend Michael Kroger, and Howard had lost the leadership.

We had spoken on the phone a few times, and soon after his election in 1990, figuring he was someone who would go places, I took Costello to lunch. His off-the-record forthrightness at that first personal encounter left even me gobsmacked. He basically declared John Hewson unsuitable for the job, and nominated John Howard as the only person who could or should be leading the Liberals.

How right he was. But not even he could have suspected then that, once reincarnated, Howard would stay such a long time as leader. Nor could he have dreamt that the price he would have to pay for the endurance of the self-proclaimed Lazarus with a triple by-pass was the destruction of his own ambition.

I spoke to Costello the day after the 2007 election as he walked to his press conference to announce that he would neither stand for the leadership nor hang around in the Parliament. I was bitterly disappointed. He was angry and hurt. The very people who had blocked him from the leadership were now begging him to stay. He didn't want to hear any of it. He'd had enough.

Costello's decision to reclaim his life outside Parliament was ultimately the right one for him. We should not — make that, I should not — continue to blame him for failing to live up to all the expectations of him.

Costello had carried the weight of leadership expectations on his shoulders for decades. I told him early on that I had not chosen to work for the Liberal Party — I had gone to work for him. It was the singer, not the song. He went pink with embarrassment.

The burden of those expectations would not have been made lighter by years in opposition. He has finally discarded them, resigned if not content, to live with himself as possibly the finest Liberal never to become prime minister.

He was never hungry enough to kill for the leadership, and if he had stayed that is what he would have had to do, either immediately or eventually. He would have had to force old friends to make difficult choices. Worse than that, he would have had to put in many more nights away from home, rebuilding and regenerating the party, and spending more time than he could possibly bear with people he couldn't stand.

And for what? To fight an election he was convinced he would lose.

He had neither the stamina nor the will to do it. Or the heart. His bitterness after the 2007 defeat ran deep and long.

Costello leaves behind a chronically unstable, under-resourced, and self-indulgent Liberal Party obsessed with testing the patience of even the strongest and most talented leader.

Malcolm Turnbull had many but not all of the qualities that a good leader needs — and patience was certainly not one of them.

Unlike Costello, Turnbull was bereft of caution. Also unlike Costello, he lacked any appreciation of the complexity of the task before him. He thought it was going to be easy. In fact, he told people soon after he got the job that he couldn't believe how easy it was. A political novice with an uber-ego is begging for trouble, and he got it. Turnbull made his millions because he was willing to take risks, but politics demands a combination of other skills.

Turnbull was different from Costello in another critical respect — apart from the fact that he is much, much richer, which drove Costello nuts.

Turnbull lusted after the leadership so badly that he was prepared to destroy Brendan Nelson to get it. Then, when his own leadership came under threat, he pressed the self-destruct button, seemingly determined to leave his successor nothing but rubble from which to rebuild. In what many Liberals saw as an unforgiveable act of betrayal, not only did he take no prisoners, but he set about slaughtering his own troops, too. I have never seen anything like

Finally

it, not even during the years of the Howard–Peacock war and the mad Joh-for-Canberra campaign. In retrospect, they behaved like gentlemen.

Turnbull was never going to go quietly. After he won the leadership, Turnbull had sent an unequivocal message to Costello that if he wanted the job, he would have to 'wade through blood' to get it. He was not about to just hand it over to Costello if he had decided to stay in Parliament. He judged rightly that Costello would not have the stomach to fight him for it, but it was one of the few things he did get right. His first mistake was in moving too quickly against Nelson. He should have waited, and concentrated on refining his political skills. Then he thought he could kill Rudd with one blow with Utegate, and instead ended up mortally wounding himself. Ultimately, Turnbull failed to convince middle-ground voters and his own MPs that he had the right temperament and the right values. He didn't consult, he didn't listen, and he didn't learn from his mistakes. Sadly — and it is sad when someone with so much promise disappoints — he failed to make himself into something other than a rich guy with an impetuous personality and a charming smile used to getting whatever he wants, whenever he wants it.

Turnbull is intelligent, engaging, volatile, utterly ruthless, egotistical, and politically opportunistic. There is no greater sin in politics, to my mind at least, than to be boring, and Turnbull is anything but that; however, his impulsive nature guaranteed a precarious existence.

Howard was not boring either. He couldn't tell jokes to save his life, but what made him interesting were his ideas — whether you agreed with them or not — and his remorseless tenacity. It was hypnotising. What helped him succeed was his preparedness to adapt.

One of the biggest challenges for any leader is to manage the broad church that is the Liberal Party (how I came to hate that phrase), and to assuage the fears of the Left as well as the Right that he is not about to destroy everything they hold dear.

Good luck with that one.

The Right especially needs to remember that, in order to win the 1996 election, their standard-bearer, John Howard, also had to shift ground to the centre. He had to apologise for his remarks on Asian immigration, he had to dispel fears that he would destroy Medibank, and he had to convince the battlers that in reforming the industrial-relations system he would not rip away the safety net.

Australian elections are not won from the Right or the Left. It's the great mass in the middle that decides the result.

Turnbull was also convinced that the electorate was well and truly over the Howard–Costello years, and that if Costello had ascended to the leadership it would have done nothing to restore the Liberals' fortunes.

Well, he would say that, wouldn't he?

While there was a grain of truth in that, it would be a big mistake for the Liberals, whoever is at the helm, to trash by design or neglect the Howard–Costello legacy of prosperity and sound economic management.

Once upon a time, not all that long ago, I would have recoiled in horror at the prospect of Tony Abbott as leader. I would probably not agree with 90 per cent of what Abbott stands for, and some of his earthier expressions make me wince. I doubt that he would ever be elected prime minister, unless he moves even further to the centre than he already has, seeks and takes advice from a much wider circle, and promises not to allow his religion to infiltrate his politics. A clever and gutsy opposition leader — and while Abbott's judgment veers into unsafe territory at times, he has no shortage of ticker — would rattle Kevin Rudd's cage like a great white shark sniffing out blood in the water. It would be worth it to see that alone. There are times when Rudd seems so tightly wound that just a tiny nudge would unhinge him.

A recovered Robb — compassionate, thoughtful, and intelligent as ever — would make a first-class leader, and provide a sound alternative to Rudd, perhaps after an Abbott reign of terror. If guts and determination count for anything — and in politics, as in life, they are priceless — Robb deserves to make it.

It is impossible to hate Joe Hockey, although his verbal tangles and personality threaten to plop him into the jolly-giant category of politician: likeable and unelectable (see Kim Beazley).

Straddling both the conservative and moderate camps, Costello would have been the best option, although Turnbull is right in believing that Costello would have had to remake himself as opposition leader. His economic credentials alone would not have been enough to enable him to succeed. And he would have had to deal maturely with every other piece of grief that goes with the worst job in politics.

Now, given that Costello cannot reconcile with John Howard and other former colleagues, he needs to reconcile with himself. He has to acknowledge, if only privately, that he made mistakes. That's the only way he will get the most out of the rest of his life.

Talented people such as Arthur Sinodinos, Mitch Fifield, Tony Smith, Michael O'Brien, Dan Tehan, Sarah Henderson, and Kelly O'Dwyer will help the party rebuild federally and in the states, from the frontline and the backline, if they are given the chance. An encouraging sign is the number of decent candidates lining up for preselections, but it will take time for their presence to be felt and for them to make a difference. It certainly won't happen until they can find a leader strong enough and smart enough to unite them and satisfy the Liberals' Saviour Complex. While they continue to tear one another to bits in public, and brawl over what measures, if any, should be taken to protect the planet from humankind, they will decay as surely as the environment around them.

I always found the debate on climate change frustrating — and still do. I suspect I am more contrarian leftie than conservative leftie on this. I find the climate-change zealots off-putting, to say the least: they make me want to turn on all the taps and lights full bore, and leave them on for days, and buy every piece of imported fruit I can lay my hands on. Then I get infuriated by the agnostics. If a system of bribes and blackmail is what it takes to induce people to look after our air, waterways, and terrain, then we should try to work out a decent and fair way to do it.

Even if you don't agree about the science, and even if you do think Al Gore is as boring as bat droppings, and a hypocrite to boot, surely you can see the sense in treating the planet with a bit of respect. Not to mention the politics of it, for God's sake. All we have to do is ensure that those at the lower end are adequately compensated, and that we do not needlessly destroy jobs. I have absolute faith that the right mechanism will be implemented, and that it will be just, because journalists will pursue the Rudd government as assiduously as they did the coalition over the GST to make sure that there are no losers — not a single one. Pardon my sarcasm.

The media remained fixated on the opposition's conflicts — even though its chances of winning the next election are worse than they were in 2007 — rather than on what the government was actually planning. Gee, I wonder if there is a connection there. I suspect the planet will freeze over again before journos start hankering for another conservative government.

I can't just blame the media, though, for the Liberals looming political Ice Age. Turnbull's success in uniting climate-change believers and sceptics against him, then trashing his own party, branding anyone who opposed him a denier even if they weren't, and handing Rudd his lines of attack for the next election was truly awesome. Nick Minchin believed in Turnbull even less than he did in man-made global warming, and had desperately wanted Costello to stay and lead. He was ready from the outset to do whatever was necessary to prevent Turnbull from remaking the Liberals in his own image. It was part of an epic struggle for the heart and soul of the Liberal Party, and is destined to last for a good decade at least. It will break many hearts and bruise many souls before it is resolved, and will ensure that the Liberals stay as they are — a C-grade opposition fighting a B-grade government.

Conservatives aren't helped, either, by the fact that Kevin Rudd has proved every bit as adept as I thought he would be, although I am still not quite sure who or what he is. He is on a new mission, desperate to find someone else's skin to slither into since he shed Howard's. So far, too frightened — or too smart — to be himself, and still uncertain about who else he could or should be, he remains, publicly at least, robotically programmed to make just the right responses at just the right time.

Rudd's complete lack of subtlety, and his reliance on a machine stuck on the spin cycle, will eventually wear people down. One day he will forget who he is pretending to be and will indulge in one of his infamous brain explosions in public, giving voters a real insight into the meaner side of his nature. But it's going to take a long time for his appeal to fade — even longer if the Liberals can't get their act together. When he does fade, Julia Gillard, an altogether more substantial character, will take over.

My first insight into Gillard came courtesy of Barry Jones. Costello, Smith, and I ran into the retiring Jones at Tullamarine Airport, and he proceeded to tell us that a talented woman had just won preselection for his seat of Lalor. Barry felt obliged to add that, even though she was of a mature age and single, she was not gay.

This is no latter-day conversion on my part. I told one senior journalist who had sought my opinion years ago that, if I were Beazley (then Labor leader), I would promote Gillard to the frontbench. He didn't, to his eventual cost. If I had still been in the gallery I would have followed my long-established practice of zeroing in on the most talented new recruits, and shared a few meals with Gillard. And Rudd, too, for that matter.

Rudd will maintain his supremacy, much like Howard did, until the Liberals find a credible leader to challenge him. Labor MPs will then admit that they never liked him, or his brutally authoritarian office, very much anyway. A former colleague of mine worked for Rudd years ago in Queensland, and swore he would never work for him again, ever, because of the rotten way that Rudd treated people. For all his faults, Paul Keating treated his staff and others who served him, from police to public servants, with affection or respect, and it was reciprocated. It's not just that Rudd works people hard — people expect that in politics — it is his manner: overbearing, impatient, and arrogant.

From what I hear, this hasn't changed much, but the few times I have seen Rudd in person, at formal or informal functions, he has been disciplined, well-briefed, and surprisingly charming. However, the harder he tries to act sincere (and, to give him his due, he does try hard), the less convincing he becomes. I find it incredibly grating, as do my friends and family — even those of them who vote Labor.

Rudd has centralised power, is badly organised and, according to journalists, has spoken disparagingly about some of his colleagues, including his treasurer, Wayne Swan, when he was going through a difficult patch. One unconfirmed story had Rudd referring to his fellow Queenslander as 'DC' — 'D' standing for 'dumb' and 'C' for that other four-letter word so beloved of Labor figures. True or not, stories like this, as well as those surrounding his obsession with his hair (hairspray has to be close at hand at all times, and car windows must always be wound up so the hair doesn't get blown around, etc.) gain currency because they fit with the already-confirmed reports of temper tantrums and foul language. Although they help build an unflattering image of the secret Kevin, they are not life-threatening while he rides high and the economy stays sound. When his popularity begins to slide, seemingly trivial traits and incidents will turn into overnight sensations. Literally.

Finally

Canberra is a small place, and Rudd is remembered from his days at the Australian National University as a dobber and wowser who has allowed decades-long petty resentments to influence his decisions, such as his vetoing of a former fellow ANU student, Hugh Borrowman — an intelligent and dedicated public servant — as ambassador to Germany. He doesn't have many, if any, real friends in the caucus. All leaders use patronage to cement alliances and, while he remains popular, his pets will stay true to him. But I can't see anybody in that caucus prepared to lay down his (or her) life for him — as Abbott and a few others would have done for Howard when the former prime minister was bleeding to death.

Maybe Rudd will be smart enough to arrange a peaceful succession. Perhaps he will look at Howard and think, *No way am I going out like that.* Then again, Howard used to look at Bob Hawke and think the same. Weird and wonderful things happen to leaders after a few years at the top. Maybe the air up there is a bit thinner, and the brain a tad puffier. One of my old leftie mates reckons that all prime ministers are mad. He should know — he worked with two of them. I think that if they're not mad when they get there, they certainly are by the time they leave.

I'll be taking a keen interest in whatever happens from the splendour of my replanted garden which, apart from this book, has been my major preoccupation since the 2007 election. I keep telling people these days that I'm more left-wing than Kevin Rudd. They're not especially impressed by this, given Rudd's small 'c' conservatism, especially on social issues.

In between yelling at the television and radio over bad grammar or wilful bias, and squishing aphids, I'll be baking goodies for my appreciative young friend Jack Kunkel, who loves everything from my Cypriot cheese bread, *haloumopitta*, to my very Anglo muesli muffins, and watching in adoration as my four nephews — Andrew, Peter, Thomas, and Christian — grow and prosper, marvelling all over again at my brother Steve's strength of character and the vitality of his new partner, Dana Forte. I discovered a recipe that approximated Vera's heavenly apple-sponge, and bake it often; each time I do, I think of her and the rest of the Abaloz family.

The garden that Vincent and I had spent 25 years creating, full of plants that my father had given me, was largely obliterated by a bushfire which swept through a badly neglected government reserve in 2005. Looters made off with most of the other plants that survived.

The one remaining twig of a rose that Andreas gave me is now thriving, as are all the other plants and bulbs that Elpiniki, my sister-in-law Marion Fraser, and my friends Denise, Lajla, Anna, Bob and Bev, Laura G., Kay, Valerie, and Steven T have donated to help with the restoration.

A couple of attempts I made to get back into journalism went nowhere.

Did I happen to mention that nothing lasts forever?

Acknowledgements

When I told people that I was writing this book, I told them my aim was to be fair but honest. Not surprisingly, there was a reflexive 'Uh-oh.' Being honest and fair often means telling people what they don't want to hear.

I hope I have achieved my objective and, if I have caused offence, I am sure the wounded parties will let me know and will, almost certainly at some point, reciprocate.

As a journalist, I used to urge people on the inside to write books to tell those of us on the outside what it was really like, what the politicians were really like, and to give an insight into the complexity of relationships and the impact they have on the political decision-making process. After a decade as an insider, I have felt obliged to take my own advice.

Long-time political staffer Liam Bathgate told me when I took on the job with Peter Costello that, while I would never eat well or sleep well again, I would never be bored.

He was right. The day I resigned as Costello's press secretary, I had my first decent night's sleep in six years. It wasn't because I hated the job, although by then I had had enough. It was relief from the relentlessly unforgiving pressure that went with it, including that which I put on myself.

I loved journalism because it was so much fun, but I loved working in government all those years, too, because I was part of something big and important.

Having the chance to do good things every day is an enormous privilege. And that's what we set out to do. We might not have managed it all the time, and I know there were days when we fell short, but we did our best. Overall, I think we succeeded.

My chief urger in all this, my companion conscience, was my sister Christina, who wanted our family's story told. I only wish she had been around to do it. She would have done it so much better, as she did most things.

In the more than ten years since Christina died, at least twice a week I have had the following conversation with our mercurial mother, Elpiniki, in Gringlish, the fifty-fifty language we use to communicate with.

'I am ready to die now. God should just take me. I have had enough.'

'Don't be ridiculous'

'No, I have had enough. Please, God, take me.'

It changed, briefly, on 16 April 2009 when my extraordinary brother, Steven, told her that he was getting married again. This was great news. Even better was that his wife-to-be, a beautiful Italian called Dana Forte, was pregnant with twins.

Almost the first words out of Elpiniki were a recantation: 'I don't want to die now.'

Elpiniki soon retreated into the more familiar territory of worrying about every little thing that could possibly go wrong. At least I know where that came from.

For a while there, the Savva family was shrinking alarmingly. Now it's growing again. And if the new additions, Thomas and Christian, turn out as well as the previous two, Andrew and Peter, then they, and we, will be very lucky indeed.

Every family has its tragedies, including ours, but we have been blessed also with our extended family: my aunt Christina; cousin Vana, who named her second daughter Elpiniki and allowed me to

Acknowledgements

become her godmother; my uncle Paul Savva and his family; Hazel and Harry Georgiou; Chris and Stella Leonidas; and Nina and Meli Kleanthous.

My childhood friends, Bruce Abaloz and Natalie Philippou; my former teachers, Joy Brown, Tom Comerford, and ER Johnson; and our Greek teacher, Sam Merambeliotis, who did his best on Saturday mornings to teach Steven and myself to read and write in our first language, all contributed in one way or another — as did my brother's friends who became mine, Carol and Peter Zeccola, Bernie and Deanna McKeown, and Rick and Shirley Radeticchio. In a way, Carol kicked off this process years ago with a taped interview with Elpiniki. The diversity of their names gives only a hint of the spread of cultures — Montenegrin, Dutch–Indonesian, Italian, Greek–Italian, Irish, and Australian.

Although I say that Canberra is not a good place to make friends, I have made friendships here, through work or marriage, that have endured for decades despite tedious no-shows along the way because of work commitments in journalism and politics.

We would have been much poorer in every way without Denis and Denise Page.

Lissa and Laurie Oakes, both of whom I met soon after I arrived in Canberra, thankfully, remain my friends all these years later. Tony Smith, Mitch Fifield, Elizabeth McCabe, Valerie and the late Wally Brown, the Hunters, the Maillers, John Kunkel, Peter Conran, Gavin Jackman, Nigel Bailey, David Quilty, David and Stephanie Wawn, Jenny Howse, Lajla Sidhu, Marion Fraser, and Laura Grande provided both physical and moral support. Jacqui Corbett, Claire Chadwick, Candice Mikkonen, Sam Cusack, Kathryn Macfarlane, and Kylie Jacobsen typed millions of words of transcripts, filled out dozens of travel-allowance forms, and helped make my various jobs easier and more fun. Everyone I ever worked with taught me something — even if it was what not to do. I remember them all, even if I haven't named them all.

Apart from all the people who spoke to me, filling in gaps in my knowledge, or refreshing my memory, there are a few who physically helped make it happen.

My thanks to Matt Peacock for his invaluable research and computer skills, and to Keith Blyth for setting up my office.

My eternal gratitude to Henry Rosenbloom at Scribe for showing faith in my project, and then for guiding me through it with his finely honed skills in both editing and diplomacy.

Finally, I would like to thank my dear husband, Vincent Woolcock, for putting up with the moody Mediterranean all these years, and for his never-ending support, especially during the writing of this, at times, painful book.

Index

Abaloz family 23–5, 30, 285
Abaloz, Bruce 25
Abbott, Tony
    2007 elections 268–9
    Badgery's Creek 251
    Costello 158–9
    Howard 188, 241, 261
    as leader 280
    Niki 183
ABC 54, 72, 86
Aboriginals 105, 145, 170
    interventions 219
    'sorry' 258
Ackland, George 30, 36
ACTU 214
Afghanistan 85, 86, 205
The Age 20, 40, 47, 99, 104
AIRC 215
Akerman, Piers 91, 92, 192–3
al-Qaeda 220
alcopops 170, 251
Alexander, Dave 171, 194
Alexiou, Andreas 46
Alston, Richard 168, 171
anaemia *see* thalassemia
Anderson, John 145–6, 185
Andrews, Kevin 213, 217
Angelli, Phillipos 10–11
Anthony, Jim 65, 66–7
Anzac Cove, Gallipoli 92–3
apartheid 59–60
APEC 75–6, 234, 252
Arbib, Mark 229
Argus, Don 197
Asian financial crisis 121
Asian immigration 80
asylum seekers 155–7, 164, 185, 210
Austin Hospital 141–2
Australasian Political Science Association 66–7

The Australian 39–42, 67
Australian Democrats 154–5
The Australian Financial Review 65
Australian Labor Party
    interest groups 120
    Keating government 98
    'Knowledge Nation' 136–8
    NSW Right 60, 61–2
    policies 77, 105
    Press Gallery 52–3, 56, 60–1
    Young Labor 38–9
Australian National University 284
Australian Rules 30–1, 33
Australian Senate 213
Australian Society for Medical Research 140–1
Australian Tax Office, use of electoral roll 2–4
Australian Trucking Association 143
Australian Wheat Board 212
Aylmer, Sean 95

Badgery's Creek 250–1
Bailey, Nigel 110, 122, 126, 127, 275
    2007 elections 252, 255, 259–60, 262–3, 272
Baird, Bruce 147
Baker, Don 52
bank mergers (Four Pillars policy) 95
Banton, Bernie 269
Barnett, David 60
Barron, Peter 49
Beazley, Kim 61, 170
    Gillard 283
    Keating 71, 73
    'Knowledge Nation' 136–8
    as leader Labor Party 128, 139, 155, 203, 220
    McKew 171–2
    in polls 205–6
Bennelong (seat) 244, 251, 266
BHP Billiton 197
Bhutto, Zulfiqar Ali 86–7

Index

Bjelke-Petersen, Joh 80
Bolkus, Nick 70–1, 105–6
Bolt, Andrew 169
Bongiorno, Paul 75, 267–8
Borrowman, Hugh 284
Bowden, Dr Don 132
Boys on the Bus (Crouse) 90
Brandis, George 146–8
Brissenden, Michael 230–1
British in Cyprus 9, 11, 45, 47
Britton, Hawker 206
Brogden, John 187
Brough, Mal 219, 228, 233, 236–8, 239, 251–2
Brown, Joy 29
Brown, Wally 131
Bruce, Susan 257–8
Brumby, John 103
Buggy, Hugh 36–7, 39
Bullwinkel, Sister Vivian 2, 5
Burke, Brian 220–1
Burnet, Macfarlane 140
Bush, George H.W. 88, 91
Bush, George W. 233
Business Coalition for Tax Reform 121
Button, John 81

Cabinet Policy Unit 141, 175, 215, 249, 253, 271
Callaghan, Mike 3, 110, 140
Calvert-Jones, Janet 98
Cameron, Clyde 64–5, 66
Campbell, Ian 221
Canberra Press Gallery see Press Gallery
Canberra Times 52
Carleton, Richard 52–3
Carlton, Jim 79
Carlton Football Club 181
Carney, Shaun 185
Carroll, Des 36
Cassidy, Barrie 83, 86
Cebon, Dr Jonathan 102, 128–9, 140–1
Chaney, Fred 51
Chang, Victor 140
childcare rebate 248, 251–2
Chimoni, Nikolas 42
Churchill, Winston 93
Clark, Philip 149
Clark, Pilita 92
clergy 164–5
climate change 209, 217–18, 281–2
Clinton, Bill 126
Clinton campaign (1992) 90–3
Cohen, Barry 67

Colebatch, John 20
Colebatch, Tim 20
Collingwood Football Club 76
Comerford, Tom 29
Commonwealth Bank 77
Conran, Peter
    assessment of 2007 election campaign 271–2
    Cabinet Policy Unit 141, 204, 208, 214, 226
    health policy 259–60, 262–3
    Niki 217, 275
    tax cuts 252
Cook, Peter 71–2
Costello, Peter
    50th birthday party 231
    2007 elections 221–3, 277–8
    Abbott 158–9
    as acting prime minister 1–2, 4–5
    asylum seekers 155–7
    budgets 100, 115–16, 140–2, 160–1, 198–9, 224, 251–2, 255
    character and judgement 178–83, 230–1, 235
    Democrats 154–5
    'enemies' 183–6
    fear of failure 242–3
    GST 119–24, 126–8, 142–4, 150–1
    Howard and 2007 elections 264–5
    Howard and budgets 100, 115–16, 198–9
    Howard and leadership 119, 145, 146–7, 161–4, 168–9, 172–3, 187–90, 191–3, 273–4
    Howard and McLachlan note 193–203, 240, 273
    Howard and quasi-coup 239–43, 245–6
    inflation dragon 135–6
    Kyoto Protocol 218
    medical research 140–1
    National Party 145–9
    New Right 277
    Niki as press secretary 106–7, 108–16, 171–5, 231–2
    Niki, relationship with 103–5, 253–4, 277
    Packer 116–18
    reconciliation 145
    republic campaign 144–5
    Rudd 220–1
    Shane Stone memo 152–4
    tax cuts 254–5, 261
    Textor 228–9, 242
    transition to leadership plan 158–60
    as treasurer 177–8, 209
    Turnbull 182, 278, 279–80
Costello, Tanya 103–4, 153, 231

Index

Costello, Reverend Tim 165–6
Court, Richard 150
Cousins, Geoff 149
Crean, Simon 61, 73, 138–9, 150, 162, 206
Critchley, Cheryl 98
Cronin, Bob 97
Crosby, Lynton (polls)
   on 1998 elections 127–8
   on 2001 elections 155–6
   on Costello 222, 264–5
   on Rudd ascension to Labor leadership 211–12, 272
   Shane Stone memo 151, 152–3
Crow, Shirley 28
Crowley, Rosemary 71–2
Cypriot migrants to Australia 12–14
Cyprus Broadcasting Corporation 46–7
Cyprus/Cypriots 7–13, 16–17, 18, 42–7, 48

Daily Telegraph 60, 96
Daley, Paul 230–1
Dandenong *Journal* 30, 35–9
Dangerfield, Sebastian (nickname) 49–50
Davidson, Gay 52
Deamer, Adrian 42
Debnam, Peter 267
Delaney, Michael 65
Della Bosca, John 268
Department of Prime Minister and Cabinet 208–9
   Austin Hospital 141–2
Department of Treasury 116, 167, 170, 174, 208–9
Devine, Frank 5
Diamantopoulos, Elpiniki (goddaughter) 22
Diana, Princess of Wales 169
Domican, Tommy 61
Doveton High School 27–9, 47
Doveton housing estate 22–3, 25
Doveton West State School 3
Downer, Alexander
   Costello 160, 188
   in fishnet stockings 96–7
   Howard 189, 196, 228
   Keating 76
   Kyoto Protocol 218
   push for Howard to go 233–43
   Stone 225
dowry system 45–6
Drewe, Robert 51
drug abuse 170–1
Duck, Colin 90

Duffy, Michael 5
Dunne, John 41
Dutton, Peter 222, 280
Dyer, Jack ('Captain Blood') 31

economy 211, 275–6
Eden, Barbara 136
Egan, Michael 179
Eggleton, Tony 80
electoral roll, use by ATO 2–4
Elliott, John 276
Emerson, Craig 84
ENOSIS 11
Essendon Football Club 181
euthanasia 101–2
Evans, Gareth 52, 56–7, 137
Evans, Ted 120
'evil eye' 23

Fairfax 84
Farmer, Pat 251
Farr, Malcolm 229
Feldman, Joe 83
Ferguson, Doug 112
Fifield, Mitch
   Costello 2, 5, 110, 137, 146, 158, 179
   HECS/Ozcorps proposal 166, 168
   Howard leadership 241
   Niki 181
   The Party Room 183
   in Senate 168, 171, 201, 281
Fightback! 120
Fischer, Tim 92–3, 267
Fitzwater, Marlin 88
Florey, Howard 140
Forsyth, Chris 51
Forte, Dana (brother's partner) 285
Fraser, Malcolm 53, 80, 247, 270
   Glen Sheil 59–60
   Soviet Union 85
   Whitlam 64–5

Gaetjens, Phil 110, 142, 158, 209
Galilee, Stephen 259
Galtos, Con 151
gambling 16, 33
Gandhi, Indira 87, 94–5, 187
Garland, Deb 42
Gawenda, Michael 103
Gazard, David 204
Geelong Football Club 81
Georgiou, Petro 32, 184

Index

Gibbs, Dr Peter 102, 128–9
Gillard, Julia 97, 189, 283
Gillespie, Dr Matthew 140
GM-H (Fishermens Bend) 15, 22, 26
Goh Chok Tong 84–5
Gorbachev, Mikhail 91
Gordon, Harry 97
Gordon, Michael 84, 113
Gordon, Sue 219
Gore, Al 90–1, 218, 282
Gorton, John 38–9
Goss, Wayne 72
Grattan, Michelle 52, 82, 99, 139
Gray, Gary 78
Greece 11, 45
Greek national anthem 46–7
Greeks in Australia 22
The Greens 52
Griffiths, Alan 85
GST
   Costello 119–24, 126–8, 142–4, 150–1
   Democrats 154–5
   on food 268
   introduction of 214, 216, 217
   Packer 117
   state revenues from 122, 124
Gulf War (1991) 91
Gurrie, Peter 66
Guthrie, Bruce 99, 102, 103

Haase, Barry 221
Hamilton, Clive 142–3
Hand, Gerry 70–1, 105–6, 136
Hanke, Ian 217
Hankin, Adam 41–2
Hanson, Pauline *see* One Nation
Harris, Steve 103, 104
Hartcher, Peter 144
Harvey, John 79
Harvey, Michael 98
Haupt, Robert 91–2
Hawke, Bob 46, 60, 61
   Barry Jones 136
   Indira Gandhi joke 94–5, 187
   Keating 73–4, 201
   London Convention 82–4
   Mick Young 68
   MX missile tests 62–3
Hayden, Bill 71–2, 95, 105–6
Hayden, Dallas 72
health policy 259–63
HECS/Ozcorps proposal 166–8, 251

Heffernan, Bill 191
Henderson, Gerard 166
Henry, Ken 208–10
The Herald Sun 74, 76, 97, 99, 137
Hewson, John 75, 98, 120, 123, 277
Hicks, David 224, 249, 272
Higgins, Chris 74
High Court of Australia 203–4
Hill, Robert 253
Hockey, Joe 251, 256, 280
Hollings, Les 62–3
Hollingworth, Dr Peter 165
Holt, Harold 29, 80
Honiara, civil unrest in 2–3
Horton, Ted 265
housing 250
Howard, Janette 124, 151, 237, 239, 248, 258, 264, 265
Howard, John 61, 84, 98, 99
   1996 elections 78
   1998 elections 128
   2001 elections 155–7
   2004 elections 247–9
   2007 elections 222–3, 249–74
   2007 leaders' debate 256–7
   2007 polling leak 229–30
   2007 Sky News leak 238–9
   climate change 217–18
   Costello and 2007 elections 264–5
   Costello and leadership 119, 145, 146–7, 161–4, 168–9, 172–3, 187–90, 191–3, 273–4
   Costello and McLachlan note 193–203, 240, 273
   Costello and quasi-coup 239–43, 245–6
   Costello's budgets 100, 115–16, 198–9
   Democrats 154–5
   GST 121–4
   as leader 176–7, 191, 212, 219–20, 221, 227–8, 233–4
   Lindsay (seat) leaflet scandal 269
   Niki 79–80, 270–1
   no-disadvantage test 213–4
   One Nation 114–15, 187–8
   Packer 116–17
   The Party Room 183–4
   policies 105, 220, 248, 252–3, 254, 259–63
   Press Gallery 53–5, 59
   press office 266–70
   republic campaign 144
   Stone 151–4, 225–7
   Turnbull 182
Howard, Richard 264, 265

Index

Howse, Jenny 272
Hu Jintao 233
Hudson, Phillip 98
Hunt, Ralph 51
Hywood, Greg 91

income splitting 252–3, 254
industrial relations
    High Court of Australia 203–4
    New Right 79–80
    no-disadvantage test 213
    polling on 205, 212–13, 256
    WorkChoices 214–17, 222, 223, 247, 272–3
inflation 135–6, 150
interest rates 257
International Harvester, Dandenong 22
Iraq 91, 112, 150, 205, 212, 249, 272

Jack, David 47
Jackman, Gavin 259–60, 262–3, 272
Jackman, Mr (teacher) 3
Jackson, Margaret 169
Jaeschke, Graham 269
Jamaica 51
James Hardie 143
Job, Cathy 137
Johnson, Mr E.R. 28, 29–30
Johnson, Lyndon 29
Jolly, Rob 38
Jones, Alan 54
Jones, Barry 136–8, 283
Jones, Bob 101–2, 129
Jones, Bruce 83, 86–7

Keating, Paul
    1993 election win 75
    Banana Republic 73
    Dr Mahathir 75–6
    flick the switch to vaudeville 73
    Hawke 73–4, 201
    Liberal tax policy 79
    MX ballistic-missile tests 62–3, 67
    Niki 46, 70, 72–8, 93
    Packer 84–5, 117–18
    Placido Domingo speech 74–5
    Press Gallery 98
    privatisation 70–1
    treatment of staff 284
Kelly, Jackie 269–70
Kelly, Paul 58, 62–3, 65, 159
Kemp, David 137, 253
Kemp, Rod 192, 203

Kennedy, Trevor 78
Kennett, Jeff 32, 181
Kenny, Chris 235
Kernot, Cheryl 56–7
Kessell, Keith 51
Kew Cottages, Melbourne 21, 22
Khyber Pass 86
Koundoros, Nikos 12
Koundouris, Georgina 13
Krassaris family 13–14, 16, 33
Kroger, Michael 145, 191, 277
Kunkel, Jack 285
Kunkel, John 217, 252, 257, 258, 275
Kyoto Protocol 218

language use 37–8
Latham, Mark
    2004 elections 256, 268
    ascension to Labor leadership 58–9, 212, 247
    as shadow treasurer 138–9
    Tasmanian timber workers 248
Laws, John 78
Leckie, David 116, 180
L'Estrange, Michael 143–4
Leunig 185
Lewinsky, Monica 126
Liberal Party
    1996 elections 247
    1998 elections 127–8
    2004 elections 247–9
    2007 elections 204–6, 211–12, 265–6
    2007 polling leak 229–30
    broad church 279
    interest groups 120
    Niki 76–7
    One Nation 114–15
    The Party Room 183–4
    policies 77, 98, 105
    Press Gallery 53, 56, 62
    Queensland Branch 151, 152
Lindsay (seat) leaflet scandal 269–70
Lloyd, Jim 268
Lombard, John 83
Lord, Jack 40
Loughnane, Brian 119, 204, 229–30, 249, 265–7, 271
Luff, David 55, 195, 229, 238, 249, 256
Lyneham, Paul 117, 118
Lyons, John 169

McCabe, Elizabeth 110, 153, 178, 180, 209–10
MacCallum, Mungo 52

Index

McDonald, Pat 41
Macfarlane, Ian 136
Mackenzie, Grahame 78
McKew, Maxine 171–2, 266
McLachlan, Ian (note) 175, 193–6, 199, 202–4
McManus, Rove 205–6
McNicholl, David 78
Mahathir, Dr 75–6
Martin, Peter 136
Martin, Ray 117, 127
Mason, Brett 146, 148
Meakin, Peter 116
Menzies, Robert 189, 270
Middleton, Jim 84, 178
migrant factory fodder 22
migrant literacy 22
Millett, Mick 76
Milne, Glenn 56–7, 72, 82, 137, 147, 193–5
Minchin, Nick 137
   Howard 189, 228, 234, 238, 240, 241
   Howard–Costello 200
   Kyoto Protocol 218
   McLachlan note 194
   relationship with Turnbull 282-3
   WorkChoices 214
Mitchell, Ben 55, 238, 256, 275
Mitchell, Neil 54, 115
Mohan, Palani 98
Monet, Claude 93
Moody, Rowley 37–8
Moore, John 3, 119
Moore-Wilton, Max 122
Morhun, Henry 27
Morris, Grahame 149, 192–3, 194
Munson, Susie 109
Murdoch, Lachlan 116, 144
Murdoch, Rupert 35, 36, 42, 63, 74, 84, 116, 192
Murphy, Lionel 65
Murray–Darling Basin 208
MX ballistic-missile tests 62–3, 67

National Farmers' Federation 145–6, 196
National Party 81, 145–9, 189–90, 199, 236
Neal, Belinda 268
Nelson, Brendan 168, 237, 278
New Right 79–80, 145, 277
Newman, Jocelyn 123
News Ltd 74, 96, 229
nicknames in Cyprus 8–9
nicknames in Press Gallery 51
Noonan, Peggy 55
Northern Territory government 219, 227

Notaras, Theo 13–14
Novak, Robert 55
Nureyev, Rudolf 41–2
Nutt, Tony
   2007 elections 226, 244, 249, 265, 270
   APEC 259
   Shane Stone memo 151–4
   WorkChoices 214–15

Oakes, Laurie 54, 76, 83, 116, 220
   Costello 112, 114
   Crean 138–9
   as a journalist 64
   Keating's piggery 117–18
   Kernot–Evans 56–7
   Niki 77, 97
   Shane Stone memo 152–4
   Truth Melbourne 51
   Turnbull 182
Obama, Barack 220
O'Brien, Michael 110, 281
Old Parliament House 49–50, 64, 69 *see also* Parliament House
Oldmeadow, Max 29
O'Leary, Tony 53, 55, 114, 238, 256, 269, 275
Olsen, John 179
One Nation 105, 114–15, 119, 187–8
O'Neill, Gary 87

Packer, James 116, 118, 231
Packer, Kerry 84–5, 116–18
Papua New Guinea 90
Parker, Derek 276
Parkinson, Tony 235
Parliament House (from 1988) 50, 68–9 *see also* Old Parliament House
Peacock, Andrew 79, 80, 85–7, 163, 172
Pearce, Chris 249
Pearson, Noel 170, 219
Penberthy, David 229
Perrett, Janine 83
Philippou, Natalie 46
political journalism 55–6, 81–2, 93–4
political lexicon 73
politicians
   imperatives for 186–7
   Press Gallery and 58, 62, 63–4, 96
Pratt, Jeanne 176
Press Gallery 4, 49–61, 74–5, 97–8, 210, 276
Price, Matt 148–9
privatisation 70–1, 77
Putin, Vladimir 233

Index

Pyne, Christopher 147, 201, 241

Quill, Frank 35
Quilty, David 214, 217, 249

radio talk shows 53–4, 56
Ramsey, Alan 56–7, 95, 187
Ray, Robert 71–2, 75
recession (we had to have) 77, 78
Redlich, Forrest 28, 30
Rein, Therese 222
Reith, Peter 61, 63, 115, 120, 123, 188, 214, 267
Reserve Bank 111, 136, 150, 184–5, 257
Richardson, Graham 61–2
Richmond Football Club 31
Richmond, Graham 31
Robb, Andrew 183, 196, 243–5, 266, 280
Rolling Stones 40–2
Ronaldson, Michael 200–1
Rothwell, Bruce 42
Rove, Karl 205–6
Roxon, Nicola 171, 178, 261, 269
Royal Children's Hospital, Melbourne 19–20, 31–2, 175
Rudd, Greg 206
Rudd, Kevin/Rudd Labor government
    2007 elections 61, 256–7, 262, 263
    Abbott 280
    ascension to Labor leadership 203, 211–12, 221–3, 272–3
    Burke 220–1
    character 210, 283
    Gillard 97, 189
    Howard, comparison with 206, 246
    inflation 136
    past, present and future 282–5
    policies 168, 170, 219, 251, 255, 259, 261
    in polls 234
    Scores strip joint 232–3
    succession 189, 282–3
Ruddock, Philip 156
Ryan, Mark 71
Rylah, Arthur 28

Savva (name) 8
Savva, Andreas (father)
    Australian food 24
    Christina 19, 25, 31–2
    in Cyprus 7–14, 42–3
    death 103
    Elpiniki goes to work 26
    love of politics 31
    migrates to Australia 13–18, 23
    Niki 21, 47–8, 285
Savva, Andrew and Peter (nephews) 125, 133, 285
Savva, Christina (sister) 108, 142
    birth 19–20
    in Cyprus 43
    death 128–33
    illness 21, 24–6, 46, 99–104
    life 31–4
    Niki 124–5
Savva, Elpiniki (mother)
    Australian food 24–5
    Christina 19–20, 25–6, 31–2, 104, 133
    in Cyprus 7–13, 42–3
    goes to work 26
    Mary 20, 21
    migrates to Australia 16–18
    Niki 47–8, 285
    sayings 93
    Steven 30
Savva, Mary (sister) 20, 21, 26
Savva, Nicki (sister-in-law) 125
Savva, Pavlos (uncle) 44, 45
Savva, Steven (brother)
    arrival in Australia 17–18
    Australian Rules 30–1
    Christina 25, 26, 31–2, 132
    family 125, 285
    Niki 19–23
Savva, Thomas and Christian (nephews) 285
Scott, Bruce 149
Shanahan, Dennis 145
Shearer, Andrew 220
Sheil, Glen 59–60
Shergold, Dr Peter 219
Shipton, Roger 276
Simons, Margaret 171–2
Sinclair, Dr Andrew 140
Sinodinos, Arthur 226, 249, 281
    2004 elections 223
    chief of staff 141, 152, 189
    Costello 198–9
    Howard 227, 270–1
    Howard–Costello 202
    McLachlan note 195
    WorkChoices 214
Smark, Peter 42
Smith, Tony
    Carlton Football Club 181
    Costello 4, 106, 110, 111–12, 114, 115, 119, 153
    Howard leadership 240–1

leadership 162, 201
  as MP 281
  'sacked' 179
  tax reform 122, 126
'so Greek' 5, 179, 253, 271
Soviet Union 85, 91
Spencer, Stephen 61
Sperling, Perry 259
Staley, Tony 245
state premiers 187
Steketee, Mike 65
Stevens, Glenn 231
Stone, Shane 151–4, 194, 225–7, 236, 239, 249
Stork, Marg 37
sub-prime crisis 257
The Sun 47, 73, 77, 85, 97
The Sun News-Pictorial 42, 64, 95, 97
Swan, Wayne 136, 177, 178, 284

Taliban 86
Tampa 155–6
tariff cuts 64
Tasmanian timber workers 248
tax cuts 160–1, 198, 252–6, 261
tax policy (double-counting error) 79
tax reform 105, 112, 119–24, 126 *see also* GST
Tehan, Dan 281
Textor, Mark (polls)
  2007 elections 256, 263, 264–5
  2007 polling leak 229–30
  on budget-night 161
  on Costello 222, 228–9, 242
  on leadership question 204–5
  on medical research 140
  on Rudd ascension to Labor leadership 211–12, 272
thalassemia 20, 32, 102
Thalassemia Society (Victoria) 32–3
Thatcher, Margaret 82
Theophanous, Charalambos 12
Timor levy 173
Tingle, Laura 63, 77, 93
Tinker, Cheryl 131
Toohey, Brian 65
Trioli, Virginia 127
Troeth, Judith 184
Truman, Harry 59
The Truth About a Journalist (Moseley) 37
Truth Melbourne 28, 51
Turkish Cypriots 45
Turnbull, David 61
Turnbull, Greg 61, 84

Turnbull, Malcolm
  ascension to Liberal leadership 278–81
  Badgery's Creek 251
  Costello 144, 179, 182
  Howard 188
  Kyoto Protocol 218
TV networks 61, 268
TV talk shows 54, 56, 117
Twentyman, Les 170–1

unions 217, 222, 256
United Nations 46
United States 88–93, 257

Vaile, Mark 189–90, 193, 199, 203, 236
Vale, Danna 251
van Onselen, Peter 230
Vanstone, Amanda 160–1, 267
Vause, John 210

Walker, John 25
Walker, Ros 30
Walker, Tony 146
Walsh, Geoff 81
Walter and Eliza Hall Institute 175
water 209
Wawn, Stephanie 272
West Gate Bridge disaster 39–40
Wheeldon, John 65, 66–7
White Australia Policy 89
Whitlam, Gough 38–9, 50–3
Whitlam government 47, 49
  dismissal 53, 64–5
wholesale sales tax 187
Willacy, Mark 145–6
Williams, Darryl 2–4, 123
Wilson, Mandy 41
Wood, John 39
Woolcock, Vincent 53, 102, 147–8, 276, 285
Wooldridge, Mary 127
Wooldridge, Michael 102, 141
WorkChoices *see* industrial relations
Worthington, Peter 122–3
Wren, John 36
Wright, Tony 230–1

Yanner, Helen 132
Yeltsin, Boris 92
Young, Mick 67–9

Zaffiris family 26
Zia-ul-Haq, General 86–7